UNRAVELLED

UNRAVELLED

REFORM THE CHURCH, TRANSFORM THE CULTURE

JON PETERSEN

Published in 2018

Manuscript prepared by Rick Killian, Killian Creative, Boulder, Colorado. www.killiancreative.com

Design by Peter Gloege, LOOK Design Studio.

Unless otherwise indicated, scripture quotations are taken from the *Holy Bible, New International Version.*® NIV.® Copyright © 1973, 1978, 1984, by International Bible Society. Used by permission of Zondervan. All rights reserved.

Scripture quotations marked AMP are taken from *The Amplified Bible*, Copyright © 1954, 1958, 1962, 1964, 1965, 1987 by the Lockman Foundation. Used by permission.

Scripture quotations marked ESV are taken from *The Holy Bible, English Standard Version*, copyright © 2001 by Crossway Bibles, a division of Good News Publishers. Used by permission. All rights reserved.

Scripture quotations marked KJV are taken from the *King James Version* of the Bible.

Scripture quotations marked MSG are from *The Message* by Eugene H. Peterson, copyright © 1993, 1994, 1995, 1996, 2000, 2001, 2002. Used by permission of NavPress Publishing Group. All rights reserved.

Scripture quotations marked NASB are taken from the *New American Standard Bible*. Copyright © 1960, 1962, 1963, 1968, 1971, 1972, 1973, 1975, 1977, 1995 by The Lockman Foundation. Used by permission. www.Lockman.org.

Scripture quotations marked NKJV are taken from the *New King James Version* of the Bible. Copyright © 1979, 1980, 1982 by Thomas Nelson, Inc. Used by permission. All rights reserved.

Scripture quotations marked NLT are taken from *The Holy Bible, New Living Translation*, copyright ©1996. Used by permission of Tyndale House Publishers, Inc., Wheaton, Illinois, 60189. All rights reserved.

ISBN: 978-0-9997491-0-4 (paperback)
ISBN: 978-0-9997491-1-1 (eBook)

Printed in the United States of America
24 23 22 21 20 19 18   (ACS)   1 2 3 4 5 6

(The seed of the Kingdom
is friends, together, praying and dreaming,
stumbling and growing.)

*Each person should live as a believer in
whatever situation the Lord has assigned to them,
just as God has called them. This is the rule
I lay down in all the churches.*

—1 CORINTHIANS 7:17

CONTENTS

PART THREE: TRANSFORMATION
The Grove Story: The Anatomy of a Transformed Neighborhood

PART FOUR: AN INVITATION TO KINGDOM MISCHIEF

INTRODUCTION

*Let us say that all things that happen must be somehow
woven into the emerging pattern of God's ultimate design.
Even the stray and errant threads can be used—or, perhaps,
especially the stray and errant threads may be required for a
particular purpose that, because of our limited human view and
understanding, we cannot possibly see or know.*

—STEPHEN LAWHEAD
The Shadow Lamp

Sometimes things have to be unravelled before they can be woven together correctly.

I've long been fascinated with the art of weaving tapestries on a loom. The vertical *warp* threads are secured in place while the horizontal *woof* threads are worked between them by the dexterity of the weaver's hand. Slowly but surely over time, the image of the tapestry is revealed almost like a photo being developed from the bottom up. When mistakes are made, the horizontal woof threads must be unravelled so they can be reworked in correctly. Sometimes threads are missed and become part of the pattern. The weaver must decide which errant threads to unravel and rework and which will make a new and wonderful design.

When I think of the Church, I often think of this process. Certain things are set immovable in the Church like the vertical warp threads that everything else is woven around: For example, the person and nature of each member of the Trinity—Father, Son, and Spirit. These are the threads that set the design and image we are to be revealing through walking out the Great Commission and following the Great Commandment.

Then there are the horizontal warp threads that we as members of the Body of Christ represent individually and corporately. The ways we organize ourselves to be the expression of Christ in our townships, cultures, and nations. How we relate to one another and the work God calls us to—the unique expression we are of the Family of God calling in the orphans and stragglers around us. When the shuttle is in the hand of elders who hear from heaven, the image of our Savior is revealed in the tapestry of our churches; but too often we have gone off on our own, woven according to our own designs. Sometimes there is much that needs to be unravelled before we can reveal the image we were meant to portray.

The Church was never meant to be an end in and of itself, but a conduit: A God-birthed, God-inhabited Family commanded to bring the reconciliation and transformation of their own lives into every sphere—the home, the neighborhood, the workplace, and the city. This internal transformation in each heart is God's norm for a deconstructed and reconstructed people. Personal salvation flows into and from the Family of God that is called to be a transformational community within all cultures as carriers of Christ's DNA.

(Like Lazarus, sometimes it's not enough to just be called out of death and into life, we also need to be freed of our grave clothes so that we can run our races unencumbered by the trappings of traditions) As Jesus said when Lazarus walked out of the tomb, "*Take off* [unravel] *the grave clothes and let him go*" (John 11:44).

It has taken me several decades of ministry (I started in the '60s) to recognize these patterns for what the Master Weaver designed them to be. While each expression of the Church is particular to its people and place, there are some techniques and principles in the weaving that carry over from church to church. If I were to sum them up into phases (I would say they are deconstruction, reconstruction, and transformation) In the last two decades I have had the privilege of working with different friends in Tulsa, Oklahoma; Kansas City, Missouri; and New Haven, Connecticut to see first-hand how God works through such phases to not only reform churches but transform cultures. It's been an incredible ride.

So in this book, I what to tell you the stories of Believers Church in Tulsa, Navah Church in Kansas City, and the Friary in New Haven, and introduce you to some amazing friends in each of those places. I want to celebrate each of their journeys back to God's design for the magnificent Family of *"My Father and your Father"* (John 20:17). I want to bring you this "good news." There's nothing better than a story to illustrate God working among us—especially when that story is about people you love: your friends.

In the following pages I want you to meet Roger Nix, Gyle Smith, Adam Cox, David Blackwell, Nathan Chud, and Ken Janke, as well as many of their co-conspirators. We'll go behind their greatest failures and witness their steady, small victories. They are some of the best expressions I know of the revealed power of the Gospel.

I first met Roger and Gyle of Believers Church in Tulsa when it was in disarray after her lead pastor stepped down because of a moral failure. Though it had exploded from a house group to roughly 4,000 in just a handful of years, the church had been built on a foundation that proved faulty. Before it's new leaders could move forward in any clear direction and with any clear conscience, they came to realize that God was committed to deconstruct what had incorrectly been built in the church's infant years. Their story illuminates some of the traditions and mindsets that had kept Believers from looking like the Church that Jesus died to establish. Captive to a hierarchical leadership structure, heroism, human vision, and a professional-like approach to ministry, together they found each other's hearts along with a biblical and relational pursuit of God's purposes. Through God's gracious tutelage, Believers shed its "church-centric" mindset to become a vibrant, healthy, disciples-making-disciples church committed to the extension of Christ's Kingdom in Tulsa and beyond.

God never tears things down for the sake of demolition alone, but always with the mind to rebuild. A business friend told me of a comparable term in the business world—"creative destruction." It is through this deconstruction/reconstruction process that God shows His creative intentions, redemptive prowess, and lavish love. The Kansas City Boiler Room (later to become Navah Church) pioneered by three twenty-somethings—Adam Cox, David Blackwell, and Nathan Chud—would come to understand the genetics of being put together by the Divine Architect from inception. Though young, these three had the advantage of not having many church traditions to deconstruct, although they still needed to discover God's blueprint for building according to His pattern. In the process of being instructed by the power of the Gospel, they found life-long friendship with one another, with God, and with the spiritual family the Lord began to entrust them with. Now, along with other churches in Kansas City, God is setting the table for great "Kingdom mischief" to be unveiled in and from that city.

Ken Janke, a sojourner and pilgrim of sorts, wandered his way into God's divine purposes for his family by planting a church that would never be built. Plunked by a loving Father into a blighted neighborhood in New Haven, Connecticut, Ken became a "dreamweaver"—an underground menace to the kingdom of darkness. From his house to his neighborhood to the economic community and eventually to the halls of city and state government, this "dangerous" man and his band of friends turned their neighborhood, then their city, up-side-right. ✗

Each of these stories is unique. The personalities, gifts, and passions represented are on all ends of the human spectrum. But one thing each of these groups seemed to discover (after comparing notes) was that "The seed of the Kingdom is friends, together, praying and dreaming, stumbling and growing." Take a pinch of friendship, a love for Jesus, a heart for the Father, and an ear to the Spirit, and the journey begins to look very similar in its genetic imprint, no matter where you start or with whom you are traveling. ✗

As you share in these stories I think you will see that we are all fundamentally clueless when it comes to "being the Church" on the earth—that we need each other more than we realize—and that we too often learn best through our mistakes. We all tenaciously hold on to "impossible" dreams, receive only incremental glimpses of the One we love, and cry out to Him for help on a regular basis. If you can believe it, this is the essence of God's recipe for success in His Kingdom. As you'll come to see, God was all over these beautiful servants—sons and daughters of the King—as they walked and stumbled through these same obstacles. ✗

Unravelled is the saga of my friends (oh yeah—and me!) innocently being taken apart only to be rewoven into the tapestry according to the Weaver's original design. Their collective stories are illustrative of the tremendous grace the Father is bringing to His frumpy bride, a grace that leads us, matures us, and will ultimately present us to Himself *"without stain or wrinkle or any other blemish, but holy and blameless"* (Ephesians 5:27). ✗

PART ONE:
DECONSTRUCTION:
The Believers Church Story

Since a spiritual community exists to be
responsive to the transforming presence of
Christ so that we can discern and do the will
of God, our practices must be consistent with
this overarching purpose. Life in community
can never be about merely getting a job
done—as important as that is. It must also
always take into account how we get the job
done and whether we are transformed or
deformed in the process.

—RUTH HALEY BARTON,
Pursuing God's Will Together

CHURCH AS WE KNOW IT

*"Go into all the world and preach the gospel
to all creation."*

—MARK 16:15

"Just how *do* we create a discipleship culture at Believers Church?"

I looked up at Gyle's question. I remember pausing and thinking, *Oh, dear. There is no quick answer to that one.*

Roger nodded and expanded, "We spend most of our time as church leaders putting out fires, counseling, or trying to keep the church programs moving forward. Is this really what we're supposed to be doing? Didn't Jesus tell us to 'go make disciples'? What does that even mean today?"

My mind whirred with years of trying to do just that as part of church staffs, missionary organizations, and as an advisor to Christian nonprofits. It filled with all the false starts, partial successes, and sudden collapses that had led to our present convictions and models. (I probably shouldn't say a "model" so much as a "path.") Over the past several years, we'd been tinkering with the handful of church plants in our 24-7 Prayer Boiler Room network

1

to see what nurtured relationships, saw people through hardships, helped individuals grow, and melded hearts together into a "church." Each group we worked with found its own expression. All the same, it felt like a biblical pattern was beginning to emerge.

Rather than speaking my thoughts, I looked at Gyle, then Roger, and said, "If you'd like, I am available to come back to Tulsa and seek the Lord with your team for an answer to that question."

I could tell it wasn't exactly the easy-to-implement, seven-step-program answer they'd hope for, but Roger and Gyle both nodded without looking at each other. It felt like they were almost desperate enough to try anything, and over the course of getting to know each other, they'd come to trust us enough to try what we'd been finding success with.

Here we go again, I thought with a smile.

Roger Nix, the pastor for the last couple of years at Believers Church in Tulsa, Oklahoma; Gyle Smith, his executive pastor; Pete Greig of 24-7 Prayer; and I were having this conversation at the ever-quaint Coffee Shop on Cherry Street in Tulsa. We'd recently met each other at a 24-7 Prayer Roundtable in Kansas City, and they reached out to Pete to invite him to Tulsa to get better acquainted. Fortuitously, I was invited along.

We'd been sitting together for some time when Gyle popped his awkward question. Both Roger and Gyle seemed dissatisfied with "church as usual." They were looking to us to help them find a truer form of what it meant to be the Church[*] in a culture where the norm was to form big congregations around big personalities.

---

[*] Throughout this book I have followed the convention of capitalizing "Church" when referring to the universal Body of Christ and not capitalizing "church" when referring to a local body or smaller subsets of the universal Church. (If "Church" is part of a name, as in "Believers Church," it is also capitalized, but, of course, just refers to that church body.) Likewise, "the Kingdom" is capitalized when referring to "the Kingdom of God," but not capitalized when referring to an earthly "kingdom."

Many have called Tulsa the "buckle of the Bible belt" because it is full of mega-churches and "star" leaders. It's a place where you can start a church and have 250 people show up to the first service, but if you don't "do things right," it's all downhill from there. Big churches there tended to have pastors who are ministry superstars and incredible church programs for every age group. And while that was the foundation on which Believers had been built, that just wasn't Roger and Gyle.

While we sat together that day, Roger told us of the mess of a mega-church they'd inherited. It had began quickly shrinking when the former pastor—a man of incredible charisma and a gifted speaker—stepped down after having an affair. Under his leadership, the church had excelled at the super church model. It exploded from inception to over 4,000 members in the last three years of the 1990s. By the time Roger and his wife, Donna, stepped into leadership in 2001, however, it had shrunk to 1,500 members. The church was struggling to find its footing again.

Roger had never been a pastor, let alone anything close to what it meant to be pastor in Tulsa. He and Donna had spent eighteen years with Impact Productions doing dramatic presentations of the Gospel across the United States and around the world. As an actor, Roger had the dubious distinction of playing the devil in "Toymaker and Son." With Donna pregnant, a newly adopted son, a circle of loyal Impact Productions friends, empty church coffers, and Believers facing a pending lawsuit, he stepped into the pastorate of Believers in obedience to God's leading. That much he knew for sure, but where to from there?

Roger was not the type of guy to be "the man" in the typical mega-church style. Despite being a former actor, he was not a "personality," but at the same time dripped with one of the truest gifts of being a pastor I've ever encountered. He wasn't interested in having a church that was a mile wide and an inch deep. That's why, when we told him about what we'd been doing in our Boiler Room churches, he was so intrigued.

Roger and Gyle wanted to create a culture of disciples making disciples, a culture of friends praying and dreaming together, permitted to stumble toward what God was calling them to become, and then to grab those dreams with both hands and follow them.

But the church Roger inherited no longer knew what it was about. The former pastor's transgression left many reeling. He, after all, was the reason most of them had started attending Believers in the first place. Several called it "the church I've looked for all of my life." The chaos that followed the pastor's resignation had the remaining church leaders scrambling to console a shocked and confused congregation. Everyone seemed to be asking, "Where can I find what used to be *here*?" Many of them also wondered, "If my pastor—a man I looked to as a role model—can't make it, how can I?" They felt betrayed, distraught, and disillusioned. In a word, they'd lost *hope*.

The day Roger and Donna took over, it felt like the former leaders handed them the keys to the building and then evaporated into the ether. Roger inherited no local elders, a grocery list of meetings to preside over, and a full schedule of church programs to oversee. The biggest concern for the paid staff seemed to be whether or not they would keep their jobs, not the welfare of the confused congregants in the programs they ran.

At the same time, the previous pastor, feeling he'd repented and been redeemed, wanted to return to the pulpit. He began quietly letting it be known he was willing to be restored when the church's leadership was open to it. The congregation, however, seemed split down the middle on whether he should be welcomed back or sued for fraud.

The environment was toxic, to say the least. However, while the church was in the midst of this, they created a prayer room and launched into a rhythm of 24-7 prayer that lasted for weeks. They took the simple prayers written on the walls of that 24-7 prayer room and began to pray them into the life stream of the church.

Roger's hope for the former pastor was restoration, healing, and reconciliation, but there was no healthy way for him to return to leadership at Believers. There was still too much hurt. So, he brought the former pastor in with his family. They prayed with them and stayed open for what God might want to do next. Roger related, "I felt tormented how I was to love him *and* see a good end to the story for the church. My desire was to see him restored, but there was too much broken trust for it to happen at Believers."

Despite their own pain, the congregation responded in a beautiful way, forgiving and blessing their former pastor. At the same time, as soon as it was clear he wouldn't be returning to leadership in any form at Believers, it was as if the church breathed a sigh of relief. There was a palpable change of season.

Soon after that, Roger asked a circle of loyal friends to launch into a season of prayer with him. They took specific prayers from that time and turned them into a series of worship services. Roger later told me those prayers and services "shifted our hearts. We started hoping again."

The following year they started "free market" small groups to help the people in the church connect beyond the corporate meetings. The groups didn't have to gather around anything much more than an excuse to get together, play games, or talk—any reason to get to know each other better. Unfortunately, the groups never really jelled into anything more than social get-togethers and the program soon fell apart.

Then in 2003 they added "Celebrate Recovery" to their repertoire, a program to help people get over addictive, life-controlling behaviors. They eventually opened it to the greater Tulsa community. Celebrate Recovery helped transform Believers into a healing church, a safe place for people to come and find a home. This was great, but it led to a new issue. Once people "recovered" through these courses in the church, what should they do after that? The church had no other "trails" to help them continue their walk with Jesus from there.

It was now three years into Roger's pastoral journey as we sat around the table in that coffee shop on Cherry Street. We shared stories, laughed, commiserated, and all fell in love with each other. As God knit our hearts together for His own reasons, we were all blissfully ignorant of the divine destiny we had just careened into. The Father was calling us into a long, fruitful journey together, praying and dreaming, stumbling and growing.

Believers was truly at a crossroads. Though the church was finally putting the former pastor's failure in the rearview mirror, they felt as if all they had done since they had come into leadership was limp along in survival mode. They had taken over a fractured vision and done the best they could with "duct tape and bailing wire" to keep things together. Though they'd accomplished many good things, they were still scarred and tentative. The events of 1999 still hung ominously over their heads. They knew in their hearts that continuing in recovery mode wasn't what God had for their future, but they also had no idea what to do differently.

Continuing to fumble forward, just doing what was next in front of them to do, no longer felt reasonable. (Although stumbling is a viable exercise when it comes to us humans, as it is how we learn to walk.) They wanted to ascertain what the DNA of their church had been from the beginning. What had the Lord dreamed for Believers at its conception? What had He planted this church to accomplish in Tulsa? And was His vision for it only limited to Tulsa? Why had He asked the former pastor to found it? Was there a way back to what God originally wanted for their church from the dead end where they now found themselves? Would the people ever recover their hope? Their focus on Jesus? How could they possibly do something new when they were still so busy maintaining the crumbling foundation of what had been built before they had even arrived?

Something was wrong. Something had to change. They needed a new plan—a new vision for moving forward.

But quite often, before you fix things, you have to take them apart first.

DECONSTRUCTING TO RECONSTRUCT

My wife Mindy and I (and our three kids) used to be missionaries in Amsterdam. While there, I learned that many of the ancient buildings were built on wooden piers and those piers were not standing the test of time. As a result, these buildings were slowly but surely beginning to sink into the harbor and canals of the city. As a result, an entire industry rose up around lifting up the buildings, digging out these old piers, and laying new foundations.

In the same way, just as He did for my friends in Tulsa, I believe the Lord is visiting us in our churches today to lift us from the ideas, practices, and traditions that our churches were originally built upon, but are now rotting in our subsoil. They are simply not compliant with His blueprint for the Church as Jesus planted it in the Gospels. They need to be dug up and replaced. That's tricky business.

For Believers Church to understand its calling and grow into the future, they had to first enter a time of dismantling—not parts of their building, but mindsets that were keeping them from being the church God wanted them to be. They needed to look specifically at what God had been up to in the years since Believers inception, so they could see what God was systematically challenging them to retain and what needed to be removed. It was time to look behind in order to bring into focus what lie ahead.

And they were asking for my help to do it. I was honored.

In my experience, you can't talk about deconstruction without celebrating God's desire to reconstruct and rebuild what He tears down. That has to first begin in our own hearts. The Lord whispered a phrase to me many years ago, "You cannot change what you do not love."

During the previous two decades, the Lord had held me accountable to the necessity of "tearing down" *in love* to make room to "build up," *also in love*, what He had really wanted from the beginning. There was some significant discussion that emerged in the late '90s that posited the need for the Lord to deconstruct much of the modern-day church construct. The unfortunate aspect of much of this discussion was that many began to tear apart their church paradigms without any notion of God's magnificent plan to rebuild and reconstruct His Church. Instead of ending up with what God wanted, they found themselves in a demolition zone wondering what was going to come down next. Rather than risk being hit by falling debris, many fled.

A friend of mine even began dismantling many of his church's outdated traditions and practices on worship, leadership structure, meeting content, and Christian training only to see his church completely dissolve. In the end, it was so summarily disassembled that there was nothing left upon which to rebuild.

Deconstructing shaky or rotting church traditions and mind-sets can only be done under the guidance of our Builder King and as an act of God's love. He only tears down in order to rebuild us into the pattern that is Christ Himself. You can't properly do the former without a vision of the latter. The three and a half years Jesus walked with His disciples were not only dedicated to deconstructing their worldviews, but also promising that He would reconstruct them with His Spirit and Word* in the future. Without the spiritual audit they went through as disciples, they could never have built the Church Jesus entrusted them to build on the revelation He would give them. ⌣

When Paul tells us *"For no one can lay any foundation other than the one already laid, which is Jesus Christ"* (1 Corinthians 3:11), He was fulfilling His apostolic ministry. He lovingly but strongly reproached the early church for allowing divisions within their assembly. Instead of living by Christ's mandate for unity, they accepted the cultural norms of factionalism and disunity (which were earmarks of Corinthian society). Cultural foundational blocks are never on the blueprint Jesus gives us for building our churches—they are just part of the window dressings. We needed to fight through to what He really wants for us, not just do what the organization down the road has had success with. But then again, success in our eyes is not always what God calls success. His plans tend to run deeper and last longer.

---

* A little more capitalization clarification: when referring to the Word of God, aka *The Bible*, I capitalize "Word"; when referring to a "word," such as when someone hears "a word from the Lord," I use lower case "word" to clarify that it bears less authority and comes as an impression from God to the individual, usually giving specific direction, explanation, encouragement, or instruction. Such a "word" needs to be judge and if it is truly from God, it will bear up over time. I know not every denomination uses this phraseology in the same way, so I thought it good to stop and explain it here to keep things clear as we move forward.

Perhaps the analogy of a tree is better in describing the need to remain connected to the original DNA of any work God births. An apple tree is birthed in darkness, grows from an emerging sprout, and begins its annual journey of spreading outward and upward into the sky. As the roots grow deeper and stronger, what were once twigs now become branches sprouting with new growth—and at their tips, the blossoms, then the fruit. ✗

When storms and blight assail the tree, the blossoms, the forming apples, the leaves, and the weakest branches suffer the most damage. However, no experienced orchard farmer, looking at the damage, would say, "Well, what a mess! Let's cut the tree down and plant a new one in its place. What we need is a new tree." No, he would assess the damage, then prune the tree back with the full knowledge that life is still in the roots and will eventually fulfill its created purpose—new blossoms and new fruit. A wise farmer doesn't discard the years of the tree's life—scrapping it and starting over—but trusts that the life is still in the tree and its future fruitfulness lies in the resident roots. This continuity of life from one generation to the next is something we, the family of God, need to fight for as we usher the emerging generations into the way of Christ and His apostles. Too many hunger for new, only to have to wait years for any fruit worthy of sharing with others; or they grow up trees so quickly that they have only shallow roots that will not last through the first heavy wind or storm. That's almost exactly what had happened at Believers Church. ✗

For those of you who are new leaders like Roger and Gyle in churches or in the marketplace (another very worthy calling of the Lord that needs solid Kingdom foundations), I can confidently say, "Don't be ignorant of your family line; don't get over-impressed with the new things going on—with the way the wind is blowing today. God is doing a really old thing, and everything He does was planted a long, long time ago." Times do change, and those changes will affect much of what we do, but they won't change our foundations. While they take a lot of work at the beginning, healthy orchards throw off nutritious and delicious fruit. Only those who faithfully stay the course can lean back in their proverbial rocking chairs and brag on the efficacy of ancient roots, and the beauty that will blossom from staying connected to them. ✗

I have seen such deconstruction and reconstruction patterns repeat themselves throughout the various transitions God has orchestrated in each of the last five decades. In the 1960s, it was a reintroduction of the Holy Spirit; in the 1970s—literally the time of "the Jesus movement"—it was a reemphasis of the kingship of Christ; in the 1980s, we experienced a renewed call to take God's Kingdom to the nations; in the 1990s, there was a reemphasis of what the Church was actually designed to be; and in the 2000s, we found ourselves introducing a seemingly orphaned generation to their Heavenly Father and getting familiar with His invitation for them to become His family. Each of these themes are being braided together in the 2010s, each central to God's ultimate mandate for the transformation of the Church into a Kingdom people. The Weaver is intent to intertwine these Kingdom realities back into the Church's fabric, bringing forth the Son's image into the tapestry of God's people. This will happen as we allow deconstruction to have its full effect on the family of God and our broken frameworks; only when they are dismantled can we, together with Him, rebuild. The Lord is pulling all of these threads through the cosmic loom once again so that the Church will reveal Christ in the pattern of the tapestry. ✓

Personally, it took me three decades of ministry before the beauty of God's deconstruction brought me joy and gratitude. I can't look back on my own journey and find a smidge of regret, resident pain, or shadowy memories, though I do walk with a pronounced spiritual limp sometimes and a well-earned humility that lets me know I don't always know better. The only thing I do know for sure is that God's presence was always with me through the best and the worst of circumstances. Always, though, after much painful deconstruction, He utterly redeemed each situation into which He led me. It was never a fast process, but it was never late either.

I have seen how wrong things can go and can now rejoice to see how they can be set right as well. Despite our mistakes and missteps, I know the Weaver leans over His tapestry, gazes upon His emerging masterpiece, and smiles with foreknowledge, confident that what He started on the earth—in us—will be completed to His satisfaction.

It was just such a journey of divine tapestry weaving that we started on that day around that table at The Coffee Shop on Cherry Street in Tulsa, Oklahoma.

NOW WHAT?

Question #1: Am I (are we) prepared to invite the Lord to lay again any foundations that are not according to His blueprint *no matter the cost?* (And be sure to count the costs first: people in the pews, income, staff morale, etc.)

> **Exercise:** Meditate on and discuss Nehemiah 1:4-11 in light of Nehemiah's response to the report he received on Jerusalem.

> **Exercise:** Meditate on and discuss 1 Corinthians 2:6-3:23. This is a seminal text for laying proper foundations in your church.

Question #2: Do you trust in God's ability to guide you? What would be some natural fears you might encounter along the way and need to confess to God before you begin? It will be a difficult journey.

> **Exercise:** Meditate on Proverbs 3:5-7 and consider the passage in light of embarking on a journey of "tearing apart" and "building back up."

Question #3: Do I (we) trust the Holy Spirit's ability to guide me (us) even though it may mean losing people, finances, and reputation? Take a little "fear inventory" and ask, "If not, why not?"

> **Exercise:** Pray Proverbs 3:5-7 together and respond to what the Holy Spirit shows you.

FRIENDS

Some men came, bringing to him a paralyzed man,
carried by four of them. Since they could not get him to Jesus
because of the crowd, they made an opening in the roof above
Jesus by digging through it and then lowered the mat
*the man was lying on. When Jesus saw **their** faith, he said*
to the paralyzed man, "Son, your sins are forgiven."

—MARK 2:3-5 (emphasis added)

Not long after our coffee klatch, I found myself in the pulpit at Believers Church. After speaking, I stayed a few more days as I'd promised to meet with their leaders and staff. They felt what they had gotten through their former season of prayer had sustained them, but now they sensed God wanted to do more, but just weren't sure how to get there. Celebrate Recovery was still going well, but the question of "What's next?" for its graduates was also still ever present.

I told them I had no formulas for discipleship or church structures and values, but that I was willing to stay and pray with them and see what God said. They agreed. Again, I had no idea what I was in for—I don't think they did either.

I know a lot of times meeting to pray is a lot of talk about what should be prayed about, and then finished with a quick, sort of grocery list of prayers: "God, I just ask you to bless my brother Tom's business, and resolve that issue with his distribution vendor; please bless Craig and Beth's marriage and provide for them financially in this trying time; please comfort sister Ellen, who just lost her husband, and be with her family in their grief; we ask that you touch Bryan's bosses heart about his need for a raise," and so on. A lot of praying together starts this way, but over the years as a pastor, missionary, and compatriot with others trying to figure out what the heaven God wants us to do with the things He's put into our hearts, I've discovered it's better for us to talk less to each other, present our petitions and requests to God, and then spend most of the time listening for what God wants to tell us about our concerns. (We'll develop how to do this more in Part Two.) This brings in the challenge of truly hearing from God and discerning whether it's Him speaking to us, our own thoughts, or last night's pizza, but like a lot of things, you get better at it the more you practice.

So, for this particular meeting, the Believers Church leadership team—Roger, Gyle, and Mark Tietsort, who was in charge of counselling and prophetic ministries, and Susan Sealy, who ran everything else—and I got together, lifted up our concerns, and started listening. Some of us got up and walked around, Susan knelt on the floor, others of us sat, a couple mumbled prayers under our breath, all trying to focus on what God had to say to us.

As we prayed together, a clear picture came to my mind of the four of them sitting under a table with their backs to each other, facing outward. They were all busy doing church work, but never interacted with each other. Occasionally, one would reach up and grab food off of the table, but nothing was in cooperation with any of the others.

It was weird.

The four people I saw under the table seemed riddled with insecurity and were frantic to juggle all of the church demands in their various departments. They lacked the confidence to move past their own weaknesses and discover the strength that could be found in walking openly from the heart with one other. Not only were they still shell-shocked from the trauma the church had been through, they were simply surviving by "doing church" the way they had seen it done before.

Then I had a mental image of them getting up, sitting in the chairs around the table facing each other, and looking deeply into each other's eyes for the first time.

When we came back together after the time we had allotted to pray, we had a lively discussion around the picture I had just seen. The team reminded me of this story years later and said I had told them, "You need to repent—*go do it!*" (I don't remember being quite so abrupt.) They reported I delivered this salvo then promptly released them to get on with the business of repentance before turning back to work on my computer. (Oh well, I'm older—and hopefully wiser and gentler—now.) Despite the abrupt nature of their encounter with this "flawed servant," they began to ask the Lord's forgiveness for not doing God's work God's way.

Gyle refers to this as "Repentance Day." He later told me, "Until I repented before the Lord, I never realized we needed to be friends as leaders—that we needed to *be* the church before we could *lead* the church."

If I was blunt that day, perhaps it was because what they were learning was a lesson that was painfully close to home.

"DON'T GET TOO CLOSE!"

As a young pastor in California in the 1970s, I attended a pastors' conference and heard to a leader advise young pastors to "never get close to anyone in ministry—or you will get hurt." I was shocked. This leader went on to suggest that our role as leaders was to "preach the Word and get the work done. If you get too close to people, they won't work hard enough and may eventually betray you. The closer you are to them, the more it will hurt you." Okay, I was a rookie, but that didn't sit right with me.

Then we encountered a "disaster" (proven later to be a divine one) at The Barn Community Church in Grants Pass, Oregon where I was pastoring a couple of years later. I'd gotten close to my elder-leaders, and we hurt each other deeply. I was tempted to think that speaker in California might have been right after all.

I made an inner vow to "never get close to people again." I determined it would be easier to just get the vision from God on my own, outline the tasks that needed to be done to fulfill that vision, and make sure we got the "right people on the bus and into the right seats" so that we could get the work of the ministry done. No fuss, no muss. We were all servants of the Lord doing the work of the Lord, we were here to obey, God had given us the vision, etc., etc. I vowed that in the next church or team I was in charge of, I would set up a strict chain of command, and for the most part, I would just preach and let my few direct reports manage the "work of the ministry."

Mindy and I left Grants Pass exhausted and deeply discouraged, but God wasn't through with us. We were almost immediately invited to join Youth With A Mission's first Leadership Training School that would start a few months later in Kona, Hawaii. We jumped at the opportunity (it was not like we had anything else to do, anyway, and a trip to Hawaii always sounds good).

Under the warm, regenerative sun, we got to know YWAM's President Loren Cunningham and his wife Dar, two deeply compassionate and spiritually insightful people. After finally opening up to Loren about the "disaster" that happened in Grants Pass, he suggested I go and sit on a secluded lava hill every day and ask the Lord for clarity on what He thought about what had happened there—an uncomfortable place for an uncomfortable task. Despite feeling initial resistance to the idea, I decided to do as advised. It turned out to be the right move.

While sitting on my patch of lava, I began to realize that I had to revoke my vow to not open my heart to people—and seek a deeper understanding of what had gone wrong. I asked the Lord to reveal His way of doing ministry to me. Not much happened sitting on those sunny rocks except enough healing to open myself up again to what I felt deep inside was right: if ministry is about people, not just "getting stuff done," it meant I would have to open myself up to being hurt by letting myself get close to others again. I think I left that place more open-hearted, but with my tail still between my legs.

Some months later, now in Amsterdam (this was in 1981), we were on the YWAM leadership team under Floyd and Sally McClung. Floyd was a man full of vision, but I never felt it superseded his commitment to the hearts and wellbeing of our team.

Not long after we arrived in Amsterdam, we came an annual Dutch national staff meeting. Despite my new openness from my lava rock meditations on Kona, I still stung from the shame of the failure in Grants Pass. I entered that meeting feeling depressed and monkish, still thinking more about what I left behind than what lay ahead. I promptly placed myself behind a pole that obscured me from Floyd's line of sight at the leadership podium. (Like that was really going to keep me out of God's crosshairs!)

During a "response" time after Floyd's teaching, he walked down off the stage, past 300 others, crawled over ten people in my row, and knelt down in front of me to look up into my eyes. He simply spoke a few words that God had given him.

"I'm going to get inside of you."

I melted.

It's hard to describe what went through me at those words. It's what I longed for from God and was terrified of all at once.

Every heart needs to be pursued past the point of comfort where love is not contingent on behavior. This love needs to be repeated until the subject of such an assault surrenders to the inner healing of God.

Under Floyd's direction, I learned what it meant to "move at the speed of relationships": guarding people's heart, listening to receive God's vision together, and releasing each team member into the area of gifting they were called of God to fulfill. I learned what it meant to put people first, and what it meant when Jesus told His disciples they weren't servants, but friends. (See John 15:15.) I soon learned that starting by building relationships not only worked better for "fulfilling the vision," it made for a happier team. Peace and the partnership of the Holy Spirit can accomplish way more than we might imagine is possible on our own. I was learning the power of being relational.

It was during that time I was first impressed by the little verse, *"He appointed twelve* that they might be with him *and that he might send them out to preach"* (Mark 3:14, emphasis added). The first thing wasn't that they went out to preach and perform miracles, the first thing was *"that they might be with him."* Yes, they got things done, but they did it in the power of tenacious brotherhood.

It is a pattern I've seen again and again throughout the Gospels.

Jesus always put people first.

A RAG-TAG BUNCH OF JESUS FREAKS

When Jesus began walking the dusty roads of His birthplace, He immediately challenged the religious paradigms of His day. In order for the Kingdom to manifest, He needed to dismantle the presuppositions of the religious/nationalistic thinking that was so prevalent in Israel's culture and tradition. He told them, *"You study the Scriptures diligently because you think that in them you have eternal life. These are the very Scriptures that testify about me, yet you refuse to come to me to have life"* (John 5:39-40). He went on to say, *"Do not suppose that I have come to bring peace to the earth. I did not come to bring peace, but a sword"* (Matthew 10:34).

Jesus came to turn over tables both literally and figuratively. He was a revolutionary of the heart and soul. Many thought He would come as a political activist to bring Israel into prominence again as a nation, but instead He came to release Israel (which means "he or she who has standing to wrestle with God"*)

---

* Wrestling with God" is an interesting terminology for what at least one aspect of prayer was meant to be. Yes, we always come to the Father with respect, but we don't bring false selves to him. Whatever our emotions, frustrations, and outrage at injustices—whether perceived or real—He welcomes us to come and argue them out with Him in the same way we might at the dinner table with a natural father we love and respect, but have a differing perspective from. It's part of learning His ways, it's part of growing up, it's part of how we make the world a better place. To bring, for example, "Father, why do you let good things happen to innocent people" into the throne room of heaven isn't disrespectful, because the King welcomes His sons and daughters coming into His presences passionate to spread the goodness of His Kingdom to all. It's just that when we do, we need to be ready to leave with a charge to somehow be part of the solution, and it may be with a challenging mission. Yes, we "wrestle" with God in such conversations, but often it's our own selves we wrestle with in His presence, and we leave the better for it because we have overcome something that was previously holding us back.

into every human heart. He came that people might once again be reunited with Him as a Father they could tussle and even argue with—someone they could have supper with and talk about politics, religion, and heart issues—nothing being out of bounds. This is the mark of the type of family the Father always planned humanity to be.

When Jesus came to unleash the Kingdom of heaven, He was permissioning every generation to insist on its own revolution, to challenge what had not been built on biblical foundations or on the image of Christ, the Cornerstone. As disciples of Jesus, we are each invited to challenge existing paradigms in ourselves and in those around us—we are to be the ones turning the world upside-right again towards the Father of us all. We are to be a revolutionary people of a radical, holy Kingdom that has no rivals. But we don't win by conquering others; we win by restoring hearts.

What was Jesus's model for building this Kingdom?

Yes, He did gather crowds, but that wasn't His purpose. If that had been it, they would have dispersed after His death as quickly as the mob shouting "Hosanna!" on the day He entered Jerusalem turned into the mob shouting "Give us, Barabbas!" just a few days later. Jesus's main work wasn't with the crowds, it was with the twelve.

His Kingdom wasn't based on performing miracles (they were demonstrations of it, not foundations), because none of those who became the "pillars" of the church—the apostles—were there solely because they'd been healed or delivered from oppression. Instead, Jesus was building something else into their hearts.

Nor did Jesus do it merely by spouting great wisdom and being a great teacher. His students scattered on the day He was crucified faster than they had gathered when He first proclaimed, "The Kingdom of God is at hand." Only the twelve and their immediate family and entourage remained. (Yes, Peter denied Him, but he was back with the twelve the day Jesus rose.) It wasn't because of what He'd taught them; it was because of who He was to them.

What *did* Jesus build His church upon?

He built the Church on the apostles—*those flawed fellows who had walked with Him day after day in the three and a half years of His ministry.* Christianity became a world-shaking force because a small group gathered in an upper room to obey the last words Jesus had spoken to them:

> "Do not leave Jerusalem, but wait for the gift my Father promised, which you have heard me speak about. For John baptized with water, but in a few days you will be baptized with the Holy Spirit. . . .
>
> *"You will receive power when the Holy Spirit comes on you; and you will be my witnesses in Jerusalem, and in all Judea and Samaria, and to the ends of the earth."*
>
> —ACTS 1:4-5, 8

What built the Church into an enduring, countercultural, revolutionary force that has plagued unrighteousness generation after generation? Jesus built it upon the twelve disciples He called one by one, the revelation that He was the Christ, and eventually the disciples they made according to that revelation in the days following the coming of the Holy Spirit. He built it upon a band of men He called "friends," their families, and the new friends they made in His name in the days and years that followed.

When we see the Church as an organization formed to fulfil a purpose or a mission, we miss the person-to-person foundation on which Jesus built Hi Church. We miss the power of what He developed in Peter, Andrew, James, John, Philp and Bartholomew, Thomas and Matthew, the other James, Thaddeus, Simon, and Judas (who betrayed Him and was replaced by Matthias in Acts 1:26). Rather than spreading His teaching far and wide, Jesus spent His entire life within the small province of Israel and created an experience for the handful walking with Him that would never leave them. He didn't create intellectual students, blind followers, or mindless servants. He created *friends*, as He called them on the night He was betrayed:

> "I no longer call you servants, because a servant does not know his master's business. Instead, I have called you friends, for everything that I learned from my Father I have made known to you."
>
> —JOHN 15:15

The disciples were never victims of Jesus's vision. He loved them and laid down His life for them. They were partners in the Kingdom enterprise because they knew and loved Him—He had won their hearts.

Note that these twelve and their family and friends—those most devoted to Jesus in the days following His resurrection and ascension—numbered only 120 praying together in unity on the day of Pentecost. By the end of that day, there were over three thousand.

And what was their first thought in response to this revival? "Oh my goodness, we need a building! Who can write bylaws? Does anyone know how to file as a 501(c)3?" No. The first church wasn't the gathering in the square on the day of Pentecost when Peter preached, it was the people who gathered house to house in the days that followed:

> They devoted themselves to the apostles' teaching and
> to fellowship, to the breaking of bread and to prayer. . . .
> Every day they continued to meet together in the temple
> courts. They broke bread in their homes and ate together
> with glad and sincere hearts, praising God and enjoying
> the favor of all the people. And the Lord added to their
> number daily those who were being saved.
>
> —ACTS 2:42, 46-47

The Church isn't an organization (perhaps why so many complain about organized religion?); the Church is people. The first step for the apostles was the first step Jesus took—they needed to get to know the new people that had joined "The Way" (as Luke first called this new faith in the book of Acts) and bond them into families. The Church isn't an institution; the Church is people gathered together here and there, relating to one another and trying to figure out how to follow Christ in whatever circumstances, culture, or conditions they find themselves. We often think of a church as having members, but the truth is that it's its members bonded together as families that are what constitute any church (a "family of families," as we like to call it). Thus, our big missionary mistake: we shouldn't be merely "planting" or "building" churches, we should be infecting people with *"being the Church"* together and in the society around them. In that way we extend the Church Family genetic wherever we go.

The difference is small, but significant. Too often we have our thinking about being the Church completely upside down.

"I HAVE LOVED THOSE YOU GAVE ME"

Traditional, transactional ministry focuses on working together to accomplish our goals, like building a structure we call "our church." (You know, the one on the corner?) Relationally-focused ministry is modeled after Jesus's choosing of the disciples to be *with* Him. It is in this "being together and loving one another" that His image is transferred. After all, if the world is to "know we are Christians by our love," how will they see that love except in how we relate to one another? It was the commitment to doing all of life together that became the soil from which rich ministry grew.

When Jesus evaluated His own ministry to the Father at the end of His life, He made little mention of His works. (Look through John 14-17 and see for yourself.) Obviously, Jesus and the Father had laid out criteria for His being on earth—there was a point to it, after all—and this is His report back to the Father of how He had done on His mission:

> "I have revealed you to those whom you gave me out of the world. They were yours; you gave them to me and they have obeyed your word. Now they know that everything you have given me comes from you. For I gave them the words you gave me and they accepted them. They knew with certainty that I came from you, and they believed that you sent me. . . . While I was with them, I protected them and kept them safe by that name you gave me. None has been lost except the one doomed to destruction so that Scripture would be fulfilled. . . .
>
> *"I have made you known to them, and will continue to make you known in order that the love you have for me may be in them and that I myself may be in them."*
>
> —JOHN 17:6-8, 12, 26

Jesus doesn't mention His miracles, healing anyone, His raising people from the dead, or the numbers of people He preached to; He simply refers to the fact that He kept the disciples as the Father requested and that those disciples had come to trust in Him. The final phrase is John 17:26 is the clincher, *"that I myself may be in them."* Christ's image in us is the goal of all discipleship—the ultimate purpose of being on earth! It is *"Christ in you, the hope of glory"* (Colossians 1:27). ✘

I recently heard Jeff Vanderstelt share an insight on this truth, "You bear in your body the fullness of Christ to enable you to come into all He intended for you. You are invited to live the life He died to save you for."[1] What is the report of our time on earth we will make to the Father when we stand before Him? The questions in the Father's eyes will be "How did you keep the Kingdom gems I entrusted to you? Do they know my Son and the Holy Spirit? Did they know how to take what they were taught and teach that to the Kingdom gems I gave to them?" ✘

When people take priority over our work, they will never be discarded, but will be "loved" into character changes and eventually become like John Mark, who Paul at one time rejected (see Acts 15:38), and then later requested to join him: *"Get Mark and bring him with you, because he is helpful to me in my ministry"* (1 Timothy 4:11). It is an invitation to rascally saints to do life together and champion their families, passions, and talents as well as be released into their unique and divinely fashioned gift mix. Like Jesus, we respect and honor those God has given us without condition, and they, in turn, fulfill the Father's destiny for themselves and corporately with us as His local body. We get things done by *being* His Family; we don't *use* the Family to get things done.

The litmus test of relationship over the transactional "getting the business of the ministry done" is often found in leaders' meetings and in what happens between those meetings. Do leaders know each other's hearts? Do they meet socially, for fun, and for prayer? Do they know each other's stories, champion them, guard them, and walk with them through the painful and disappointing seasons of their lives? Do they function in cooperation or in competition? Are they being assigned responsibilities, asked to volunteer to fulfill a needed task, or are they being skillfully released into their God-given gifts? Are meetings taken up with business, ignoring one of their own sitting there absorbed in personal pain, or do we first check in with each other, loving one another as the first step in everything we do? ✗

When conforming to the pastor's or leader's vision is the basis of unity, we undervalue the people of God entrusted to us. They become like replaceable cogs in a machine. The result is almost always disastrous. If Jesus called His disciples His "friends," then it is both possible and imperative that we embrace the same relationship with those we are called to work together with in our families and communities. And I don't mean just friendship like the world thinks of it—like a group getting together to BBQ before the big game or those you hang out with to be social—I mean friendship like the covenant-bond David and Jonathan shared together. The dedication that we don't just separate because we disagree, but we will fight through to truth together, dedicated to each other because we are dedicated to Christ. (Again, this is a topic we will touch more on in Part Two.)

Don't get me wrong, there is a lot of work to do and it is a joy serving the Lord to equip the saints and accomplish the expansion of the Kingdom in our churches and cities. But in the process of doing that, we can't forget that the whole nature of the Kingdom is people-oriented, inclusive, and about the fruit *they* bear, not the number of programs a church runs efficiently or the money that comes in each week. Leaders who reach their mid-forties and have not been detoxed from the "drivenness of achievement" will either experience damage from the resulting fallout, or will submit to the Father's beautiful journey in maturing as His sons and daughters—a far better option than being slaves to *the* vision" we must accomplish at all costs.

The revelation that church needs to be relational runs counter to almost all the information on leadership that is out there for ministers. It's a tough switch, not because minsters aren't "people people," but because cultivating relationship takes time and is hard to quantify—and our modern world likes to use things that are more easily measured as a gauge for "success." Quick church growth in numbers of attendees each week or dollars brought in look like signs of life and can easily be mistaken for fruitfulness— and don't misunderstand, they are things that are important to the lifeblood of a church that will last—but we have to put first things first and see what such numbers are built upon. At the same time, the quality of foundational relationships in both the church leadership team and the general congregation are much more difficult to measure. All the same, there are also much more important things to the mission of being the church that God has called us to than numbers alone, as well as much more telling measures for how solidly a church will remain relevant into the future.

NOW WHAT?

Question #1: Is your heart closed, partially open, or open to any of the primary people in your life? How aware are you that they have been given to you by the Father to love as He loved you? Have you ever put your tasks above the needs of those around you? Ask the Holy Spirit to reveal any areas of your heart that are resistant to seeing those around you as He sees them.

Question #2: Are you a part of a team of friends or a cluster of "church workers"? Do you know each other's stories? How often do you pray for each other, pray together, study the Scriptures together, and listen to God for direction?

> **Exercise:** Jesus established the pattern for expanding the Kingdom. Meditate on John 15:15 and ask the Lord to show you any new alignment He wants to bring to you.

Question #3: Do you regularly practice "hearing the Lord" for affirmation and guidance with the primary people in your life?

> **Exercise**: Many of our elderships and pastoral teams have benefited immensely from reading, discussing, and applying the principles found in Ruth Haley Barton's book, *Pursuing the Will of God Together*. I highly recommend you and your team increase your "listening to God" skills by interacting with this very salient book. Don't be in a hurry to deconstruct unhealthy relationships and decision-making patterns. This will take some months.

Question #4: Have you asked the Lord to give you conviction on anything you are thinking (mindsets, theologies, etc.) or practicing that did not originate from His Word or direct instruction? Have you simply been relying on other models of church or "leaning on your own understanding"? If you answer "yes" to any of these questions, ask the Spirit to reveal what response He is requiring of you. Take adequate time personally to let the Holy Spirit lead you into a season of hearing His correction and responding to it. You will be healed and prepared to move forward.

WHAT HAVE WE CREATED?

*By the grace God has given me, I laid a foundation
as a wise builder, and someone else is building on it.
But each one should build with care.
For no one can lay any foundation other than
the one already laid, which is Jesus Christ.*

—1 CORINTHIANS 3:10-11

Not long after the "under the table" episode, the Lord gave me another, rather bazaar picture for the Believers leadership team as I was praying for them. I saw a large circus tent and to my amazement, there were the four illustrious leaders of Believers Church all acting as ringmasters, replete with top hats and showing off a rascally little circus monkey. The cavorting monkey had the crowd mesmerized by its performance and the audience was raucously clapping their hands, yelling, and asking for more. The ringmasters were visibly frustrated, though. They were having a difficult time bringing the monkey under control. The monkey wasn't only dominating the audience, it was dominating them!

Realizing this, I looked closer at the monkey. As I did, I noticed a dark gleam in its eyes. "Huh," I observed, "that little monkey is evil." The whole performance was a charade. It wasn't to entertain the crowd, it was to keep the ringmasters occupied, thinking their "show" was a success because of the reaction of the audience—and therefore distracted from the real work they were supposed to be doing.

I remember thinking, "No wonder the team is not living 'heart to heart' with each other and is constantly on the verge of exhaustion." I had a hunch they were being driven to perform for the church because that's what good pastors do—make people happy by entertaining them and meeting their perceived needs. I was soon to find out from them how they had become ringmasters to a "church circus" none of them realized was controlling them.

A week or so later I was back at Believers with the crew working through an exercise I'd conceived in response to my circus monkey vision. I asked them to take sticky notes and write the names of whatever programs and activities they were responsible for and then to put them on the big wall of their meeting room.

After nearly an hour, we stepped back and looked at the wall, covered floor to ceiling with sticky notes. It was staggering. There had to be at least a small hint of pride at all they were accomplishing. It was impressive.

As we stood there, I asked, "Now, which of these did God tell you to start?"

Everyone looked around at each other blankly, then back at the wall, then at me.

"But this is what churches do, isn't it?" Susan asked. "People come because we meet needs through the programs we run every week."

"Maybe," I said, "but which of *these*"—I said, pointing their attention back to the wall—"did God actually tell *you* to begin? Which ones are bringing more of God into your midst?"

They all just stood and stared at the wall.

"I think we should pray again," Roger said.

Everyone nodded their heads.

A CHURCH VISION DOESN'T LAST BEYOND YOU IF YOU DON'T RECEIVE IT TOGETHER

For years I felt the pressure as a leader to be the one to supply the vision for the church or ministry I was a part of. I had to have some big inspirational vision from which all we did as a church flowed. I've frequently heard God's people say in frustration, "What we need around here is a clear vision of what we are doing." What that usually means is "I need to know what I am supposed to be doing—what activities and responsibilities should I devote myself to? I need to know where I fit."

We should have a vision, but it shouldn't be based around the "ministries" or programs the church needs to direct, or some certain kind of impact we're supposed to have in our communities. Those are secondary things, at best, not the main event. Our vision instead should be Jesus and His Kingdom, pure and simple: *"looking to Jesus, the founder and perfecter of our faith"* (Hebrews 12:2 ESV). (In Part Two, we'll dig deeper into what God's vision is for His Kingdom Church and how the Gospel itself is the vision God has outlined for us. For now, let's just talk about vision in its more traditional sense.)

Today, I believe the Lord is deconstructing the presuppositions of most of our endeavors. We have become immersed into a formula of "The leaders get the vision, which then defines our tasks. As we do our task, if things go well, we organize our relationships around getting the work done together and, maybe, become friends in the process. And if things don't go well, at least we can say, 'Well, the *work* got done." (I call this the "Vision–Tasks–Relationship" construct, or "V-T-R" for short.) This is, at best, an old wineskin (like Old Testament old).

What I believe God is calling us to today looks more like the pattern Jesus laid out for us: "Let's come together to hear God's instruction over the Word and in prayer. As we do, let's join together in heart and mission. Do we know what He wants and what each of us cares about? What are the shared values that bind us into a community?" Then, out of that, we will "pray and stumble" after a vision of what God desires for our church, each supplying our part of the puzzle. That allows us to consider each of our gifts and callings and see where those fit into accomplishing that shared vision. This then gives us a framework for exercising and growing our gifts as we walk out the vision as friends and experience the appropriate blessings of God as a result. (This I call the "Relationships (and shared values)–Vision (of and from Jesus)–Gifts" construct, or "R-V-G" for short.))

Though vision is key to each of these constructs, its source and nature in each is quite different.

In "Vision–Task–Relationship," we often see *the* leader "get *the* vision" for the church, line up the tasks and roles, then deploy the people into fulfilling *the leader's* vision. This is a strong reflection of an Old Testament leadership pattern: like Moses going up the mountain to get the plan for the people of Israel. In the New Covenant, the construct goes through a major renovation: everyone has at least a partial responsibility to hear from God for themselves, their families, and their communities. (Note that I'm not saying the "one man" vision model means the leader didn't hear God; I think they often do, but they often hear it alone. They should bring their "God-given vision" before others to confirm it, pray it through, and establish unity in expressing it. Any word and direction from God should come through accountability and con-firmation of elders and those recognized as being more spiritually mature in the congregation.) ⌁

When Nehemiah had people laying bricks to form Jerusalem's new wall, the purpose was not only to reconstruct a wall, but to also rebuild a people. A shared vision provides a guide for unity—something to rally around—not just a task list of work to be accom-plished. It's not about something to *do,* but something to *become.* The vision is really secondary to the unity formed through getting and making it happen *together.* The vision still gets done—and the vision is a good thing—but each of us also grows tremendously towards who God has called us to be in the process. No one should remain the same—or regress in their relationship with God and/or each other—when everyone is engaged in the mission of the church as one. ⌁

In the "vision first" construct we often hear, "Get the work done, fulfill the vision!" If you subtract vision and task from this first equation, or one or both aren't fulfilled, where does that leave the people? Probably discouraged and disenfranchised, especially if the vision is never realized or they are not sure of their real role in the overall plan. (Or what if the leader who had the vision is sud-denly gone? Then you end up with something like what Believers was experiencing—a congregation chasing a vision that had no foundation and "doing church" to keep the church alive, trans-forming neither lives nor impacting their city. After all, a family is made up of fathers and mothers, sons and daughters, children and grandchild—you don't run it like a corporation.) ⌁

Too often people's acceptance into their roles within the church has been on the basis of loyalty to the leadership. If you aren't in line with their vision, you're either removed or ignored. Disagreement can even be seen by some leaders as rebellion.

There's no creation of unity; there's only conformity. Vision alone cannot produce heart-level harmony.

In the "Relationships–Vision–Gifts" framework, people's hearts are preserved no matter what happens to the church or ministry vision. They know they are loved unconditionally no matter how they perform or how "loyal" they are to the church leadership. In fact, frisky dialogue and disagreement over the vision is key not just to getting the vision right, but to melding hearts together through hammering out its details. There has to be mutual "loyalty"—perhaps "trust" is a better word—so that healthy conflict is both welcomed and a positive force in the local body. In this way, we relate to one another as a family that unconditionally loves each other, seeks to understand the vision Jesus has for the family in general (the biblical vision), and then champions the God-given gifts each individual contributes towards fulfilling the vision. As this happens, spiritual authority is a byproduct not a pecking order and is released in the process of fulfilling the tasks necessary to accomplish the vision from Jesus.

If individuals are acting as knuckleheads and can't seem to keep from causing trouble, they become candidates for "intense discipleship," not discarded for failing to comply with the leadership's vision. There's little to no "hiring and firing" as usually happens when people have to perform to accomplish the vision of a leader. (Except of course for huge breaches of trust like infidelity, embezzlement, or criminal activities, but that's not what we are talking about here.) In the "relationship first" construct, you don't really need to go looking for people to fill roles inside the church from outside of the church—it is much more likely that "home-grown" leaders emerge to take oversight of the ministry responsibilities needed in the church rather than hiring outsiders to fill "staff" vacancies. Loving spiritual fathers don't discard sons like executives discard their underlings. That's not how family works.

We see this demonstrated in Acts 13, when the leaders of the church were ministering to the Lord and the Spirit spoke and gave direction, vision, and assigned new roles.

> Now in the church at Antioch there were prophets and teachers: Barnabas, Simeon called Niger, Lucius of Cyrene, Manaen (who had been brought up with Herod the tetrarch) and Saul. While they were worshiping the Lord and fasting, the Holy Spirit said, "Set apart for me Barnabas and Saul for the work to which I have called them." So after they had fasted and prayed, they placed their hands on them and sent them off.
>
> —ACTS 13:1-3

They didn't appear to be in a "vision meeting," but a "worship service." They simply came together and the Spirit spoke. It was corporately hearing God together that led the church into the great first-century explosion of Christianity across the Roman Empire that happened after Saul became Paul and the first apostle who hadn't walked with Jesus.

In the conference of Jerusalem in Acts 15:1-20, the first big disagreement of the early church was hammered out, and those in attendance heard the wisdom and put their stamp of approval on the final consensus. Leaders were speaking their opinions and leading out of their gifts, but they were ultimately moving in "one accord," not being pressured solely by the power of the apostolic presence in their midst. The passage ends with the proclamation, *"It seemed good to the Holy Spirit and to us"* (Acts 15:28). He, the Spirit, is the validator of all direction being issued from heaven's throne. It's always best to lead with what He thinks.

BECOMING A VISION PEOPLE

We need to be careful not to create a network of busy saints who aren't necessarily becoming disciples of Jesus. The anemia of some believers makes them dependent on doing church work to slake their need for approval, but often leaves them ineffective in bringing the presence of God into their everyday lives at home and work. This dichotomous tension has worn God's people out and left leaders frustrated with the lack of spiritual depth and hunger in their congregations.

When Jesus first called disciples in Matthew 4:19, He invited them to *"Come, follow me . . . and I will make you fishers of men"* (NASB). The invitation came in the following order:

1) *"Come"*: an invitation to leave your current dependencies and allegiances,

2) *"Follow me"*: go on a journey of investigation with me (Jesus), and then,

3) *"I will make you. . ."*: I (Jesus) will transform you by being with you in order for you to realize your destiny.

These disciples were being offered the opportunity to be made capable of fulfilling God's vision for their lives. It was a call first to a relationship and then second to a mission: displacing darkness with light and establishing His Kingdom supreme over all others. Again, people before enterprise!

I have spent a massive amount of my life sitting in leaders' and elders' meetings. The most successful have been those where, after issues were discussed, they were parked, and God was inquired for clarity on the rightness, timing, and specifics of the thoughts on and plans for addressing each.

In contrast, too often leadership teams are comprised of gifted men and women who bring their business or professional acumen into the equation without surrendering all aspects of decision making to King Jesus and the Spirit's guidance in the affairs of *His* Church. Their agendas are organized according to the Ol' "sandwich" approach: *A quick prayer at the beginning and a quicker prayer at the end, with all the bologna in between.*

Overconfidence in our intellects, experience, or our positions and prominence is a sure way to invite ultimate failure in the works of our hands. We must rely on Jesus, even when the way forward seems self-evident to our natural minds. We are under-shepherds who were never conscripted to run a church organization, but rather were entrusted by the Chief Shepherd to know and execute His will for His people. ✄

I recently asked an elder of a local church how often their leadership team prayed and studied Scripture together to ascertain God's will and direction for their church. He paled; the concept seemed foreign to him. All I got was a blank look.

To live under the blessing of a Kingdom-centric church, we as leaders have to surrender to the Head, "leaning not on our own understanding, in all our ways acknowledging Him," and letting Him "make our paths straight." (See Proverbs 3:5.) To do otherwise is absurd. After all, we are "headless" without Him!

GETTING BACK TO THE HEART OF CHURCH

After our time of prayer and discussion, the Believers team realized there were a number of activities they had embraced because "that's what the church was doing when we got here." Some they knew the Lord had started, but they were quite sure

His blessing was no longer on many of the others. They then boldly began identifying certain programs and activities that focused solely on pleasing people and meeting needs they'd never been told to meet. What were the things they were doing that were bringing people closer to God? Slowly they began to separate the wheat from the chaff.*

As I watched them moving sticky notes around and making a small pile of rejects on a table behind them, I realized they were no longer sitting under the table, but were face to face, working together under the headship of Jesus. I also realized the circus tent was coming down, the ringmasters were fading into the background, and that berserk little monkey was no longer entertaining the crowds. That day began the slow disengagement from a corporate church framework to a more biblical and relationally-rooted partnership in being a spiritual family. ✗

After that visit, I began rotating into Tulsa three to four times a year to meet with the core team and walk with them through the long, deliberate journey from chaos to clarity and from dysfunction to healing. Though they seemed unsettled, I could see they were a team that the Lord Himself had put together—and as I saw that, I fell in love with them anew. We were all in need of the Lord's presence and revelation, and the process of pursuing answers to our questions not only knit our hearts together, but also gave each of us new perspective on what God was trying to do within our own and each other's lives. At the same time, Believers leadership was gradually transforming from a religious hierarchy into a shared leadership journey.

---

* I'm going to tell you here, that if you are interested in winning a popularity contest with your church, this approach will not work. If you are out to be "well pleasing" to the Lord, however, this is a sacrifice you'll have to make.

Gyle once said of this, "These changes kept us humble and dependent on Jesus and eventually broke the circus mentality we had lived under since our inception." They came to realize that they didn't have to engage in the relentless pursuit of a "workable model" for being the successful, corporate American church that everyone seemed to expect them to be. It led them back to Acts 1:13, 14—*"When they arrived, they went upstairs to the room where they were staying. . . . They all joined together constantly in prayer"*— right where the Holy Spirit found—and *founded*—the Church on the day of Pentecost. It was in this same posture of praying and ministering to the Lord that the Spirit Himself spoke major direction in an environment of relational unity throughout the rest of the book of Acts.

It taught the Believers Church team to pray over every major issue to get the Lord's direction for His church. They came to call it "prayer and stumbling," an apt term for moving from one paradigm of church to another. They'd pray, they'd try something, it wouldn't work, and then they'd pray again until they were sure what they were doing was inspired by God or they'd correct it if they found it wasn't.

The church had been riddled by a performance mentality at every level. The team felt the Lord showing them that the inoculation against such proud and self-serving attitudes could only be the presence of the Lord Himself in every affair of the church. In the coming years, they faithfully cultivated a "culture of presence" where the presence of the Lord became the determining factor for whether an event was successful or not, rather than human expectations and traditions. The result was that the Spirit was changing the leaders and the people, not through "sexy" activities that seemed like good ideas—nor through powerful sermons, slick worship, or gleaming personalities—but through His presence!

Believers Church was moving away from being a church corporation—run by a board of directors and a "CEO" pastor—to being a corporate church—a body of believers who heard Jesus's instruction and pieced His vision for them together as a family. Jesus was truly being honored by sons and daughters, and brothers and sisters, as the Head of their church.

NOW WHAT?

Question #1: Do you operate on the Vision (from leader)/Task/ Relationship paradigm or according to the Relationship/Vision (from God)/Gifts paradigm?

Exercise: Take ample time to discuss your own modus operandi for making decisions and from where you ultimately get your direction for making big decisions.

Exercise: Reflect on the difference between putting people in "slots" to get jobs done vs. discovering people's God-given gifts and deploying them into the vision God has revealed to you together for that person. Are you more organizational or relational in your approach to training and deploying staff and leaders?

Question #2: Are the foundations your church or ministry have been built upon based on God's revealed pattern from Scripture—or on the traditions and ideas passed down to you? Are there any activities in your church that were not initiated by God's direction? Are there other activities whose time is up and yet continue to exist?

Exercise: Perform your own sticky notes exercise. Simply put each personal and ministry activity you are engaged in on a sticky note and pray over each, asking the Lord to confirm if it was truly His idea or yours. For those that remain, ask the Lord if it is to continue. You will also want to ask Him what is missing on the notes that He wants you to add to your calling.

Question #3: What, if any, Scriptures and materials have you intentionally engaged in to determine what God's plan is for your church ministry or business endeavors? What biblical framework has God revealed to you? What non-biblical frameworks have you embraced, if any, and what is the Lord's opinion of those? What will you do about them?

BECOMING A BODY

For just as each of us has one body with many members, and
these members do not all have the same function, so in Christ we,
though many, form one body, and each member belongs
to all the others. We have different gifts, according to the
grace given to each of us.

—ROMANS 12:4-6

As the Believers leaders became friends hammering out a common vision together, they began to wonder about where each of them fit in the grand scheme of accomplishing it. That led to a process of determining their individual gift motivations in order to reshape their efforts around each of their personal callings. Their daily focus became less about the maintenance of church activities and departments and more about "what is God calling each of us to do?"

Congregations tend expect their "pastor" to do most of the pulpit work, but in this process, the team recognized that Gyle had a stronger teaching gift than Roger. Roger, on the other hand, had a strong trans-local convening gift both in Believers Church and in the city—he was a better "ambassador," so to speak. Mark flowed more in the prophetic gift and excelled in his counseling role, while Susan, as the consummate friend, trainer, and organizer, was adept at overseeing the life group leaders. Their diversity made a nice four-pillared base, but they needed more help, not just from their staff, but from fathers and mothers in the congregation as well.

When Roger took over as the senior pastor in 2001, there were no "resident" elders in the church. He invited an advisory group from the outside to function as elders for a time, but they needed to establish a permanent, in-house eldership as a spiritual infrastructure. The first elders' board met once a month and heard the reports of the core team members. They were informed, but not engaged very deeply in the ministry of the church—these team leaders were not much more than a sounding board. Believers needed elders that were more directly invested in the fabric of relationships within their body.

Still referred to as the "pastoral team," Roger, Gyle, Mark, and Susan redefined themselves as "vocational elders" and merged with the rest of the eldership as it was. This meant all the decision for the direction and operation of the church would no longer come from just "paid staff" but out of the eldership. This removed the distance between those who "worked in the church offices" and "those who sat in the pews." Once this "partition" came down, questions arose about what it really meant to be an elder. (Jesus was about to perform another major overhaul.) More assumptions needed to be deconstructed so that they could be put back together more biblically and soundly.

More time-honored traditional walls were about to fall.

WE ARE ALL "MINISTERS" WE ALL HAVE A MISSION

I vividly remember the shock of answering a knock on my door in Amsterdam and seeing none other than Jack Hayford standing there with a large grin on his face. I had met Jack—Pastor of Church on the Way in Van Nuys, California and a nationally recognized speaker—on numerous occasions during the Leaders' Conferences in Mount Hermon, California in the 1970s. He simply said, "Anna and I couldn't be in Amsterdam and not bring a greeting to our brothers and sisters in YWAM."

We spent the next two days hosting the Hayfords—praying, talking, and laughing while the ladies fulfilled their perfunctory "shopping ministries." Jack was a father-in-the-Lord to me, but I never felt a clergical distance or a "Let me instruct you in the ways of the Lord, sonny" attitude. He was devoid of the latter and lived at sea level with me for those two days—he always had. When he left, I remember praying, "Let me be like that when I'm older— no pretense; no leader/follower split—just brothers in the Lord." Because he demanded no perks that authority usually required, I gave him authority in my life by virtue of the honor I knew he deserved.

The early church never entertained the idea of their leaders being a professional, educated, and superior group of individuals. Although John refers to the Nicolaitan Heresy in the book of Revelations, the clergy-laity split only came into full bloom around the third century under Constantine. When the church become Roman, meeting "house to house" was forbidden and the basilica was anointed as the formal place of worship. The leaders of the basilicas were set apart from the people and given positions of honor and preeminence. (Of course, things for the Celts in Ireland were a little different because of Patrick, but that's a different story.) These new church leaders—and they alone—were "appointed of God" to tell their "uninformed" congregants what the Bible said. They soon became intermediaries between God and the masses. Even the Reformation didn't entirely eradicate this strong line between appointed leaders and God's precious sheep.

Is there a difference in those called to lead and those who aren't? Yes, there are different callings and functions in the Body of Christ, but we begin all relationships in God's family as equals in value, knowing that all are loved by the Father and all are able to—and are expected to—hear the voice of the Chief Shepherd. This goes for husbands and wives, parents and children, leaders and followers, Jew and Gentile. As Paul wrote:

> But God has put the body together, giving greater honor to the parts that lacked it, so that there should be no division in the body, but that its parts should have equal concern for each other.
>
> —1 CORINTHIANS 12:24-25

and

> There is neither Jew nor Gentile, neither slave nor free, nor is there male and female, for you are all one in Christ Jesus.
>
> —GALATIANS 3:28

There was no longer to be any middle management between God and man—no more "we'll go up on the mountain to hear God and then come back to tell you what He said." All now had a direct line to Jesus, and through Jesus, to the Father and the Holy Spirit.

> For there is one God and one mediator between God and mankind, the man Christ Jesus.
>
> —1 TIMOTHY 2:5

The cross of Christ leveled the playing field for all human relationships. This enables us to see each other in the light of the value the Father assigns to each person we meet, well before their behavior or "authority" steps in to differ. In this, we each become responsible to hear God for ourselves and for our own God-given missions, even though we walk them out together.

Paul's magnificent testimony (beginning in 1 Timothy 1:12) was from a man that realized his selection by Jesus as an apostle to the Gentiles was due to one peculiar fact: he was the worst person God could find. How's that for a leadership selection requirement? He was noted as the "chief of sinners" (see 1 Timothy 1:15) so that God could lavish His mercy on him and display His unlimited patience through Paul's life for all to see how God functions and redeems. A leader's life is to be a display of his need for God and the subsequent "rescue jobs" designed to reveal God's mercy and redemption through that leader. ✗

Oh, and what is the fundamental prerequisite and mark of *apostleship*? The reception of mercy and the greatness of God that results in the surrendered life of the leader—not power, authority, anointed teaching, and/or dazzling testimonies. These things are not the goal of leadership, but the fruit of brokenness which is the ultimate goal or proof of the calling and blessing of God. Again, Jesus is our example.

> For we do not have a high priest who is unable to empathize with our weaknesses, but we have one who has been tempted in every way, just as we are—yet he did not sin. Let us then approach God's throne of grace with confidence, so that we may receive mercy and find grace to help us in our time of need.
> —HEBREWS 4:15-16

Leaders in the Church are not exempt from severe difficulties, but are given the privilege of living through the pain of life in the presence of God's people so that God gets the credit for the image of Christ that emerges out of those dark tombs. Ministry success often clouds the imperative to "take up your cross and follow me." (See Matthew 16:24; Mark 8:34.) The cross and the subsequent resurrection is the insurance that only God gets the credit for the fruit of a leader's life. There is no room for personal advancement and human boasting—all boasting is in the redeeming power of our amazing God. The cross of Christ is the ultimate instrument of deconstruction! ✄

Paul mused that the gifts of apostleship were to be left for dead, stoned, have boats sink under you, to be misunderstood, bitten by snakes, as well as experience other example of extreme "bad days." (See 2 Corinthians 11:23-30.) Why was this? Because he and the other apostles knew their calling was to *always carry around in our body the death of Jesus, so that the life of Jesus may also be revealed*" (2 Corinthians 4:10).

A priest, by definition, stands before God and man to bring the affairs of the "footstool" to the "throne's" attention. Jesus the High Priest provided the ultimate sacrifice, opened the way to the Father, sat down in power, then anointed each of us, as Peter declared, "a royal priesthood." (See 1 Peter 2:9.) All Christian leaders—in the business world as well as the Church—blaze the way for other priests to learn how to function in every domain of culture. Paul invited the churches to imitate him as he imitated Christ. Brilliant! What's happening here? The image of Christ, our pattern, is being passed on from fathers to sons and from generation to generation. ✄

What Paul had to say on this isn't quite finished. To complete the priestly paradigm, he instructed Timothy to teach the church "*that petitions, prayers, intercession and thanksgiving be made for all people. . . . This is good, and pleases God our Savior, who wants all people to be saved and to come to a knowledge of the truth"* (1 Tim 2:1, 3-4). Paul is calling the whole priesthood, not just those appointed leaders, into the high calling of dispensing the will of the King over every earthly authority and over every human heart—completely inclusive of all of earth's residents. ⚰

Heaven wants its kids back and the Father wants all inferior kings to know that His son, Jesus, reigns. This was why Paul was so insistent on going to Rome—because it was high time that Caesar knew that there was a new King in town—and it wasn't him.

Do you see the beauty and inclusive nature of all of God's people accepting the mandate as priests in dispensing the heart of the King to every human heart in this broken world? Paul was an apostle and priest before God, commissioned to create other priests who knew how to span heaven and earth under the Kingdom mandate. This is the hill we leaders in church must be willing to die on.

Likewise, Jesus appointed leaders to "equip" the "priesthood of all believers" (see Ephesians 4:11-16) and built His church on a plurality of elders and leaders, spiritual fathers and mothers, who would oversee the affairs of the people of God. In a plurality, there most often is a key facilitating leader amongst the elders, and a beautiful array of diverse giftings, some more publicly displayed than others. We see this in Paul's last visit to Jerusalem where most of the apostles seemed to have dispersed, though James was present and appeared to be the leader amongst the elders, *"The next day Paul and the rest of us went to see James, and all the elders were present"* (Acts 21:18). They go on to make a corporate recommendation to Paul on how to navigate the shark infested waters of Jerusalem's "Judaizers" and local religious leaders. (This is the same James that facilitated the conversation of leaders at the Jerusalem Council in Acts 15.) ⚰

It was clear to the early church apostles and the church elders that they were not in need of a "star," a "head honcho," or a "senior pastor"—they already had one! Jesus, the Head of the Church, the Apostle of our Faith, the Bishop of our souls, the True Prophet, the Master Teacher, and supplier of all life to His Body, the Church. These leaders were content to form an assembly of elders and overseers who were responsible to get direction from the Head and dispense it in love and clarity to the growing members of His Body. It was not so much authority as responsibility, similar to that of parents caring for a child who they love and want to raise to become healthy, contributing members of the Kingdom and loving parents themselves.

If you read Ephesians 4:11-16 carefully, you will see that the traditional "offices" we refer to as ministers—apostles, prophets, evangelists, pastors, and teachers—aren't really "ministers" at all—they are "equippers" of the ministers—they are gifts to the Body of Christ. We should not call the people in the pews "members," we should call them what they really are: *ministers.* These are the dreamers of God's dreams—people on mission—and the fivefold gifts of Ephesians 4:11 aren't there to rule and reign, they are there to make sure the ministers in the pews have everything they need to fulfill the missions God has sent them on. We are solo agents either, thus the concept we will talk about again and again throughout this book is of the Church being a family of "families on mission."

This mindset should cause us to re-evaluate the use of the word "ministry." In the clergy/laity tradition, clergy were the ministers who were called to do the "ministry." It is not uncommon for people to say, "I have a call to the ministry," or "I can't wait to quit my job so I can enter 'the ministry.'" Yes, there are those that are called to full or part-time engagement in equipping and leading God's people. Yes, they do have a ministry, but that's not exclusively what that word means. Those of us they are equipping are also ministers in our homes, workplaces, cities, and nations. It's when we put "the" in front of "ministry" and we speak of it as a noun—a role for a select few—rather than as an active verb—"ministering" or "serving"—that we get confused. *All* are called to be equipped in ministry in some form or another, while a few have the ministry of equipping other ministers—those called as specific gifts to the Body in Ephesians 4:11: *"the apostles, the prophets, the evangelists, the pastors and teachers"* as well as the "under-shepherds" (the elders) in every church.

This is how the Church, the family of God, grows. This is not the "church growth" that was prevalent in past decades, growth that was measured by numbers and activities. Paul explained that the "equippers" (again see the list in Ephesians 4:11) existed

> to equip his people for works of service, so that the body of Christ may be built up until we all reach unity in the faith and in the knowledge of the Son of God and become mature, attaining to the whole measure of the fullness of Christ.
>
> —EPHESIANS 4:12-13

Growth in Christ and doing His work are the measure of Kingdom growth. The clergy/laity distinctions in the Church bear the responsibility—in many case—of growing the Church institution, but leaving the people feeling less than *"being heirs together of the grace of life"* (1 Peter 3:7 KJV). Today we seem to have leaders focused on maintaining and supporting the Church as an *organization*, which has the potential of turning into that three-ring circus run by the evil monkey. We suddenly get more concerned about raising money to repair the roof or replace the air conditioning than empowering the people in the pews to be Christ in the community. (Not that roofs don't need repair and air conditioning doesn't need to be replaced now and again, but it's a matter of planning so we can keep first things first.)

All of God's people, leaders, and saints alike are equal in value but different and unique in calling and function for the building up of the Church in love. Operating within roles and on authority alone—a church divided into "leaders" and "followers"—never truly works. When a leader operates out of a sense of entitlement due to their positional role or displays an air of authority, they are more likely to inspire the creation of followers than other leaders. They will not likely see the potential in younger believers, nor champion them and become committed to helping them fulfill the dreams God has placed in their hearts.

This creates resentment and spiritual constipation in the Body of Christ—gifts are squelched and generational divisions ever hamper the maturing of believers. Rather than deconstruction and reconstruction every couple of decades, they throw everything out and start over again—each new generation rejecting what was built by the previous—a strategy that is good neither for the wine, the wineskins, nor the vineyard in developing a thirst-quenching "product."

CREATING AN "INCLUSIVE" UNITY

I was concerned that Believers Church was not properly aligned with the biblical injunction to appoint elders and train them to oversee the affairs of the church. After much discussion and biblical reflection, the Believers leaders began to go much deeper with the group of elders they had appointed. Gyle taught a series entitled "What is an elder?" that generated a heated and healthy discussion on the nature and practice of what elders did and didn't do as well as who they should be. Traditions were being challenged, and they were moving forward into a shared understanding of the biblical order in the household of God. That biblical framework helped them understand that if elders were to oversee the affairs of the church, they would have to be engaged in various domains of oversight commensurate with their God-given gifts. Various elders began populating the ministry "clusters" that included the core team, staff members, and various leaders in the church with gifts in discipleship, mission and training, etc. Elders were never meant to be advisors, but actively engaged leaders according to their giftings—compassionate overseers in their respective "fields" as they looked after the "affairs of the church."

During this process of examining the Scriptures together, the vocational elders—Roger, Gyle, Susan, and Mark—were impressed more deeply by the biblical significance and imperative of elders in the church. After a couple of years of biblical reflection, they realized that they and the greater elder board had inherited a different vision for the church. There were still vestiges of the church organization as the core of their activities rather than seeing the church as a Kingdom people scattered throughout their community. They all had a genuine love for one another, but weren't "of the same mind" about the mission of the church.

So the vocational elders invited all of the eldership to go through a biblical studies course together. Roger later reported, "Every one of the elder couples said 'yes' and we've been searching the scriptures together weekly on Wednesday nights ever since."

As members of the eldership have come and gone over the years, the current group seems to be hand-picked by the Lord and are now engaged in various aspects of discipling people from house church oversight—what they call "life groups"—to counseling, prayer, healing, and prophetic ministry to the ongoing process of training newly emerging leaders. The greatest testimony to their being true elders is their tenacious commitment to pray together for the church, its people, and its affairs, while also being dedicated to hearing the voice and desires of Jesus first and foremost.

This deconstruction/reconstruction process began to release both the team and the congregation from the pressure of "playing" church as defined by anything other than what God was doing in their hearts and who He was inspiring them to be as a result. There was a tangible shift as Roger, Gyle, Susan, Mark, and other leaders began to operate in their gifts rather than just fulfilling positions and roles. The eldership became more energized, more supportive of each other, and more unified as a team. The effects in the church were apparent as the performance mentality was being evicted and people were beginning to feel loved unconditionally and released into their own gifts and missions, no longer simply performing church functions. ✗

The natural result of discovering and championing the gifts and callings in the eldership was that individuals grew in their passion to see the church experience the same freedom. This new impetus finally opened the door to being able to focus on creating the "discipleship culture" Gyle had first asked Pete and I about some eight years before.

NOW WHAT?

Question 1: How do you resonate with Paul's statement that he was an apostle because he was the chief sinner and selected primarily to reveal the redeeming nature of God's character through his life? What is the basis of your leadership? Have you had feelings of entitlement due to your "position"?

> **Exercise:** Consider the question, "for what purpose did God call me?" Note the difference in the answers between being called to "be" something or to "do" something. Yes, Paul was called to do the work of an apostle to the Gentiles, but his main motivation was that he was called to be like Jesus and model that to the church. *"Be imitators of me, as I am of Christ"* (1 Corinthians 11:1).

Question #2: Do you see yourself as the "minister" and the people of God as the "members"? What do you believe the Scriptures teach regarding leaders as being "equippers" of the "ministers"? How could that become more evident in your thinking and practice in your ministry?

Ask the Spirit to reveal God's plan for the Church and Kingdom from Scripture. A major ingredient in this mindset shift is a fresh understanding of the revealed plan of God from His Word together with your team. Too much solo study will lead to opinions and conflicting information without the transformational effects God brings when He reveals the understanding of His Word to a multi-gifted huddle of friends.

> **Resources:** There are many good resources you can avail yourself of, but I recommend the BILD studies, series III: *Unfolding the Great Commission* (Acts); *Laying Solid Foundations in the Gospel* (1 & 2 Thessalonians); *Catching God's Vision for the Church* (Ephesians); *Living in God's Household* (Pastoral Epistles). Find these and other excellent resources at store.BILD.org.

Question #3: What, if any, Scriptures and materials have you intentionally engaged in to determine what God's plan is for your church? What biblical framework has God revealed to you? What non-biblical frameworks have you embraced, if any, and what do you feel is the Lord's opinion of those as you reflect on them now?

Exercise: Ask the Spirit to reveal God's plan for the Church and Kingdom from Scripture. A major ingredient in this shift is a fresh understanding of the revealed plan of God from His Word in fellowship with your team or house group. Document how your thoughts change as you learn in concert with others you are connected with and trust.

DISCIPLES MAKING DISCIPLES

And the things you have heard me say in the presence
of many witnesses entrust to reliable people
who will also be qualified to teach others.

—2 TIMOTHY 2:2

Impressed by the injunction of Jesus to "go into all the world" to "make disciples" and "disciple nations" (see Matthew 20:19-20; Mark 16:15), the Believers team realized that most church training was falling short of equipping God's people for their work in their "worlds"—their neighborhoods and marketplaces both locally and trans-locally. Believers was doing "sacred" church work, but had viewed the everyday responsibilities of their members as "secular" endeavors. The realization that they had created this artificial division led them to begin an intentional search for a biblical framework for "making disciples" who engaged the culture, rather than just training up people to call themselves Christians. ⊂

Jesus was not a Christian, after all, and never asked us to make people Christians. The word was actually assigned to believers in Antioch (see Acts 11:26) and it is unclear what the source was— or whether it was meant for derision or as a simple descriptor of followers of Christ—"little christs." Up until then, followers of Jesus had simply been known as part of "The Way." (See Acts 9:2; 19:9, 23.)

Today, in my opinion, "Christian" has become too nebulous a term. Many who call themselves Christians are not *disciples* of Christ. It's become too much about what we believe and not enough about what we do and who we are becoming. We are too obsessed with the "point of sale" conversion experience of saying "the prayer" and don't pay enough attention to what it truly means to make Jesus Lord of our lives. Do we just "agree" with Jesus like a political platform, or are we actively working to be transformed into His image? (See 2 Corinthians 3:18.) The difference is huge.

This is the distinction Roger and the team wanted to make clear to their church, so they decided to go back to the Scriptures and see what the pattern was for the early church which the faith was so contagious. Is there something they did then that could be the key to creating a culture of disciples making disciples in the same way today?

GOING TO CHURCH IN THE FIRST CENTURY

The Church was birthed on the day of Pentecost as recorded in Acts 2. It was right in the midst of the rule of the Roman Empire over Israel. It was birthed surrounded by occupying forces. Not only that, but the Romans were famous for absorbing other cultures into their use of language and custom. In fact, the Greek word which we translate as *church—ekklesia—*was hijacked from Athens and incorporated into Roman society. The origins of this word give some interesting insights.

Within the [Greek] city-state *ekklesia* consisted of all the citizens who had retained their civil rights. The *ekklesia*'s powers were almost unlimited. It elected and dismissed magistrates and directed the policy of the city. It declared war, and it made peace. It negotiated and approved treaties and arranged alliances. It chose generals, assigned troops to different campaigns, raised the necessary money, and dispatched those troops from city to city. It was an assembly in which all members had equal right and duty. As the Roman Empire rose and supplanted the Greeks, the Romans adopted the term into Latin. . . .

(*Ekklesia* described anything that might be happening within a community that requires an assembly. This assembly could be social, governmental, or religious. It could be legal or illegal. . . .

The concept that distinguishes biblical usage from classical Greek usage is the emphasis that it is *God's* assembly. *Ekklesia*, therefore, means "God's people, called together by God to listen to or act for God." The emphasis is on the action of God, which has the force of a summons (as from a judge). The biblical *ekklesia*—the church—is a body of people, not so much assembling because they chose to come together, but assembling because God called them to himself—*not assembling to share their own thoughts and opinions, but to listen to the voice of God.*[2]

Some would have us believe that the *ekklesia* is simply those "called out" by God to be His Church and that there is no framework that organizes the *ekklesia*. Paul makes it clear to the Ephesian elders in Acts 20:28 that there is a need for fathers and mothers to step up and guide the younger: *"Keep watch over yourselves and all the flock of which the Holy Spirit has made you overseers. Be shepherds of the church of God, which he bought with his own blood.*" Here we can see the "assembly of Saints" needs to be shepherded, have overseers (elders) and apostles, prophets, evangelists, pastors, and teachers as equippers of the *ekklesia* (back to Ephesians 4:11-13), both in the universal Church and the local church on the corner. The *ekklesia* of God was to be an assembly "called out" of the world's system by God to be His "called together" family, a community on Kingdom mission (we'll discuss this concept of "being on mission" in more detail in the next section). It doesn't give us permission to construct the church willy nilly or to "do what is right in our own eyes." (See Proverbs 12:15.)

In Hebrews 12:22-23, the writer describes *ekklesia*'s scope and supremacy on earth:

> But you have come to Mount Zion, to the city of the living God, the heavenly Jerusalem. You have come to thousands upon thousands of angels in joyful assembly, to the church [ekklesia] of the firstborn, whose names are written in heaven. You have come to God, the Judge of all, to the spirits of the righteous made perfect.

The scope of the *ekklesia*? Greater than anything the Jews or Romans could comprehend. For the Romans, this is the "one that got away." For the first time in the empire's strident history, they were wholly unable to absorb the *ekklesia* into their cultural web—this *ekklesia* was conceived and created out of "different stuff." The Christian *ekklesia* was

> *called out of the Roman and Judean system to come together into a separate civil community.* It meant a politically autonomous body of Christians under no king but Jesus; under no other jurisdiction but that of Jesus.

No man ruled them! Only Christ. And that was the reason these same Christians ran into trouble with kings and rulers; were arrested, crucified and martyred. They dropped Caesar as their King and took up Christ.[3]

This new body both served the practical and spiritual needs of the Roman system, but defied Caesar's claim to earthly supremacy. Just as Jesus had instructed His disciples that the rulers of this world "lorded it over" their citizenry, He declared that they would be known by their servant spirits to rulers and citizens alike. Paul and Silas were accused of turning *"the world upside down"* (Acts 17:6 ESV). How were they achieving this? Luke reports in verse 7 that those *"Jason has welcomed them into his house. They are all defying Caesar's decrees, saying that there is another king, one called Jesus."*

> They were announcing another King. Not Caesar! . . . They were forming civil bodies that no longer looked to Caesar as their King. . . .
>
> They were dethroning rulers in the minds of the people and alienating them from the mental hold Caesar (the world and their governments) had upon them. . . .
>
> They were putting forth the call of God to whomever would hear and obey, and those whose hearts responded to the call became citizens of Christ's Kingdom and joined themselves to the ekklesia, a common unity of believers.[4]

When we comprehend the supremacy and nature of the *ekklesia* in this light and juxtapose it to our current understanding and practice of *church*, it should leave us with a hunger and determination to see the Church returned to God's original design and purpose.

Jeff Reed, President of BILD International (an organization whose goal is to create "well-established church-planting movements"[5] around the world) has written a number of helpful "encyclicals" to their global church network leaders. In one of them, "The Churches of the First Century," he outlines the challenge being faced in the Western church:

> The West is in significant decline and its institutions are a significant part of the reason for this failure. Western Christianity has become highly individualistic; the churches, full of traditions, are far removed from their first century roots; and the church's missionary and theological education enterprises are in many ways in significant tension with the "way of Christ and his Apostles." This "way" is set forth in Acts and Apostles' letters to the churches that make up much of the New Testament.[6]

Because of this decline, many have become engaged in the pursuit of the historical church, trying to rediscover our foundations and see what helped them grow so quickly. Reed suggests that one of the first questions we need to ask is, "Why was the first church so successful?"

> We must understand why these churches were so strong and the secret of why they so successfully multiplied across the Roman Empire until they turned the entire world of that day upside down. The simplicity of the churches and the complexity of their movement are hard to see today because we are blinded by the clutter of our ways: our institutions, our traditions, and even our expectations of what it means to go to church.[7]

Reed describes the shape of these first churches, what he called "small, simple gatherings":

By *small, simple gatherings*, I mean small, simple meetings of new believers that were called churches; simple, met in homes on the first day of every week, around an evening meal, celebrating their new life, inviting friends, co-workers, relatives, etc. They were in essence kerygmatic ["proclaiming" or "preaching"] communities. They all looked like this. And they multiplied around the world.[8]

For nearly 300 years the church met in these small groups until Constantine began encouraging the erection of basilicas. This shift from small to big has stayed with us over the centuries, from small groups in homes to corporate gatherings in buildings. As I looked at these things together with the Believers leadership, we realized the concepts and accepted norms around "big" and "small" church were primary areas where deconstruction and reconstruction needed to happen if they were to be the church God was calling them to be.

Looking closer, though, we had several questions about the details. What exactly did the early church do when they got together? What were their rhythms? What were their practices and what did they believe their mission was? We found three basic themes that ran throughout the New Testament.

1. They Gathered Around the "Lord's Supper"

The gathering itself was referred to as the "Lord's Supper"—and sometimes as a "Love Feast"—and became the vehicle for branding the church that Paul utilized globally. At the "meal," they would collect food and other provisions to send to other house churches, the poor in the group and in the city, and sometimes they sent it on to a church network elsewhere in the world (e.g., Ephesus).[9] This gathering was rich in dialogue around the apostles' teachings, fellowship (partnership in the enterprise of the Gospel), the meal (including remembrance of Jesus's death and resurrection), prayer, and discussion of church issues. It is interesting that they often began the meal with the breaking of bread, went on with the service, and ended with the sharing of the cup (pretty similar to what happened at the disciples' last meal with Jesus in the upper room). It is thought that the average size of these gatherings were fifty to seventy people, while yet others were much larger when wealthy members renovated their homes specifically for regular use. The largest of these recorded "homes" had room for gatherings as large as 1,135 people, but large groups like that were the exception.[10]

What happened to this tradition? The full meal was replaced by a ceremony only including the cup and the bread. George Barna and Frank Viola give this overview of the shift in the centrality of the Lord's Supper:

> In the first and early second centuries, the early Christians called the Lord's Supper the "love feast." At that time, they took the bread and cup in the context of a festive meal. But around the time of Tertullian, the bread and the cup began to be separated from the meal. By the late second century, this separation was complete. . . .
>
> By the fourth century, the love feast was prohibited among Christians! . . .
>
> With the abandonment of the meal, the terms *breaking of bread* and *Lord's Supper* disappeared. The common term for the now truncated ritual (just the bread and the cup) was the "Eucharist."[11]

The Supper was no longer a community event. It was rather a priestly ritual that was to be watched from a distance. In time there was an increasing sense of awe and dread ("examine your hearts") associated with the table where the sacred Eucharist was celebrated.

What we were left with, over time, is bite-size crackers or small pieces of bread, a wee glass or communal chalice of grape juice (or wine if you dare), a sober and pensive countenance (thank you, John Calvin), and in some cases, clerical robes and religious musings in Latin. These traditions were passed on into medieval Catholicism and all the way through to our Protestant forefathers. Notice the drift from family to hierarchy, from relational to transactional—these "sacraments" were removed from the daily and communal and given the air of elevated ritual. But being removed in this way and confined to the "house of God" created a rift between the "sacred" and the "secular" that was never intended by any directive of the Scriptures. ◁

2. Preaching, Teaching, and Dialogue

Barna and Viola call *the sermon*: "the bedrock of Protestant liturgy."[12] Preaching and teaching were critical to these early communities, but they've come to mean something significantly different in many of our church cultures over the centuries. Preaching generally had the proclamation of the Gospel in focus while teaching refers to how to live "the faith." (Peter's sermons would be classic examples of preaching the *Kerygma*—proclaiming of the Gospel—and Paul's letters are prime examples of the *Didache*—"the teaching," "the instruction," or "the faith.")

In Acts 19:8-10, Paul left the synagogue with his adherents and moved to the Hall of Tyrannus where he "argued" or "dialogued" [*dialogomenos*] with the people about his presentation.[13] (The same word is used in Acts 20:7: "*On the first day of the week we came together to break bread. Paul spoke [dialegamai] to the people and, because he intended to leave the next day, kept on talking until midnight."*) Paul was breaking bread with a gathering of believers and holding a discussion with them. It appears that much of the apostles' doctrine or teaching in the early church was not merely dispensed through a monologue or sermon in front of a gathered audience, but through a dialogue together in what's termed the Socratic method of learning. ⟨

No wonder they were drawn to small groups and they multiplied so quickly—*they were all engaged!* Every member was being engaged, their questions and fears discussed, and their misconceptions addressed. The Gospel wasn't being dispensed to them in the form of information from behind a pulpit on a stage, it was being absorbed into their spirits from teachers that sat face-to-face with them and invited them into a *dialogue* regarding what Paul referred to in various ways as the *Didache*: "the faith," "the instruction," "the teaching," or "the deposit."

3. In everything—all together!

We see the same "all inclusive" spirit in Paul's instructions to the Colossians that we see in the reports of the early church from the book of Acts:

> Let the message of Christ dwell among you richly as you teach and admonish one another with all wisdom through psalms, hymns, and songs from the Spirit, singing to God with gratitude in your hearts.
> —COLOSSIANS 3:16

Look how inclusive these groups seemed to be, as they "taught and admonished" one another and sang all manner of music to the Lord with each other. There is no mention of this being called a "worship service" with a professional worship pastor leading them into a mostly predetermined list of songs, all in preparation for the sermon. In fact, Paul described such gatherings as being Spirit led, with each person bringing something to add to the gathering:

> What then shall we say, brothers and sisters? When you come together, each of you has a hymn, or a word of instruction, a revelation, a tongue or an interpretation. Everything must be done so that the church may be built up.
>
> **—1 CORINTHIANS 14:26**

The beauty of this text reveals that the presence of God was designed to be demonstrated in the Body more than it is in "the meeting." It is difficult for each member to build the others up if they are only "worshipping" in a public service and not also choosing a hymn to sing, giving a word, sharing something they'd learned, or proclaiming a prophecy to one another. All of my life I've heard the "older set" complain of the loudness of the music—it's a generational phenomenon. But it isn't the decibels that are the main concern, it is that the "saints" can't hear each voice and identify the unique contributions so that each one may build the others up. The church isn't supposed to gather for "performances"—it's supposed to be something more communal. ◄

In the current framework of church today, however, it is the "professionals" ministering to the people of God—a congregation gathered into an audience—but not a participating family with which the Word and song are exchanged to the building of each other up in Christ. It's almost always only "one way" (stage to pew) and still reflects the old clergy/laity construct that has been dominant since the third century, while smaller "home" groups lend themselves more to the "building of each other up." (Note I'm not going binary here—as in hoping we choose small over big or vice versa—I'm just suggesting a refocus on the biblical value of participation by all.) ✂

While home groups allow more exchange, the dynamic of corporate gatherings creates an experience of God's presence that is different from what can be achieved in smaller groups. Singing corporately must thrill the heart of God and His presence is awesome—*understood*. I believe the Lord is shifting the emphasis away from such a heavy diet of being blessed by "the presence" of God in corporate settings where people may be tempted to substitute this for the biblical injunction to let Immanuel (God with us), the habitating Christ, give each of His members a unique contribution to be shared with the others. There are many believers who are missing this ingredient in their spiritual diet and are longing for a more intimate manifestation of Christ's presence through the exchange of the life of Christ in His Body. ✍

All of these beliefs and practices of our earliest parent church came not under a church hierarchical framework, but an apostolic one—passing down heritage through a family framework. It wasn't about filling out an organizational chart, but equipping sons and daughters, and then grandchildren, to lead into the next generation. Jesus is still building His Church on the foundation of the apostles and prophets. What then do we see needs to be deconstructed? *Attitudes, beliefs, structures, and practices that were never in the DNA of the apostolic, disciple on disciple, founding of the Church as the Family of God.*

With the current resurgence of small groups and "house churches" (see, for example, Francis Chan's efforts at wearechurch.com and Jeff Vanderstelt's network at saturatetheworld.com), some have thrown out the corporate gatherings as, at best, irrelevant, or at worst, totally unscriptural—not so fast! It is true that we are more likely to have attenders than disciples in our current configuration where "big church" is our primary focus. But it's also easy to get distracted by the forms and miss the intent of what we are discussing here. In our studying of the Scriptures and other readings, we don't find that "small house groups" are a cure all. Believers Church itself had tried small groups before I connected with them and they didn't work. "Life Groups" were first launched in 2002 as an opportunity for their fragmented people to simply get together and do something at least somewhat spiritual. They called them "free-market groups." As you may remember reading earlier, anything went, from ice cream socials to flag football. They soon realized, however, that not much was taking place and the buy-in was low. People didn't need *another* activity to attend. There was really little intentional discipleship taking place in these groups either, so they were eventually disbanded. Social clubs were not to be on the menu.

As we studied the issue and prayed further, we came to believe this first effort missed its focus and purpose in building relationship around the right practices and didn't create a rhythm of fellowship that fed into and was celebrated in the larger meetings. (Note, once again, God will have different rhythms between small and large gatherings for different groups and communities. He likes different "gift mixes" to have "different expressions," quite often uniquely relevant to their communities.) There is no one size fits all way to do this. We must first plug into the Word and Spirit of God for direction and correction, just as the Believers group did—and just as they experienced, there are no overnight solutions! (Remember, they had eight years of work that needed to be done before they could even start doing eldership right!)

The current challenge with the prevalence of "big church" is the weight we give it for discipling, gathering, and equipping

God's people for the "work of ministry." In the same way we have reduced becoming a Christian to being converted by "praying the prayer" and buying into the belief statement of our church, we have reduced "growing in Christ" to learning and assimilating certain tenets and beliefs, but not having certain competencies that are critical to doing the will of God on the earth such as hearing and recognizing what God is speaking to us, discerning God's will for our lives and communities, and acting with grace and favor in carrying out heaven's mandates for walking out our missions. (Probably because those are far more difficult, involved things to learn.) Because of this false construct, "big church" tends to focus on information download, but carries little nurturing, assurance, or accountability that anything learned will be lived out in the lives of the people being taught.

Now, my friends, don't get nervous, please: *Big* can be very good! I believe there is a case to be made for gatherings to be a place of public witness, corporate worship, and the presence of God as a waystation for new people transitioning into and discerningly decentralizing their commitment into the smaller groups. Such gatherings can also be a place for a "bigger story," for vision casting as a whole body, and Gospel proclamation through the exegeting of Scriptures to the gathered large group of small-group participants and those wishing to join them. Each church will have to discern God's will for them individually in how they knit their tribe of the Church together to impact their city and region.

I love big gatherings where the presence of God is thick and the teaching of the Word is rich; but I also love when small groups of God's people are all engaging the Word, in fellowship, celebrating the Lord's Table, praying, and being "on mission" together to make significant changes in their communities. The latter strengthens the former, while if we're not careful, the big gathering can inoc-ulate people against the desire and commitment to be actively engaged in the smaller "family-style discipleship," small-group communities throughout the week. I think there is a place for the interplay of both.

So what do we do? What does it really mean to be "the family of God"? How do we plug into that as well as the mission God has for our unique church communities? How do we pray and stum-ble along together to the point we have finally learned to walk—to *"keep in step with the Spirit"* (Galatians 5:25 ESV)—as Paul told us to do?

DOING LIFE TOGETHER

As the Believers leadership team and I continued pursuing God in these matters, we noticed disciple making was almost exclusive-ly done within the context of these early church house groups or "spiritual families" rather than the popular idea of "one-on-one discipleship" pervasive in church culture today. Just as Jesus had chosen a community of twelve—and their families—in which to disciple, the early church made disciples in the context of coming together to share meals and "break bread" from home to home. Inspired by these realizations, the Believers leadership set out to redefine both discipleship and the nature of their cell groups.

So even before they did eldership training in the fall of 2006, Roger and the eldership decided to start small groups up again with the caveat they would screen the group leaders first. They put them in teams of mature couples or two couples and a single person. They focused the instruction on helping people think of their "upward, inward, and outward" commitments to God, the church family, and unbelievers. By the day of the grand opening of new life groups, they'd set up twenty-three groups with hundreds of people signed up to participate.

These groups were really strong for the first two or three years, but over time, the original leaders began to wane in their commitment. The team attempted to recruit new leaders, but it proved untenable, though they did the best they could. In evaluating this attrition in numbers and commitment, they determined they needed to be more engaged in training leaders for the groups. They commenced a one-year course designed to lay biblical and practical foundations in the life of the group leaders. They "really didn't want to do that first year again."

Discouraged, but not deterred, the core team came across Mike and Sally Breen's book, *Family on Mission*. This key book examines the Father's desire for a family, Jesus's mission to acquire that family, and the Spirit's work in securing those sons and daughters for the heavenly family. (Father, Son, and Holy Spirit together—the Trinity—might, after all, be best be understood as a family united in purpose.) The Godhead was on a mission, as it were, to see God's love for all creation birthed in the new community of faith—a "family on mission." The book celebrates Jesus, having been rejected by one family that had become severely ethno-centric, but birthing a new family that would take the mission of the Father to "all *creation*" (Mark 16:15, emphasis added).

They handed the book out to staff, training classes, elders, and included a teaching series based on it for the whole church. This simple, inspiring book, with the help of the Holy Spirit, seemed to encourage the people to become a more "missional" church. Classically insulated and with little burden for their neighbors and workmates, people began to see that the DNA of the Kingdom included scattering God's people into their city as salt and light.

(See Matthew 5:13-16.) Eventually people realized that evangelism, discipleship, and missions were not departments of "church central," but the DNA imbedded by Jesus in every house group to be a "family on mission" in neighborhoods, workplaces, and communities. They were beginning to leave their "sacred/secular" moorings and drift into the pleasant waters of engaging all of culture as a community of faith.

The results of this "shift in gears" was that Believers began to move from yet another "sacred" church activity to embrace the organic process of equipping disciples to passionately live out and dispense the Gospel as a sanctifying aroma wherever they went. "Church" was spreading outside the four walls of their building.

This left the team with a dilemma: "We don't really know how to do training," they confessed. It was an honest realization that the Lord seemed to respond to. In 2009, 24-7 Prayer hosted a week-long retreat in England with Neil Cole, author of *Organic Church*. Adam Cox, from the Kansas City Boiler Room, shared with Roger how they had taken Neil's teaching and created D (for "discipleship") Groups. These were simply gender-specific groups of three that would meet weekly to read Scripture, share their hearts openly, and pray for one person in each individual's world that didn't yet know Jesus. New groups were formed by one person leaving an existing group and joining two others to replicate the process. Adam shared that implementing this really boosted their community's commitment to discipleship.

The idea infected the leaders at Believers and before they knew it, a similar process started accidentally. Gyle had a meeting with a young chap that wanted to leave the church, so he explained D Groups to him and asked if he wanted to start one. He did, and the young man caught fire. Then a number of new groups grew out of the fruitfulness of that first experiment. They didn't try to keep track of all the groups or turn them into a formal program of the church; they trusted the Lord to turn it into a viral movement. At one point nearly ninety men were involved. The eldership was learning to release control and let God move on the people. Through various starts and stops, the DNA of discipleship was beginning to get into the bloodstream of the church.

Even though the Lord was using "models" like D Groups, Believers Church was still slowly being disentangled from its former traditions and methodologies as it stumbled toward a more biblical framework for laying foundations into the lives of God's people. One of the major shifts in thinking was the move away from the idea of "building the church" to "extending the Kingdom." This deconstruction of the western mode of thinking and practice was boosted by Ben Pasley's little book *TOM and the Goldfish Bowl*. The book makes an appeal for the Church to move away from T.O.M.— the "Traditions of Men"—and be more aware of what God was calling them to become. It is a call for leaders to empower their people to move from traditional paradigms of church to equipping God's people for the work of *their* individual ministries—from mobilizing people to do church activities to a culture of discipleship.

Both in the church and around Tulsa, people began to remark, "The leaders at Believers Church don't seem to grab for power, they just want to empower others. Nobody's ever done that before!"

NOW WHAT?

Question #1: Are the ingredients and rhythms of your church or ministry reflective of the three practices? (See pp. 66-69.) If so, are they resulting in creating a "discipleship culture" in the church or simply seeking to produce "good Christians"?

Question #2: What is the Lord showing you about returning to some of the values and practices of our founding fathers in the first-century church? Invite the Holy Spirit to speak into your journey!

Question #3: Are your "small groups" an appendage—a department or "ministry"—or the engine of discipleship in your church and ministry? (Assuming you have small groups, that is.) Do they reflect the spirit and the ingredients of the example seen in Acts 2:41-47? Meditate on this important church "DNA" text.

STUMBLING AND GROWING

*"What shall we say the kingdom of God is like, or what
parable shall we use to describe it? It is like a mustard seed,
which is the smallest of all seeds on earth. Yet when planted,
it grows and becomes the largest of all garden plants,
with such big branches that the birds can perch in its shade."*

—MARK 4:30-32

One of the great—and scary—things about vision is that it's never limited by current circumstances. As deeper personal growth started to take root in Believers Church through the eldership and life group "dialogues," Roger started getting the picture of duplicating these conversations even further—aka "church planting." God began to plant in him the dream of being more than one gathered family of believers, but rather a hub for reproducing the family ethos of being God's people throughout Tulsa and the nations.

Susan recalled a funny discussion she, Gyle, and Roger had one day over lunch.

> I was freaked out by the idea of being a "hub church,"
> because we weren't doing enough training or discipling
> of our own church people. I couldn't imagine expand-
> ing beyond our own borders yet. We were sitting at a

restaurant and talking about something—I can't remember—and Roger started pounding on the table and saying, "The purpose of Believers Church is to be a church-planting church!" This came as a shock to Gyle and I, as this topic hadn't really come up before. Roger must have gotten a random prophetic inspiration or something—I'd never ever heard that statement before!

For this, the question emerged, "Can we even transplant ourselves here locally in Tulsa?" They were a little gun-shy to attempt training leaders again, but they felt the conviction that God wanted them to try. With the Lord's help, they began lining out a means of developing leaders that would carry their culture of discipleship, be missional in their neighborhoods, and impact new groups of believers. It would be a multi-generational plan—a seed planted for their legacy. The *"going to church services and activities"* mindset was quickly dissipating in the light of their newfound revelation of God's plan for Believers. It was time for what they were learning to infect others and start transforming their lives as well.

Fortunately, this thinking was already being discussed and practiced by others like Jeff Vanderstelt and Soma Church in Tacoma,[*] 3D Ministries, and even Believers new "cousins" at the Kansas City Boiler Room (whose story we'll tell in Part Two). There were a number of biblical ingredients that marked the new DNA in the reformation of all these church into families of families:

1. Sonship and daughterhood in Christ as the primary identity of the Kingdom family—the first aim was always to help individuals move from being orphans and servants to sons and daughters of the Father.

---

[*] Jeff has more recently become pastor at Doxa Church in Bellevue, Washington, but his Saturate network is still going strong.

2. Discipleship, defined as collective biblical discovery and the "life-on-life" experience of being vulnerable with one another in the process of reflecting the life of Jesus and His disciples—*"just as Christ loved the church and gave himself up for her to make her holy, cleansing her by the washing with water through the word"* (Ephesians 5:25-26).

3. A team/family-based approach to everything. The day of the individual "Lone Ranger" hero of God was over, and God was emphasizing the power of a multi-gifted family unit dispensing a variety of talents to reach each heart, neighborhood, and domain of life.

4. Gifts, rather than titles and roles, would be the basis for all leadership responsibilities.

5. The "family on mission" was a reflection of the early church devoting themselves to *"the apostles' teaching and to fellowship, to the breaking of bread and to prayer"* (Acts 2:42) as rhythms of life that included men, women, and children who were committed to reaching their neighborhoods with the Gospel.

6. The nature of all families is that they grow, multiply, and move beyond the walls of the nuclear family home. The mentality of *feeding Christians* was giving way to *equipping disciples* to get the DNA of Kingdom into their hearts and help them prepare their "offspring" to grow up, leave the home, and replicate family life in new geographical assignments.

7. Training leaders at all levels, both formally and informally, to bring and sustain life in the house groups.[14]

The desire to graft these principles into the Believers DNA created yet another turning point for the church. It wasn't just about being a hub, it was about instigating a virus that would spread to form other hubs—it was about manifesting and expanding the Kingdom wherever the people of Believers Church went, even if they moved away to other cities or nations. It wasn't about just being the Church in Tulsa anymore—it was about being a Kingdom people.

BECOMING KINGDOM PEOPLE

Church life for many of us as believers has dominated our consciousness for most of our lives: we attend services, go to prayer meetings and Bible studies, go on outreaches locally and abroad, support kids' groups, youth groups, participate in business meetings, building committees, and any variety of church-related programs. We have sometimes over-focused on teaching the "what we believe's" and the "how-to's" of the Christian walk rather than teaching God's people to "know Him" and walk out His eternal plan as a member of the family of God. In other words, getting out of the Christian ghetto—that space behind the doors of our churches were we all speak the same Christianese and spend a lot of time talking about what we value and what's wrong with the world outside—and into the trenches on the frontline in that outside world to live out the claims of the Gospel through His power.

This "Christian isolationism" feeds "keeping the church as we know it going" and creates a cycle that is exacerbated as we saw Roger and his team struggle with in their years of pastoring Believers Church. We hire professional staff to run the respective "ministries" the church needs to attract new members with minimal time invested in intentionally discipling those God has already entrusted to us, and we failed to enjoy the mandate to *"entrust to reliable people who will also be qualified to teach others"*

(2 Timothy 2:2). This is the old Vision-Tasks-Relationships mindset that demands sustaining *activities* and *programs* for people rather than sustaining *people* (Relationships-Vision-Gifts) for God's enterprise both inside and outside our church buildings.

As a "minister" over the past five decades, I've seen God shifting the church from a centripetal force with the church organization at the center (outside moving in like a whirlpool) to a giant centrifuge with all energy radiating out from a Kingdom center. The Church, redeemed and empowered by their King, uses their weekly rhythm of gatherings to reenergize, reequip, and bring their concerns about the outside in before the Throne. The two figures below depict the conflicting constructs of these two paradigms: What I call the "Church-centric Mindset" and the "Kingdom-expanding Mindset."

Notice in Figure 1 how all the energy moves in the direction of the church—thus a church-centric or "church as the center" paradigm. (I am defining church here as the institutional or organizational center of Christian activity in any community, not as the universal Church as we've discussed it in previous chapters.) Christians who serve "the church" as an entity are expected to

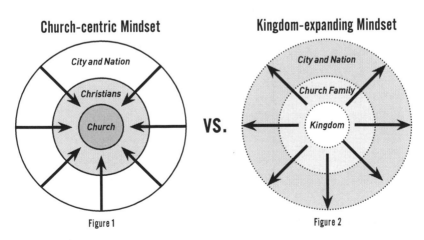

Church-centric Mindset

City and Nation

Christians

Church

VS.

Kingdom-expanding Mindset

City and Nation

Church Family

Kingdom

Figure 1

Figure 2

invite the non-believer to church, where it is hoped they will "get saved" and instructed in the Christian life. Even most mission endeavors are designed to bring converts into the Church-first construct, starting by building a building and appointing a pastor and elders to set up the bylaws and organize as an institution. The Church is seen as the vortex of life—most all of the movement being towards the local church as the center of all activity.

In Figure 2, life starts with the Kingdom coming into the human heart, then restoring "creation's design" to the individual and to the collective family of God, who then takes those paradigms into the unredeemed aspects of every sphere of life. Instead of life centering around a location, programs, professional staff, and being led by a head or senior pastor, the energy comes from "equippers," spiritual fathers and mothers, brothers and sisters, developing the image of Jesus in every believer for the work of their service in all of life. The church organism is then the mechanism by which God's Kingdom people are equipped as a spiritual family to sanctify their neighborhoods and workplaces for Kingdom activity—a holy family engaged in the enterprise of establishing the freedom of God's Government wherever they have influence.

We have often preferred teaching "the multitude" on Sunday rather than modeling the life of Jesus as disciples Monday through Saturday. The local church shouldn't be a place to gather as much as a place from which people formed in His image go out into the world to radiate His light.

Our current church-centric structures mitigate that goal. "There just isn't enough time to do everything we need to do as a church," we say, not realizing that there is always time to do God's work according to His plan. We keep repeating that mantra because we've built our lives around a church construct that is fundamentally unfriendly to a community lifestyle that effectively changes cultures. People are exhausted with life as it is and are sincerely trying to include church demands around crazy activity schedules and work pressures, further segregating them from the beauty of integrating Jesus into all of life. And this doesn't get any easier as our churches pull from broader and broader areas as cities grow. What if leaders encouraged and equipped God's people to take Jesus to the soccer match and the department meeting instead of being enlisted to sign up for yet one more activity held in the church building? (And why don't we move such activities into small groups in the areas where people actually live?)

Dispensing biblical beliefs in the local church through pulpit-to-pew sermons has superseded biblically modeling a Christ-centered way of life that impacts our neighborhoods and cities. How are we leaders modeling the life of Christ to those we are "doing life" with? And that said, who are we actually "doing life" with? Do we interface with our congregations only in meetings or during periodic counseling appointments according to carefully guarded calendars, or are we out in the world being salt and light? Are our meeting agendas only focused on getting the business of the ministry done, or does it include sufficient time to share our hearts with each other, pray for each other, ingest the Word as a habit, and sincerely hear from heaven?

Instead of being able to say as Paul, *"Be imitators of me, as I am of Christ"* (1 Corinthians 11:1 ESV), church leaders can become so busy teaching believers how to be Christians, keeping "church central" running, making sure the programs are on track, and the fires at bay, that we overlook the need to grow closer to Christ in community ourselves and fulfill the missions He has called us to as individuals. Like the old saying goes, "We get so obsessed with the work of the Lord, we lose touch with the Lord of the work."

The results are telling: the statistics for divorce, abortion, drug and alcohol abuse, and infidelity in the Church are nearly the same as those for the general culture. The low biblical and spiritual intelligence of many church attendees has inoculated them against the beauty of a life fully surrendered and governed by the mandates of our King's heart. Instead we adhere to a "political platform" of beliefs that we see as setting us apart from—making us better than—a world "going to hell in a handbasket." This also leaves Kingdom disciples longing for genuine community and harboring no desire for the exhausting good works of "churchy" Christianity—our "service days," outreaches, or other "one-off" activities we organized to pretend like we are engaged with our neighborhoods and cities. We should be doing these things anyway as part of our normal rhythms of "doing life" together rather than being driven to do them as a cumbersome duty. Things that, once done, can be check off the list until next quarter. That's not living transformationally; that's just playing good Christian.

As a result, there has been a wholesale migration out of the traditional church structures leaving many stranded on a lee shore, unsure of where and how to belong to a loving spiritual family. There are many others who have remained in their churches who are inclined to leave, but feel obligated to stay, not seeing any alternative on the horizon. These "exiles" that have left are good people whose souls could no longer stand the pressure of feeling inauthentic. Mindlessly fulfilling religious requirements had left them feeling hollow and unsatisfied in their dream to see the church be what God intended it to be.

Richard Greenleaf, author of *Servant Leadership: A Journey into the Nature of Legitimate Power and Greatness,* saw a sizable problem in relying on institutions rather than helping each of us to "grow taller and become healthier, stronger, more autonomous."[15] As he put it:

> *Love* is an undefinable term, and its manifestations are both subtle and infinite. But it begins, I believe, with one absolute condition: unlimited liability! As soon as one's liability for another is qualified to *any degree*, love is diminished by that much.
>
> Institutions, as we know them, are designed to limit liability for those who serve through them. . . . [A]ny human service where the one who is served should be loved in the process requires community, a face-to-face group in which the liability of each for the other and all for one is unlimited, or as close to it as it is possible to get. Trust and respect are highest in this circumstance and an accepted ethic that gives strength to all is reinforced. Where there is not community, trust, respect, and ethical behaviors are difficult for the young to learn and for the old to maintain. Living in community as one's basic involvement will generate an exportable surplus of love which the individual may carry into his many involvements with institutions which are usually not communities: businesses, churches, governments, schools.[16]

It is my prayer that we go to the "lost sheep" of the family of God. There are two types: those that have left the church in frustration or disgust, and those who are still in the church construct seduced by a system that shows them no alternative but to keep the traditions unchallenged. I long to see both of these "types" restored to the family of God, the community of faith, not the harsh entity that has caused so many to continue dutifully to "that's all I've known" or leave with broken hearts and inner vows to "never return." I'm not suggesting they go back to an old paradigm,

I'm praying that in the near future we can provide loving sheep pens that bring them into the type of biblical community their hearts long for.

RELEASING GIFTS INTO SOCIETY

One of the primary results of creating a missional discipleship culture is the validation of everybody's gifts and callings. Once validated, they no longer feel like "laity," but a disciple of Jesus whose home and vocational life are equally honored and sanctified. They leave their home each day commissioned as an ambassador of the Kingdom to the greater world around them. In partnership with other believing families, they become extended "families on mission": the way the heavenly family designed us to be.

For decades, we have defined "ministry" as church and mission work, and all other endeavors we've labeled "secular." I've had Christian business leaders tell me they were saving enough money to be able to free themselves to "someday quit my job and *do ministry*—you know, *like you do.*" Why would we want people to leave banking, media, roadwork, and other vocations—take them out of their places of influence—and send them somewhere to become volunteer or vocational ministers instead—something they were never called to in the first place? If they haven't learned to be ministers where they are now—to be *missional* in the marketplace or the neighborhood—what would qualify them to be fruitful in any other place?

The difficulty is that we leaders have not adequately honored callings outside the walls of the church and equipped those in the pews to be the ministers God's called them to be—to bring the beautiful Kingdom of God into any of the seven mountaintops of cultural influence: family, government, arts and entertainment, media, business, education, or even religion (on a society level, not just in the Church).

We've allowed people to be discontent with their "secular" jobs—thinking going out into the world to work makes them second-class citizens to those "working in *the* ministry"—and let them believe that nothing they do really matters unless it is in the church or in missionary activity. *Poppycock!* We need a wholesale invasion of rabid Jesus freaks and Kingdom disciples commissioned into the social and geographical assignments God has entrusted to them rather than the evacuation of those same good people from the places God has planted them. (This is something we will explore in much more depth in Part Three of this book: "Transformation.")

Over the years, I've enjoyed publicly calling the people of God to embrace their current assignments at home and at work as their calling of God to be His ministers and do His ministry wherever they've been planted. Before I share this message in any particular church, I clue in the elders and leaders as to what is coming after the teaching. We summon large amounts of oil and liberally dispense it upon the people of God as they come forward to receive a blessing from their shepherds to be inaugurated as "ministers of the Gospel" in their neighborhoods and workplaces.

The testimonies, as a result, are truly stirring. We hear things like, "I hated my job until I got God's perspective on it," or "I had never once prayed for my boss or associates, but since I started, amazing things are happening." My favorite is, "I've just invited Jesus to be the CEO of my company."

One sister told me she had taken up my idea to find other believers at work and cashed in on the promise *"where two or three gather in my name, there am I with them"* (Matthew 18:20). The peace of God came into that workplace. God knows we need His presence as we work as much if not more than when we gather together on Sunday morning.

One paint contractor in Kansas City excoriated me for an idea that I posed in a training session I was hosting for business leaders: "If Jesus told us to bless our enemies, surely that would hold for blessing our competitors." He laughed and said, "Do you know how utterly ridiculous that is to a professional business leader? If we don't outbid the competition, we don't survive."

Without preamble or argument, I suggested, "Give it a shot."

Surprisingly, he did.

He gathered his sons in their corporate offices and they discussed it. They chose to pray for their fiercest competitor, a large commercial paint contractor. What they received from God in prayer was that this father should call the competitor and tell him he was praying for him, then ask if there was anything he needed God to do that he had no control over. When my friend called, he was startled to discover that his competitor's wife had just served him with divorce papers. The man was utterly broken.

Backtracking, my friend first apologized for the times he had been too prickly in his dealings with this competitor and then asked if he and his sons could pray for the restoration of his marriage. After forgiving my friend for his un-Christ-like behavior, the competitor offered a massive contract to him stating he thought my friend's company could do a better job!

My friend and his wife responded to his competitor's pain over his impending divorce by hosting the other couple for dinner. A healing journey began. Amazing as these first steps were, it was only the start of a new era for this family of painters. Their once "secular" job-site now became a "sacred" embassy of Kingdom activity.

CONSTRUCTING NEW "FOUNDATIONS"

Roger and the team realized there were several paradigm shifts needed in their people before they could see this personal empowerment and growth begin to take root in their fellowship. If there was anything they had learned over the years of this process, it was that passive mindsets can become "norms" that needed to be dismantled before God can rebuild more solidly on biblical principles. The team responded to this need by hosting Wednesday night electives to try and draw out hungry-hearted people. They had learned that not all people are ready to be trained, but that they should focus on those who are so hungry for God and His ways that they would drop their nets, come, follow, and allow Jesus to make them into what He had always dreamed they would be.

These "Foundations" courses on Wednesdays revealed a significant hunger in the community. Susan reminisced,

> Earlier, people only wanted to get involved in groups if it involved food or flag football or things like that. I was tormented over the spiritual hunger I felt for teaching, because our people had no outlet for growth. This training was not yet as cohesive and comprehensive as it would become, but it aimed at the felt needs of those wanting to grow in Christ. Topics offered were on "The Book of Revelation," "How to Witness," and "Prophetic Training" (hearing the voice of God and encouraging God's people with it), amongst other topics, but no other discipleship tools were ready to be rolled out at that point.

Gyle remembered a conversation with Joe Steinke, US Academy Director from the Boiler Room Network, about the Antioch School in Kansas City.[*] He remembers how it

> fired my imagination. In 2012 it was in my heart to start an Antioch journey in Tulsa, so we prayed and you guys said, "Go for it!" So we entered into a biblical studies journey for training leaders offered by Antioch. That was four years ago, and we're still growing in numbers and biblical understanding that is translating into our daily lives and in our home groups.

As the house groups at Believers Church became healthier and more aligned with reproducing "family on mission," there were also various "house churches" sent out as autonomous communities who remained connected to the "resource church"—Believers—for guidance and training. These communities are beginning to fully live out the claims of Christ together and are beginning to multiply throughout various neighborhoods in Tulsa. Believers Church was becoming a family of "families on mission."

---

[*] The Antioch training material was developed by Jeff Reed of the Biblical Institute for Leadership Development. As a full-degree granting program, it offers materials for every level of church life from *First Principles* for house groups, the Antioch Core Course for leaders, and a wide range of biblical studies resulting in Masters or Doctoral degree for those so inclined.

NOW WHAT?

Questions # 1: After looking at the chart at the beginning of the chapter (p. 82), would you describe your church's predominant mindset as "Church-centric," "Kingdom-centric," or some combination of the two? (If the latter, where are you one or the other?) How about your team and key leaders? How about the members of your church? And you?

> **Exercise:** Bring any church-centric ideas and practices to the Lord and ask Him to give you both conviction and direction on how to receive His perspective on these various grids.

Question # 2: How do you use the word "ministry" individually or as a team? Where did this idea originate in your histories and how do you feel about it now? What is your ministry calling and how are you helping others discover theirs?

Question #3: If you are engaged in teaching, are you primarily focused on equipping God's people for their calling, or more aimed at meeting perceived needs and performing the tasks and ministries required to fulfill the vision of the church itself? Ask the Lord to counsel you on this important distinction.

TOGETHER

*The gospel is bearing fruit and growing throughout
the whole world—just as it has been doing among you since
the day you heard it and truly understood God's grace.*

—COLOSSIANS 1:6

Blending strong personalities and coming into unity on anything is an art form that constantly evades us mere mortals.
You have the introverts and extroverts, the A and B personality
types, the "black and white" thinkers, and the ever popular "fly
your space ship around the moon a few times before you come
in for a landing" folks. Then there are the "risk takers" and the
"overly cautious" variety salted in with the "brainy" mental types
juxtaposed with the "sensitive feeler" variation—all of these people very different—and throwing them together can lead to some
rather uncomfortable confrontations. Ah yes, and varying spiritual
gifts that, without partnership and moderation, can skew our per-
ceptions of reality. Now toss in a dose of yet unredeemed humanity,
psychological and spiritual strongholds, emotional and cultural
baggage, along with different convictions and biblical perspectives,
and you have a recipe for disaster—unless Jesus is the Chef.

Over the last decade plus, I have watched Roger, Gyle, Susan, and Mark (who has since moved to California) bump up against all manner of differences, strong disagreements, disappointments, and dismal failures. I've also watched them win battles, champion each other, and reflect a Christ-like manner to become, though at times somewhat broken, still quite beautiful people. All in all, I've witnessed them becoming relational artists who *"keep the unity of the Spirit through the bond of peace"* (Ephesians 4:3). They did all that by coming out from under that table, looking each other in the eyes, and learning how to create harmony out of their differences. The only way for them to do that was by each taking hold of their own transformational journeys.

CONFORM OR TRANSFORM?

In some of our earliest days in ministry, Mindy and I served a church in Gallup, New Mexico. It was there I experienced the pain of being removed from two separate ministries simultaneously, because we were of a different mind with our leaders on the person and work of the Holy Spirit. We were told we had to sign a letter of agreement with the church and mission boards that "you will not fellowship with those who disagree with our doctrinal statement" or we would have to leave. We were being told that unity with our brothers and sisters was in a doctrinal belief system, not in the person of Christ Himself. We were encouraged to read various theologians and listen to certain teaching that would convince us that they were "in the right" theologically. I was asked to choose between God's leaders on points of theological persuasion rather than study to learn from various, conflicting perspectives. Oddly, being in agreement on the person and work of Jesus was something we all shared, yet this was never a topic we were encouraged to study.

The Corinthian church seems to have suffered from this same mindset. Paul told them, *"I hear that when you come together as a church, there are divisions among you"* (1 Corinthians 11:18). They were fluent in the spiritual gifts, but were at odds and partial to certain leaders over others—probably even certain doctrinal emphases. Paul chastised them, saying,

> Brothers and sisters, I could not address you as people who live by the Spirit but as people who are still worldly— mere infants in Christ. I gave you milk, not solid food, for you were not yet ready for it. Indeed, you are still not ready. You are still worldly. For since there is jealousy and quarreling among you, are you not worldly? Are you not acting like mere humans? For when one says, "I follow Paul," and another, "I follow Apollos," are you not mere human beings? . . .
>
> *By the grace God has given me, I laid a foundation as a wise builder, and someone else is building on it. But each one should build with care. For no one can lay any foundation other than the one already laid, which is Jesus Christ. . . .*
>
> *Don't you know that you yourselves are God's temple and that God's Spirit dwells in your midst? If anyone destroys God's temple, God will destroy that person; for God's temple is sacred, and you together are that temple.*
>
> —1 CORINTHIANS 3:1-4, 10-11, 16-17

This is some of the strongest language Paul uses in all of his writings (and remember he wrote more than three-quarters of the New Testament). He was underscoring the perversity of disunity in the Lord's temple and warning them to lay the proper foundation in Christ or "God will destroy you"—meaning the leaders who lay temporal foundations. This is deconstruction at its most severe! In essence, he's saying, "get unity right so God doesn't have to judge you." Heavy stuff!

The presence of the gifts of the Spirit amongst them was overshadowed by their comparison of leaders—and a number of other issues Paul confronted them with—but most importantly, the division in the Body these brought. Since divisions and factions were the norm in Greek culture, they thought nothing of having them in their church. However, God's way is unity. The greatest moves of God in the book of Acts were always when the people were in "one accord." (See Acts 1:14; 2:1, 46; 4:24; 5:12; 8:6 for examples.) Paul was clear that God would deconstruct this practice in their midst. They needed to grow up by growing together. The presence of miracles and supernatural gifts is not a sign of maturity.

Kingdom unity is only found in linking ourselves to and through the person of Jesus Christ. Unity is relational more than it is informational or transactional—task-centered—otherwise there's no room for diversity. We have historically unified around "agreed to" doctrines, ministry vision, or charismatic personalities rather than being in authentic relationship under the leadership of God's Son as members of His family. God is not the author of confusion or division. Over the centuries, denominations formed around some beautiful truths the Lord wanted to emphasize for His people. Too often certain truths (grace, fathering, the Holy Spirit, etc.) became the basis of unity for a few, but left others outside the circle to gather around their own pet doctrines. Yet Paul didn't say we should have a unity of beliefs, but that "*in him* [Jesus] *all things hold together*" (Colossians 1:17) until we come into a "*unity of the faith*" (Ephesians 4:3 ESV). If we hold onto Him as our only unifying principle, then He will lead us into all truth.

Paul's letter to the Ephesians was a brilliant masterpiece in this respect. In it he first lays out the fact that the Father wanted to be one with us and sent Jesus to bring us into His family with all the benefits of being His children and heirs (Ephesians 1:1-23). With Jesus as our King, we are the younger brothers and sisters—princes and princesses, if you will—in God's household. In Chapter 2, we see that God and man were separated, dis-unified, *"but because of His great love for us, God, who is rich in mercy, made us alive* [together] *with Christ"* (Ephesians 2:4-5 [insert added]). Paul uses the preposition *"with Christ"* or *"in Christ"* numerous times in the epistles to establish that we are unified with the Father through Christ by the power of the Spirit. We are recipients of "Trinity Unity."

Paul tells the Ephesians that they who were separated, dis-unified, from God and His covenants have now become included and unified will all believers through Jesus our Peace Maker, our Shalom. (See Ephesians 2:8-18.) He goes on to describe the effects of a unified people, a dwelling place of God in the Spirit (see Ephesians 2:19-22) and the vehicle for manifesting the wisdom of God to all spiritual and natural powers in our cities. (See Ephesians 3:10.)

In Chapter 4, Paul then switches gears and focuses on our part in maintaining *"the unity of the Spirit through the bond of peace"* (Ephesians 4:3). What is the basis of our unity then?

> There is one body and one Spirit, just as you were called to one hope when you were called; one Lord, one faith, one baptism; one God and Father of all, who is over all and through all and in all.
>
> **—EPHESIANS 4:4-6**

The unity that the Father provided through the work of Christ Jesus is the basis of unity for all believers, but that still begs the question, "What are the essential beliefs of someone adhering to the Gospel of Jesus Christ?" What are the beliefs that distinguish being in the Kingdom vs. having allegiance to someone or something besides Christ? I believe Paul identified the "essentials" of the Gospel in his first letter to the Corinthian church,

> Now, brothers and sisters, I want to remind you of the gospel I preached to you, which you received and on which you have taken your stand. By this gospel you are saved, if you hold firmly to the word I preached to you. Otherwise, you have believed in vain.
>
> *For what I received I passed on to you as of first importance: that Christ died for our sins according to the Scriptures, that he was buried, that he was raised on the third day according to the Scriptures, and that he appeared to Cephas, and then to the Twelve.*
>
> —1 CORINTHIANS 15:1-5

Over the next three centuries much discussion and wrangling focused on this issue of the essential tenets of citizenship in the Kingdom of God. Eventually, in the fourth century, a manuscript emerged which in time became known as the Nicene Creed. It was written to establish the essentials of the faith and to fend off various thoughts and trends that were emerging in the fourth century that were in conflict with Scripture and apostolic truth.

The Nicene Creed is considered by many church traditions to be a reliable statement of faith for the global Church. It has always been amazing to me to see the scope of its acceptance. Every time I read this creed I am reminded of its beauty, simplicity, and resonance as our shared "essential beliefs."

We believe in one God, the Father, the Almighty, maker of heaven and earth, of all that is, seen and unseen.

We believe in one Lord, Jesus Christ, the only Son of God, eternally begotten of the Father, God from God, Light from Light, true God from true God, begotten, not made, of one Being with the Father. Through Him all things were made.

For us and for our salvation He came down from heaven: by the power of the Holy Spirit He became incarnate from the Virgin Mary and was made man. For our sake, He was crucified under Pontius Pilate; He suffered death and was buried. On the third day He rose again in accordance with the Scriptures; He ascended into heaven and is seated at the right hand of the Father. He will come again in glory to judge the living and the dead, and His Kingdom will have no end.

We believe in the Holy Spirit, the Lord, the giver of life, who proceeds from the Father and the Son. With the Father and the Son, He is worshiped and glorified. He has spoken through the Prophets.

We believe in one holy catholic [universal] and apostolic Church.

We acknowledge one baptism for the forgiveness of sins.

We look for the resurrection of the dead, and the life of the world to come.

Amen.[17]

The Moravians (a religious order from Bohemia [now part of Germany]), echoing the *Unitas Fratrum* ("United Brethren"), had as their motto, "In the essentials [of the Faith] let there be unity; in the non-essentials, liberty; and in all things, charity."

Once we stray beyond the bounds of the "essentials"—as stated by Paul and illustrated by the Nicene Creed—we get into the realm of the "non-essentials." This does not mean they are not important, but that they are not a point that should cause Christians to separate from one another—they have significance for the balance of our beliefs, yes, but are not essential for unity in Christ.

I find two things fascinating about maintaining unity. First of all, the very nature of a disagreement in the church means we need a mediator. Instead of separating over non-essentials (eg: women in ministry, church structural issues, methods of baptism, what we should and shouldn't eat and drink, how we have communion, what the gifts of the Spirit mean to us today, etc.), what if we remained together and humbly invited the head of the Church to mediate His own family?

Secondly, I don't believe unity means that we all work together. We are a body and Jesus constructs the parts and gives them assignments as He sees fit. My big toe and my earlobe have never actually met. (Um, okay, maybe when I was twelve weeks old, but that doesn't count *and* messes up my analogy.) Even in our cities, we have the shared genetic of Jesus, the call to be unified and pray across our regions—but each part must know its function and to whom it must be connected to achieve God's directives. Although I have witnessed certain endeavors of the whole church in a city, by and large, our unity is not in being in the same place at the same time, but, being of the same mind—attached to those in the city church, for example, to partner in praying and listening with them "in the unity of the Spirit" for the voice of the same King.

I have been blessed by the Lord to be assigned to a band of Jesus-loving rapscallions in our humble movement called the

Boiler Room Network (part of the 24-7 Prayer Movement). We are male and female, our leaders span nearly thirty years from youngest to oldest, are from various church backgrounds, and from different cultures and socioeconomic backgrounds. We have wildly differing political views, contrary views on raising children, disagree about church structure and polity, discipleship practices, and most serious of all, a total disagreement as to which adult beverages should be featured at our various gatherings. (A cause for mutiny, methinks.)

But we do agree on two essential things—that first, Jesus is Lord, and second, we have been placed by Him in the family of God by divine design. He is our vision and only by Him do we "consist and hold together." (See Colossians 1:17 AMP.) Because we love Him, we love each other (though I'm not always certain why), and that love is enough to eclipse our constellation of differences. We are truly friends who would and do go to battle for each other.

CHANGING MINDSETS

As you've read along so far, you may have noticed I've outlined several areas where a church-centered mindset sets us at odds with a Kingdom-expanding mindset. If we are to love one another as Kingdom Family, we need to be aware of what we are accepting out of habit vs. what God is trying to build in us and through us. The list in the following chart is not complete, but hopefully, will give you and your team of Kingdom mischief-makers ample ammunition for conversation, prayer, and renovation as you search for God's plan for your congregation, community, and nation.

Church-centric Mindset	Kingdom-expanding Mindset
TRANSACTIONAL People serve the ministry *"Do ministry together"*	**RELATIONAL** People are the ministry *"Do life together"*
CHURCH VISION MOTIVATES Leader-initiated, hierarchical	**"WORD OF THE LORD" MOTIVATES** Spirit-initiated, familial
CLERGY/LAITY SPLIT Education, Knowledge-based *"Leadership is here to show you the way"*	**PLURAL LEADERSHIP / PRIESTHOOD OF BELIEVERS** Equipping, Character-based *"We are all here to equip you to be all God has destined you to be"*
SACRED/SECULAR SPLIT Church as a sacred organization to be maintained *"Go to church, serve the church"*	**SANCTITY OF ALL LIFE** Church as a people to be developed *"Be a family, multiply into all culture"*
EXCLUSIVE UNITY Conformative *"Be like us"*	**INCLUSIVE UNITY** Transformative *"Be like Jesus"*
NATIONAL CITIZENSHIP Temporal, tribal perspective	**HEAVENLY CITIZENSHIP** Eternal, global perspective

We need to prayerfully consider which cultural paradigms we have slipped into that are holding us back from building our churches on more solid, godly foundations. I trust the Lord to grant you revelation in their application to you and your team's particular setting in how God has called you to serve. Discussing these is a great place to come together and find common ground will building the friendships and relationships that will be the backbone of impacting your city and region.

THE TAPESTRY'S TRUE IMAGE

When Christ is our basis of unity, we can handle a lot of disagreement and discuss it freely without throwing each other in the waste bin of arrogant religious "purity" and perfectionism. We should rejoice in all the truth represented in our various denominations and church traditions, humbly acknowledge Jesus as our unifying factor, then reject the denominationalism that has preferred our theological persuasions over our oneness in Christ. It is the messy art of being brothers and sisters in the Kingdom Family.

This is a beautiful glimpse into the Weaver's ultimate design for the tapestry that is His Church—the image and pattern of Christ in us, His people. This is juxtaposed to the Church's history of personality differences that often come with the very gifts and callings God has planted within church leaders. It is often difficult, for example, for someone with a prophetic calling—someone focused on holiness before God—to be able to effectively communicate what is on their heart with someone who is more pastoral—someone who feels that the highest calling of God is to love people despite their behavior. The prophetic person will see the pastoral as too lax while the pastor will see the prophetic as too harsh and dogmatic. On the other hand, the evangelist will be the person focused on the simplicity of the Gospel, longing to see the people of God impassioned for the lost, while the teacher will tend to find all of these perspectives overgeneralized and shallow—"people need to be taught the fullness of what it means to lay down our lives and follow Jesus," they say. Those with an apostolic bent may be zealous to lay firm foundations in the Church, even if it takes years, while those called as missionaries will want to "just get on with the work."

When all of these "trans-local" gifts—apostle, prophet, evangelist, pastor, teacher—are present together as local elders in a church focused on Christ first, powerful things happen—powerful disagreements as well as powerful work for the Kingdom. It is this fighting to unify diversity that God had in mind when He designed the various ministry gifts, callings, and "offices."

So, what ties all this diversity of gifts and callings into one Body under the Headship of Jesus? *Hearing God together.*

We see a beautiful example of this listening to God by observing how the early church leaders positioned themselves to be before the Lord (I know I've shared this verse before, but it bears repeating):

> In the church at Antioch there were prophets and teachers: Barnabas, Simeon called Niger, Lucius of Cyrene, Manaen (who had been brought up with Herod the tetrarch) and Saul. While they were worshiping the Lord and fasting, the Holy Spirit said, "Set apart for me Barnabas and Saul for the work to which I have called them." So after they had fasted and prayed, they placed their hands on them and sent them off.
>
> —ACTS 13:1-3

The basis of their unity wasn't just brotherly affection for one another, it was hearing from the King, the ultimate unifier. Be it elderships, marketplace ministers, or city-wide pastors, the goal isn't to respond to needs, conjure up great acts of justice, or place believers in prominent places of authority (even though all of those things are worthy aims), but to be before the King to get *His* instructions on how to impact the city and the culture *His* way. When denominational or doctrinal preferences are not allowed to eclipse the centrality of Christ, He, the Head, will be "in our midst" and direct His people. Then, and only then, do we get the real work of God done.

FIGHTING TO LOVE

How does a team achieve this level of unity? Face to face, in prayer, and with a commitment to honesty and a tenacious refusal to let anything separate them from each other.

Over the years the leaders at Believers have developed a culture of praying together with the other elders that has saved their posteriors, released peace to them, and given them wisdom in navigating the treacherous waters of raising up a Jesus-loving church family. The prayer has always been two-way: sometimes asking, more often listening.

I was recently with them during a rousing disagreement regarding new direction and a new division of labor. After some emotional pugilism, some verbal sparring, and a very long silence, we stopped, prayed, got clarity, heard the Lord's instruction, did a little repenting, and moved on. In the early years, the resolution of a spat like that took much longer. Now, years later, they've learned to love each other, trust each other, and not move forward without receiving instruction from the Head. There's still learning for them of course, but it's hard to look at them as the same people I saw sitting under that table facing away from each other more than a dozen years ago.

Learning how to become a body has had a radical effect on Believers Church, its maturity, its release of new leaders, and ultimately the presence of God in their midst. Everyone is welcome, and all maladies are accepted. They have emerged out of the cocoon of self-absorption and are taking flight into the felt-needs of the city God has assigned them to. They aren't perfect—yet—but they are growing up into all things in Christ.

WHAT NOW?

Question # 1: What is the basis of the unity that you experience in your church environment? Is it based on a commitment to the leaders' vision, or is it based in the person of Christ Himself and His instructions to all the people of God? (Remember, even if the vision fails, you should still have each other.)

Question #2: How would you define the love, unity, and commitment of your own heart towards those in the family of God He has assigned to you?

Question #3: Being that "keeping the unity of the Spirit in the bond of peace" is our mandate as believers, what principles and values are in place in your life to guard the unity God desires for you and those in your life? (E.g., comparing leaders, grumbling, church hopping, gossip, lack of generosity, lack of truth telling, ministry pride, etc.)

INVITING THE EARTHQUAKE

*Therefore, since we are receiving a kingdom that cannot
be shaken, let us be thankful, and so worship God acceptably
with reverence and awe, for our "God is a consuming fire."*

—HEBREWS 12:28-29

oth Ishmael and Isaac were fathered by Abraham. Ishmael
was the human attempt to circumnavigate the promise that
they—Abraham and Sarah—would have a son. Recognizing it was
not "humanly" possible, they proceeded to hatch a plan to see the
promise fulfilled in a different way. After Ishmael's birth by Hagar,
lo and behold, this ancient couple did conceive. The Angel of the
Lord had prophesied it and Sarah laughed at it, but Paul tells us
that Abraham had a different response:

> *Without weakening in his faith, he faced the fact that his
> body was as good as dead—since he was about a hundred
> years old—and that Sarah's womb was also dead. Yet he did
> not waver through unbelief regarding the promise of God,
> but was strengthened in his faith and gave glory to God,
> being fully persuaded that God had power to do what he had
> promised.*
> —ROMANS 4:19-21

Abraham loved both sons as did God. Ishmael was the fruit of Abraham's loins and God promised, *"I will surely bless him"* (Gen 17:20). God went so far as to say, *"I will make the son of the slave into a nation also, because he is your offspring"* (Genesis 21:13). But, at the same time, God told Abraham Ishmael had to go. It was Isaac, the son produced by a miracle of the Spirit of God, that would receive the inheritance: *"You will call him Isaac. I will establish my covenant with him as an everlasting covenant for his descendants after him"* (Genesis 17:19).

As we look back on the church-centric and the Kingdom-expanding mindsets and consider the "sticky notes" exercise, we need to ask the Lord, "Are there any Ishmaels in our house?" We can be so in love with our own creation, as was Abraham, that we resist the Father's command to *"get rid of the slave woman and her son"* (Gen 21:10). Paul explains this to the Galatian church in this powerful text:

> Now you, brothers and sisters, like Isaac, are children of promise. At that time the son born according to the flesh persecuted the son born by the power of the Spirit. It is the same now. But what does Scripture say? "Get rid of the slave woman and her son, for the slave woman's son will never share in the inheritance with the free woman's son." Therefore, brothers and sisters, we are not children of the slave woman, but of the free woman.
>
> —GALATIANS 4:28-31

That little phrase, *"the son born according to the flesh persecuted the son born by the power of the Spirit,"* is the crux of the battle we face when seeking to reconstruct and reform the church from the DNA of Ishmael—handed down by our own human traditions—instead of the covenantal genes of Isaac—those things either birthed by the Spirit or upon which the Spirit breathes life. Although these two sons grew up side by side, there was never peace in the family until the human-inspired son was sent away. The time came when a separation had to be made and the son of human effort had to be evicted. When the time for this separation comes in our ministries, we will find ourselves in the fight of our lives—hell will break loose (those nasty religious spirits seldom give up easily) before heaven takes residence amongst us. Illuminating traditions and "sacred cows" is best battled on our knees, replete with massive doses of humility, willingness to repent, the guidance of the Holy Spirit, and a circle of friends who hunger to see the Church truly be formed by the "power of the Spirit" and nothing less.

I'm not a big proponent of leaning too heavily on the "how to's" of living for Christ—I've always felt that this is ultimately the role of the Holy Spirit instructing our hearts—but am more interested in a relationship with Jesus as a person and with the community of faith that invites the Holy Spirit to clarify, direct, dismantle, and rebuild only according to God's blueprint. Christ alone can make our churches living, fruitful organisms!

At the same time, I believe there are often questions we can ask God that allow Him to guide us—that reveal keys to transitioning from hierarchical structures and manmade traditions to being a Spirit-led church and body of believers.

You may we wondering, "OK, can I (we) really embrace the change from church-centric thinking to kingdom-centric mindsets and practices?" Yes, you can. There is a caveat, however. Paul, in addressing the dysfunction of the Corinthian church stated strongly, *"For no one can lay any foundation other than the one already laid, which is Jesus Christ"* (1 Corinthians 3:11). If in any way we have not built God's Church on His plan, with His "mind," and according to His Word—then we've done it our way, not His! This isn't a little thing needing a little tweak, a small adjustment, or another conversation—*this realization should land us on our faces.* It is a serious thing to be entrusted with God's people and plans and to stray from Him being the Pattern, the Builder, and the only recipient of praise. Be prepared for some seriously beautiful repenting as the Spirit of the Lord is invited to convict! I encourage you to enter this process of evaluation and change in a spirit of great humility and sobriety.

WHEN THE WALLS BEGIN TO CRUMBLE

If we are to be the Church God has called us to be, we must invite the whirlwind of the Holy Spirit to be the General Contractor (and Demolition Expert) of our church renovation programs—one to be performed from the inside out. As we are told in Hebrews:

> See to it that you do not refuse him who speaks. If they did not escape when they refused him who warned them on earth, how much less will we, if we turn away from him who warns us from heaven? At that time his voice shook the earth, but now he has promised, "Once more I will shake not only the earth but also the heavens." The words "once more" indicate the removing of what can be shaken—that is, created things—so that what cannot be shaken may remain.

—HEBREWS 12:25-27

What needs to be shaken in our churches today are the cultural traditions and the "good ideas" we have allowed to take root in our congregations and which have left no room for the "God ideas" upon which we should be building. This is not a matter for shame or condemnation, it is simply the pattern God has followed in every generation to call His people back to Himself. It is His process for preparing new wineskins for the new wine He wants to give us, so that we can become the people He has uniquely called us to be—both corporately and individually. What needs to happen is that our mindsets need to be upgraded; our paradigms need to be shifted heavenward.

When the walls are crumbling and the dust is thick in the midst of deconstruction, there is a strong temptation to try to stop the avalanche. My recommendation? Get out of the way before you get pulverized by the things God has no intention of rescuing.

Notice how Abraham responded to his own "crumbling walls." After hearing God's command to sacrifice his son, he simply "saddled his ass," walked toward the sacrificial hill, and at the base of the mountain, turned to his mates and said, *"Stay here with the donkey while I and the boy go over there. We will worship and then we will come back to you"* (Genesis 22:5).

It was at the point of obedience that God interrupted his murderous—but obedient—arm and said, *"Now I know that you fear God"* (Genesis 22:12). Every vision, every manmade institution (the Ishmaels), and even also the "Isaacs" (promises of God), have to be sacrificed on the altar with faith (trust) and worship in our hearts—pretty much everything we are doing, protecting, and afraid to lose. It's the only smart thing to do—only then will we, eventually, inherit the promise. Only after we lay these things before the Lord can we know which are right to continue with and which will only hinder us down the road. If we don't, even God given visions can become the focus rather than staying in relationship with God Himself and constantly seeking the voice of heaven. "Good" is ever at conflict with "best." Never take your eyes off the Lord of the Work.

If you are amongst the throng of those who were not able to avoid the "crumbling wall" and became a victim of falling rubble, you are in good (and very bruised) company! If perhaps you were fired, removed, ignored, abandoned, betrayed, belittled, or shamed, you are a candidate for a very powerful principle. "Bless backward!" This simply means we don't carry the offense forward into any new assignment until those painful memories are brought to the foot of the cross, forgiveness dispensed, and forgiveness and transformation received. We are exhorted to *"Be kind and compassionate to one another, forgiving each other, just as in Christ God forgave you"* (Ephesians 4:32) Jesus extended forgiveness during His entire pilgrimage on earth, most notably to those that put Him to death: *"Father, forgive them, for they do not know what they are doing"* (Luke 23:34).

If we fail and are unwilling to forgive those who have offended or demeaned us, we move into the next assignment with a high probability of forming ideas and doing our work infected by a "theology of pain," thus changing our beliefs and practices in order to protect our broken hearts. Unforgiveness colors everything and distorts our vision of reality. It then quickly moves on to infect those we are "ministering to" through our contaminated human spirits.

I have watched numerous new church plants be founded by those who left their former church assignment carrying residual pain and determined to "Do things differently this time!" I have watched as God assigned those leaders triumphal vision for their new endeavor, but then their unhealed past hurts quickly attracted other "pain carriers," and they had to sit back and watch as their dream "mysteriously" turned to a nightmare. No surprise—they hadn't appropriated the painfully beautiful healing balm of their Father—a spiritual unguent combining forgiveness and reconciliation! He gives us "redemptive eyes" for those who wronged us—if we but simply ask!

This then begs the question: Once we have deconstructed certain things under the guidance of the Holy Spirit, what are we to reconstruct? Well that's all about finding our Gospel Identities in the family of God, as we will explore in the next section: The story of the planting of Navah Church in Kansas City.

NOW WHAT?

Question #1: What "Ishmaels"—things of "human ingenuity"—have you constructed or inherited or have become "sacred cows" in your life and ministry?

Question #2: What "Isaacs"—things that the Lord has originated or promised for the future—have you not relinquished at the foot of the cross?

> **Prayer:** Meditate and pray over this amazing scripture: Hebrews 11:17-19.

> **Exercise:** After considering this text from Abraham's life, consider what personal and collective fears you may be harboring that prevent you from laying both "dead works" and precious promises at the foot of the cross—one to die forever and the other to be brought back in His miraculous way and time as He sees fit.

Question #3: Have you ever been hit by or buried under the rubble of church warfare? Are you (we) still carrying any unresolved or residual pain from past experiences? Have you experienced the joy and peace that comes from forgiveness and a full reconciliation with those that you offended or were offended and wounded by?

> **Exercise:** Insure that each team member has had a chance to bring each infraction or remaining wound into the light and received grace for their "imperfections." Give each other time and space to "bless backwards"—a most redemptive and wonderfully painful thing—one that hurts so good!

Question#4: Review this summary of the opposing mindsets we discussed in Part One in the chart back on page 99. Which of the church-centric paradigms have you embraced and assumed to be the norm? How does the Holy Spirit want you to respond? (Pray and discuss!)

PART TWO:
RECONSTRUCTION
The Navah Church Story: Finding Our Gospel Identities

God's work in Jesus Christ

grants us a whole new identity,

and this new identity leads to

a whole new way of living.

We do what we do

because of who we are.

. . . Being precedes doing.

—JEFF VANDERSTELT,
Saturate

GOD'S "PLAN A"

Although I [Paul] am less than the least of all the Lord's people,
this grace was given me: to preach to the Gentiles
the boundless riches of Christ, and to make plain to everyone
the administration of this mystery, which for ages past
was kept hidden in God, who created all things.
His intent was that now, **through the church,**
the manifold wisdom of God should be made known
to the rulers and authorities in the heavenly realms,
according to his eternal purpose that he accomplished
in Christ Jesus our Lord. *In him and through faith in him*
we may approach God with freedom and confidence.

—EPHESIANS 3:8–12 (emphasis added)

When Adam Cox and David Blackwell met, they were in their early twenties and hungry to see what God wanted to do with their lives. Not quite sure of how to explore that, they decided to start praying together regularly each week.

Oh, the power of small beginnings.

That Adam and David met at all is somewhat miraculous all on its own. Just a few months before they met, Adam was in another city preparing to go to South Africa with Youth With A Mission when he happened across a set of cassette tapes by Mike Bickle from Metro Christian Fellowship in Kansas City. The message was about having a "Passion for Jesus." Despite his newly found hunger for anything and everything Jesus, this was language he'd never heard while growing up in a staunchly conservative Methodist church. As the Methodist founder John Wesley once put it, Adam found his "heart strangely warmed" in response to the words he heard Pastor Bickle speak—"set on fire" might be more accurate. Adam felt like he had to meet the man who'd spoken these rousing words and sit for a time in his congregation listening to whatever else he might have to say. Adam wanted to cancel his plans to go to South Africa, but felt the Father say go and then return to Kansas City. So he went to a Discipleship Training School in Muizenberg, South Africa, then returned to Grace Training Center.

As it turned out, before he even left, it seemed like his new plans were a bust. Not long after reaching out to Metro Christian Fellowship for information about their church and to see what help they could provide him when he relocated, they replied with a letter informing him Mike Bickle was no longer leading the church and that a guy named Floyd McClung would be replacing him. (Yes, the very same Floyd McClung that had delivered God's words to me at that staff meeting in Amsterdam. Small world, heh?) Adam had heard of Floyd through his YWAM connections and rather than dampening his enthusiasm to move to Kansas City, it fueled his anticipation instead, even amidst what were now jumbled expectations.

It was just after arriving in Kansas City that Adam met David Blackwell. The year was 2000. As Adam described him, David as a twenty-year-old "sight to behold—he was so incredibly 'Chicago' and over-the-top passionate." Both from elsewhere and looking for connections, Adam and David became fast friends. It was soon after that they had made the pact to pray together every week. As they did so, an odd thing happened. The only way Adam could describe it was they got the sense that "God liked our friendship. Every time we prayed, He seems to turn up."

Adam was still new to these kinds of "God impressions," but was beginning to get more used to them. He had grown up picturing God being very distant, sitting idly, far way in outer space. That changed dramatically on July 5th, 1998. Adam describes it as the day he first met Jesus for himself.

That day, Adam had come forward in response to an altar call for those wanting to know Jesus more personally. As he approached, a man laid his hands on his shoulders and prayed for him. Adam told me that as he did, "my whole body began tingling and I was filled with the presence of the Holy Spirit. I couldn't stand up, so I fell down on my back." Unalarmed and with a slightly mischievous smile on his face, the man leaned over and told him, "Whatever you've ever wanted to say to God, you can tell Him now." When Adam opened his mouth, languages came out he'd never even heard before. As he was "blubbering," sobbing, and laughing all at once, the Lord broke in and spoke to his heart: "You've tasted the world's love and it's broken your heart. Now you're going to taste My love—and I'll never leave you."

As the meeting ended, Adam still lay on the floor. God continued to speak with him. "I called you from your mother's womb to preach the Gospel," the Father told him, "and I put you here to lead." Rather than leaving him there on the floor, a group eventually carried him back to his cabin and laid him on his bunk.

Nothing was the same for Adam after that.

Adam had no idea at the time what it all meant, but he also knew it was something he needed to pursue. It was the first time he'd felt that fire in his heart.

He was now carrying a vision to see the whole world know that God is real and that He really loved people—each and every one.

He felt as if he was being called to be a modern-day revivalist like Wesley or Finney and speak to thousands of people at a time. He was consumed with the thought, "How can I take what is inside of me and put it into other people?"

CONVERTED TO THE CHURCH

As Adam and David settled into Kansas City and prayed together, one day, out of the blue, Floyd approached Adam and asked if he wanted to go see a movie together. Adam agreed.

As Adam and Floyd walked together after the film, Adam shared his vision of speaking to thousands of people and leading them to Jesus. Floyd listened to his vision to "minister to crowds" without saying a word, then gently planted a different seed. "You know, Jesus's way was to spend most of his time with twelve people—called the Church. Vision of revival is great, but the delivery system is the Church making disciples."

These words stirred something quite different in Adam. He went home, got on his knees, and asked God about what had just happened. He sensed the Lord say to him, "Tonight, everything is going to change. Before Floyd saw you, I saw you, and I loved you before you did anything." He decided to look through the book of Acts to see how they had done it. Acts 2:42-47 was as far as he needed to get.

> They devoted themselves to the apostles' teaching and to fellowship, to the breaking of bread and to prayer. Everyone was filled with awe at the many wonders and signs performed by the apostles. All the believers were together and had everything in common. They sold property and possessions to give to anyone who had need.

Every day they continued to meet together in the temple courts. They broke bread in their homes and ate together with glad and sincere hearts, praising God and enjoying the favor of all the people. And the Lord added to their number daily those who were being saved.

Despite Peter speaking to a large crowd on the day of Pentecost and seeing 3,000 come to Christ, Adam saw the norm of spreading the Gospel wasn't big meetings, but rather adding to their numbers daily by eating *together with glad and sincere hearts, praising God and enjoying the favor of all the people.* Adam realized that the Church was God's "Plan A"—and there was no "Plan B." As he read these Scriptures over again, the Lord emphasized to him, "You don't understand My Church or see her beauty. I want you to realize your dream through My people." That day Adam laid down his own dreams of ministering to thousands and opened his heart to allow the Father to teach him to see the beauty of the people of God he saw around him every day.

It was after this that Adam and David began asking new questions in prayer: "If the world is supposed to be redeemed through the Church, how will that happen? What does that look like?"

While they knew Jesus spoke to (and in some instances fed) thousands, those who rocked the world after His resurrection were not those crowds, but the core group He'd spent most of His time with—the twelve and their entourage—and those whose lives they would eventually touch, including Paul.

That was a massive paradigm shift for Adam: that God's plan for the earth was to be realized through the Church and through making disciples—not through speaking and converting stadiums full of people. God's design was to spend *time* with a few—*a lot* of time, doing life together—not giving altar calls to masses. He made disciples of them, and they would go out and make disciple of others. That was Jesus's way. Adam determined that day to make this corrected dream a reality, and that it would be in partnership with his new friend and prayer partner, David.

It was together with his friend in prayer Adam would come to understand what the Gospel he had been called to preach really meant. But before he was able step out in that realization, God would have to teach Adam how to see himself through the eyes of his Father in heaven—and the extent to which accepting the whole Gospel changes everything. God needed to form "a Gospel Identity" in Adam and David.

THE GOSPEL WE PREACH

Adam, who had just begun his journey into discovering God's plan for himself and the church he would one day plant, was being led by the Father into the greatest reconstructive power available to each of us: The Gospel of the Kingdom. Not only did Adam get ruined by God's love for him that day he lay on the floor in 1998, but that love would become the trademark of the church he would help found alongside his future wife, Juli, and their friends. He was called to lead as the Lord had told him he would that day.

Had poor old Humpty Dumpty had the Gospel, he would have been summarily reconstructed—verily, "put together again"—after his fatal fall. There is nothing as reconstructive to the Church as the Gospel of the Kingdom. The design of the church was that it would be the family in which we could return to fellowship with our Father in heaven. When this is not the central aim, we flounder. Although it is sometimes our structures that need some reconsideration, it is primarily our thinking and practices that need the most attention. Paul declared, *"For I am not ashamed of the gospel, because* it is the power of God that brings salvation to everyone who believes" (Romans 1:16, emphasis added). While Christ's Godhood, human birth by a virgin, life, death, resurrection, ascension, and eternal reign is all central to our message, the Gospel must also include that He accomplished what He came to the earth to establish: the formation of new tribes of God's people on the earth called churches. This Gospel relates to everything we encounter in life.

Just after Paul's declaration here that he was not *"ashamed of the gospel,"* he reiterates what the Gospel is meant to produce:

> For in the gospel a righteousness from God is revealed—a righteousness that is by faith from first to last, just as it is written: "The righteous will live by faith."
>
> —ROMANS 1:17

We are invited to *"seek first his kingdom and his righteousness"* (Matthew 6:33) as magnificently revealed in the Gospel work of Jesus, a righteousness that we live out by faith in the work of the Father, Son, and Holy Spirit. We are returned to the Family of the Father, established in the Kingdom of the Son, and appointed emissaries empowered by the Spirit. This is our "Gospel Identity."

When Jesus came proclaiming the Kingdom, He related it to what His Father had "told him to do" (see John 5:19), then later He told His disciples that they were to wait for the promise of the Spirit before they did anything. All three members of the Godhead were as engaged in this "re-creation" through Christ as they were in the initial creation. Jesus was the originator of a "new race" of Adam's failed progeny and the instigator of a "new family." The Gospel of the Kingdom was "new stuff" (in Christ) where "old things" (in Adam[*]) have passed away and "all things have become new." (See 2 Corinthians 5:17.) The Gospel through Jesus invited believers into a new "righteousness," a place to stand from which to move the world, by shedding their "sin consciousness" for a "righteousness consciousness" in the Godhead.

The common view of the Gospel of salvation is contained in a larger biblical narrative of the supremacy of the Godhead and the ever-expanding work of God's Kingdom in each individual person and people group. Christ's birth, death, and resurrection were supreme acts of His love for us, but were never seen by the early church to be relegated to a "personal private salvation" devoid of the participation of the Father and the Spirit to bring God's full identity back into "everything" through Christ's sacrifice.

The Father wants His earth, His temple, returned to Him and manifesting the full image of His Son. Thus we are destined to become the sons and daughters of God that the earth longs to see manifested: *"For the creation waits in eager expectation for the children of God to be revealed"* (Romans 8:19). We are not merely to *wait out* our time on this "spinning mud heap" (as Voltaire described it) until Jesus returns to save us from this lost and pathetic world. We are, instead, to actively immerse ourselves in our Gospel Identity thus personifying the Gospel of the Family and the Kingdom, winning hearts, cities, and nations under the banner of the Creator God—a massive reconstruction job!

In other words, heaven starts now, not when we die. Peter broadens our understanding of this salvation to include the point, the process, and the result of its power:

---

[*] Just to be clear, this means the Adam of Adam and Eve from the book of Genesis—the first Adam—not Adam Cox. ☺

In his great mercy he [**the Father**] has given us new birth into a living hope through the resurrection of Jesus Christ from the dead, and into an inheritance that can never perish, spoil or fade. This inheritance is kept in heaven for you, who **through faith** are shielded by God's power until the coming of the salvation that is ready to be revealed in the last time. In all this you greatly rejoice, though now for a little while you may have had to suffer grief in all kinds of trials. These have come so that the proven genuineness of **your faith**—of greater worth than gold, which perishes even though refined by fire—may result in praise, glory and honor when Jesus Christ is revealed. Though you have not seen him, you love him; and even though you do not see him now, you believe in him and are filled with an inexpressible and glorious joy, for you are receiving the goal of **your faith**, the salvation of your souls.

—**1 PETER 1:3-9** (emphases added)

He declares that He gave us *"new birth"* until *"the coming of the salvation that is ready to be revealed in the last time."* Yes, salvation for us was in the past, but it's completion waits for us in the future. Peter describes the journey in between our beginning and end points of salvation in verses 6-8 of this passage—it is trials *"of greater worth than gold"* that grow our love for this invisible God. He punctuates the destination of the journey by describing the "goal of our faith": the eventual *"salvation of our souls."* The Gospel is more than a point of entry, it is the enduring process of God until we *and creation* are conformed into His image.

To reconstruct the image of Jesus into the tapestry of our lives and ministries, we have to set and weave the threads of the tapestry together into the Designer's pattern by embracing our Gospel

Identity in the realms of the Father, the Son, and the Holy Spirit. In the chart below, you can easily identify the threads of each member of the Trinity in the Church: the Fathers reclamation of His Family, the Son's establishment of His Kingdom, and the Spirit's transformational presence in all of society.

Our Gospel Identity[*]

Who God is	What He Has Done	Who We Are	What We Do
FATHER	Sent His Son to adopt us into His family.	Sons and daughters in the Father's family.	Love one another as a holy family under the authority of the Father. (A heart issue.)
SON	Established His Kingdom on earth as a Servant King.	Servant-heir subjects of the King—princes and princesses (the younger siblings of the King).	Serve the least among us and one another in the name of the King. (A matter of practice.)
HOLY SPIRIT	Sent to manifest the Kingdom on earth and fill it with the presence of God.	Spirit-equipped and empowered ambassadors/ missionaries/ emissaries of the Kingdom.	Proclaim and demonstrate the Kingdom for all to see.

Our task as leaders is clear: we are invited to labor "night and day" under the power of God until His Church grows *"to become in every respect the mature body of him who is the head, that is, Christ"* (Ephesians 4:15).

This is what I mean when I refer to our "Gospel Identity." The attributes of each member of the Godhead has influence on who we are in Christ. It is our commitment and desire to see every one of

---

[*] I am deeply indebted to Jeff Vanderstelt, leader of Doxa Church in Bellevue, Washington, for his scholarship and practice of what is shown in this chart (any alterations are mine).

God's people in our churches alight with the understanding of the Gospel and see it invade every corner of their identity. A.W. Tozer postulated

> The history of mankind will probably show that no people has ever risen above its religion, and man's spiritual history will positively demonstrate that no religion has ever been greater than its idea of God. Worship is pure or base as the worshiper entertains high or low thoughts of God.[18]

If that's true for anyone, it's true for us in the Church. How can we expect to get what God has for us—and do what He's called us to do—until we know the provision of the Godhead and who we are in Christ?

TRYING ON EXPRESSIONS OF "PLAN A"

Before Adam got a chance to feel settled in Kansas City, David had to move back to Chicago. About that same time, though, Nathan and Marisa Chud arrived from Alaska. Barely turned twenty themselves, the Chuds were newly married and had driven straight to Kansas City on a similar quest as Adam and David's. They were just as excited about pursuing God in prayer as he and David had been. As a result, it wasn't long before Adam, still single, found himself a "third wheel" to this pair of newlyweds, spending a great deal of time together and developing a rhythm of prayer with them.

The three began praying together every morning and hanging out nearly every day. As they did, they began dreaming about an "Acts-like" church, breaking bread in homes and eating together *"praising God."* Then they were given the opportunity to lead a "life group" for Metro Christian Fellowship and they jumped on it. With great enthusiasm and little experience, they began the journey of discovering God's plan for the Church by starting to build godly relationships within a small group atmosphere. Slowly and awkwardly, they stumbled towards a form they felt represented the *"house to house"* churches of the book of Acts.

These young future leaders had come to a time at the turn of the millennium when it was ripe to investigate fresh thinking regarding the new forms and functions of the local church (as I mentioned before, there had been a lot of talk and speculation about this in the late '90s). More importantly, it was time to reconnect with the historical threads of the first church, to examine the seminal DNA of "being God's Kingdom" on the earth: What does it really mean to accept the Gospel of Jesus Christ? How does it change who we are? What does it really mean to be sons and daughters of the heavenly Father?

NOW WHAT?

Question #1: How have you (we) defined, applied, or taught the Gospel Identity and the "righteousness" embedded in it? (See Romans 1:16-17.) How well do you, your family, and your friends know it, walk in its power, and are equipped to share it in your world?

> **Exercise:** Take time to review each box represented in the Gospel Identity grid and reference the corresponding scriptures in Appendix A. Consider the level of knowledge and application of it in your life, your leadership, and your church. Are you living in the beauty of your Gospel Identity with whatever fluency you are able to deliver to your spheres of influence? Invite the Lord to bring revelation and show you how to walk it out with others, instill it in God's people, and make it the foundation you build your life and ministry upon.

Question #2: How do you respond to Adam's conviction that "the Church is God's Plan A and there is no Plan B"? How is the "Church" with all of its denominations, mission agencies, and para-organizations meant to interpret such a statement? What implications could this have on how you do ministry with the Church being the base of all local and international missions?

FOUND IN THE FATHER

And we know that in all things God works for the good of those
who love him, who have been called according to his purpose.
For those God foreknew **he also predestined to be**
conformed to the image of his Son, that he might be the
firstborn among many brothers and sisters.

—ROMANS 8:28–29 (emphasis added)

avid, who had by then had married Molly, moved back to
Kansas City in the fall of 2002 and rejoined Adam and the
Chuds. They immediately started "doing life" together, eating
meals, opening the Word, and inviting people into this rhythm of
life. They were together so much that they got the crazy idea of
moving into the same house. So, they prayed a short prayer asking
the Lord to confirm this direction.

In the echoes of that wee prayer, while out on a prayer walk
one day, Nathan came across a flyer advertising a house for sale on
the east side of Kansas City. The band of friends decided to drive
over to check it out. The place was a disaster: broken windows,
trash up to their knees, and the ever-popular, circa-1970s, orange
shag carpet. Despite its condition, they still felt led to speak to

the owner, and when they did, he offered to let them fix it up in exchange for rent. Within a week, they'd begun working on the house and moved into BCC (Blackwell, Chud, Cox) on March 1st, 2003.

THE FATHER—WHAT HE HAS DONE: SENT HIS SON TO ADOPT US INTO HIS FAMILY

I remember holding my father's hand as we walked down the halls of an orphanage in Karuizawa, Japan. I was five, but can clearly remember the hopeful little faces peering out of the doorways, wondering if we would stop and choose one of them to be in our family. (God was not answering my prayer for my "mommy" to have a baby for me to tease—and never did!) Dad was there to help find families for these post-war children born in Japan. The look of pure joy on their faces when they were selected by a family is also still a vivid memory. They were chosen, wanted, and included into the love, rights, and privileges of their new families. Their names were changed, and a new identity given—all because they were chosen.

As odd as it may seem, the prosperity of the last few decades has created its own kind of "orphan" generation. Whether it is addiction to work, entertainment, handheld devices, some mind-altering substance, some other cause for family "abandonment," or just living in a culture where people seem to slowly drift further and further away apart with each coming day, we have more disconnected people in our societies today than ever before. This has produced a sort of orphan spirit in those that come into our churches where people have that same wide-eyed desire to be adopted that I saw in the faces of those children in post-WW2 Japan. The problem is, rather than nurturing them into a relationship with their Father and their new brothers and sisters, we seemed to have turned our churches into orphanages instead of families.

Think about that for a moment. In an orphanage, dozens, if not hundreds, of children can be the responsibility of one adult. Scientists are now studying the effects on babies in Romanian orphanages from the 1980s and 1990s who grew up with very little attention given them by caregivers—left to cry themselves to sleep every night of their early lives. Their physical growth was stunted, they had difficulty forming attachments to others, and their minds were poorly developed among other shortcomings. They are examples of orphan dysfunction at its worst. Kids need attention and physical touch if they are to grow up healthy.

Now think of the way most churches operate. There's little to no nurturing connection between people who show up on Sunday mornings. Our interactions with one another are shallow, at best, and artificial and insincere, at worst. We show a more carefully curated persona there than most do on social media. We want to be liked, we want to be seen as good people, we want to be shown approval, we want to be looked up to, so we only show people our best behavior. Or we go to the other extreme and become walking sponges, sucking the life out of every interaction with our "woe is me" demeanors. Neither are real or healthy (dare I say "hypocritical"?) and neither hold the fulness and live God wants for us.

I think this largely happens because, even though we're saved, we have little idea who we are because of it.

Identity is a tricky thing because so much of it is absorbed rather than consciously chosen. As children we learn that we have worth because we are loved by our parents, then we must learn how to share that worth with others, namely our siblings first and foremost. In my family, for instance, there were certain things that went along with being a Petersen, from our Danish roots to the Japanese influence of my upbringing. There's a certain heritage, but there are also individual talents, interests, and giftings that make us who we are and help us know what God designed us to accomplish. The foundation of all of that goes back to knowing we are loved and that we have a support system that we can rely upon. It's the place from which we push off and launch ourselves into the world hoping we impact it for the better.

The trouble is those with orphaned spirits don't have that launchpad that is built through being constantly exposed to a love-filled environment. Add to that the fact that finding our identity also demands that we achieve, excel, and set ourselves apart from the pack in some way, and things can get pretty muddled. Hurt people tend to strike out in self-preservation that only hurts others. Trauma breeds more trauma. If you speak with any person who's been part of adoption or foster care, you know abandonment and broken childhoods aren't repaired easily. You can't just tell someone they are loved. They have to sit in it for a while before it starts to soak in. Actions speak louder than words. The cycle that creates messed up, broken people doesn't fix itself. It takes serious, supernatural intervention. It take reconnecting with the Father of us all.

That's why coming out of a misshapen past is rarely fixed just because we have a "come to Jesus" moment. (Sometimes God does do instantaneous works of transformation, but those are rare exceptions.) He tends instead to choose a path of patience and connection to grow up His kids. That demands a process of personal redefinition and the formation of a new self-worth that isn't defined by the past but is reformed in the present. That demands being formed in the family of God, something we cannot do until we first find our new identity in relationship with the loving Father of heaven and earth.

Perhaps this is part of why Jesus said,

> "Who is my mother, and who are my brothers?" Pointing
> to his disciples, he said, "Here are my mother and my
> brothers. For whoever does the will of my Father in heaven
> is my brother and sister and mother."
>
> —MATTHEW 12:48-50

And why He said there was a reward for those who *"left houses or
brothers or sisters or father or mother or children or lands, for my
name's sake"* (Matthew 19:29-30). He wasn't saying he was against
families; He was calling people up into Family with a new Father.

As we come to Christ, the first thing we need to realize is that
we have a loving Father in heaven, and then we need to be adopted
into a family environment where we can be nurtured and grow up
into relationship with the Father and our new brothers and sisters
in Christ. We can't leave people in an orphanage environment if they
are going to grow up in Christ, we need to put them into families.
We can only find meaning in relationship with one another. It's
one thing to know we've been adopted into a new family; it's quite
another to live it out to the point we're transformed into the image
of our new Big Brother. This is what God calls us to when He invites
us into His household—God sent His Son that He might get His family back, and that His Family would transcend our broken world.

We see in John's Gospel the relationship between the Father
and the Son, and it is to that relationship that we have been invited
to model in our lives. It is the cosmic order the earth's inhabitants
are invited into.

> "Father, the hour has come. Glorify your Son, that your
> Son may glorify you. For you granted him authority over
> all people that he might give eternal life to all those you

have given him. Now this is eternal life: that they know
you, the only true God, and Jesus Christ, whom you have
sent. I have brought you glory on earth by finishing the
work you gave me to do. . . .

*"I have revealed you to those whom you gave me out of
the world. They were yours; you gave them to me and they
have obeyed your word. Now they know that everything
you have given me comes from you. For I gave them the
words you gave me and they accepted them. They knew with
certainty that I came from you, and they believed that you
sent me."*

—JOHN 17:1-4, 6-8 (emphasis added)

The entire work of God's Son was that His disciples would
know the Father as He did and that they, like the Son, would
bring Him glory *"on earth."* The whole earth! The Father has
rescued and adopted us as His sons and daughters and sent
Jesus to secure the dreams that He's held in His heart for all His
children. In John 17, Jesus is reporting back to the Father at the
end His life that He has secured the hearts of the disciples who
have "accepted" who He is and who they are in Him—that they
are sons and daughters of God. Then, near the end of this prayer,
Jesus shifts the focus from those who were with Him to those yet
to come:

"My prayer is not for them alone. I pray also for those
who will believe in me through their message [the Gospel],
that all of them may be one, Father, just as you are in me
and I am in you. . . . So that they may be brought to complete unity. Then the world will know that you sent me and
have loved them even as you have loved me."

—JOHN 17:20-21, 23

This is too wonderful. Jesus prays that all His kidnapped and enslaved children (both "lost" and now "found") will know the Father together and find a place to "soak" in His love. This is the motivation for preaching and sharing the Gospel with people: "Father has been thinking of you, wants you, and has provided for you by sending His son to set you into your place in His forgiven Family." Our Father loves the world and all of its inhabitants with the same love that He loves His own Son and His Son's original disciples. For many of us, this was probably the first truth we learned about God,

> For God so loved the world that he gave his one and only Son, that whoever believes in him shall not perish but have eternal life.
>
> —JOHN 3:16

To help us break from our identity as "foreigners and aliens" to God, orphans set adrift and alone, He sent His Spirit to convince us of our new standing in the Father's Family—the Spirit of God is the Spirit of adoption into the Family. A revelation and reception of the work of the Spirit to adopt us comes at the point of salvation and puts us in right standing with God. Trying to rid ourselves of sin, shame, and guilt in order to come into our sonship and daughterhood just isn't the biblical order. We receive the Father's work of calling us into His Family through Jesus, and the Godhead then begins to cleanse us from any unrighteousness that may be clinging to us like barnacles on a ship. You don't "get right" before you get loved in a family; your family loves you and gives you a safe place to be nurtured, try on different expressions of who you are, and grow. God's love comes before our effort. You can't will yourself into His Family, you're just born (again) into it. Then you need to start soaking in His love to change your DNA and identity from your old self into the image of a son or daughter.

As we got a glimpse of in Part One, the seeds of the Kingdom are sown with friends praying and dreaming, stumbling and growing together—a revelational journey with the people God places in our lives to realize the dreams He has for us. Over the next fifteen years, this "praying and dreaming" Kansas City crew discovered how "friends, together, praying and dreaming" turn into a family that enjoys a lifestyle of prayer that engenders more dreams. Then as they walked out those dreams together, they became a people on a mission; alive with God's passion and intent on making disciples from those they encountered each and every day. During this early season before they even looked like a church, the Father was laying the foundations in them for multiple expressions of His Church that would extend the Kingdom of Christ into multiple aspects of life, even though they were clueless about this future at the time.

The first thing God needed to plant in their hearts was that they were called to be sons and daughters of a loving heavenly Father—brothers and sisters with Christ in the Kingdom Family. They began to consider what the Father provided for the members of His Family, what identity we've been accorded due to that provision, and how that new identity informs what we do for those in our spheres of influence.

This is the Gospel!

MEETING A "RATHER ODD FELLOW"

About three months after moving into BCC, the friends happened across what Adam likes to refer to as "that rather odd fellow from England"—Pete Greig. Pete had invited Floyd to meet at a 24-7 Prayer conference in England, and when Floyd agreed, he invited Adam, David, and Nathan to be his bewildered companions. While savoring a perfunctory curry together (Brits have a thing for curry), Pete shared the story of 24-7 Prayer. (This story was later chronicled in Pete's book, *Red Moon Rising* and continued in his book, *Dirty Glory*.)

What Pete described was this incredible culture of friendships and people with a passion for God who didn't take themselves too seriously. Pete told them, "It's like me and my mates went out to build sandcastles on the beach and this massive wave overtook us. Now [having been smacked by this wave], I find myself as the accidental leader of a worldwide prayer movement called '24-7 Prayer' that is calling the Church to pray and care for the poor."

Adam, David, and Nathan just sat there with their jaws dangling precariously over their curry. They weren't thinking about joining the 24-7 organization, they were thinking, "This is already our story. We're friends and we've prayed together since the moment we met." They dreamed together—greatly inspired by the stories Pete had shared with them—to see places changed and transformed by Jesus. This brought them courage and hope to believe that they would see their dreams manifest in the same way someday. And, of course, that was only the beginning of their connection to Pete and his viral prayer movement.

This little cadre came back inspired, but with new questions: "Okay, what does this look like for our lives? How do we live this culture of prayer, family, mission, and justice?" This began their deeper, more determined exploration into the dreams God was planting in their hearts.

NOW WHAT?

Question #1: What identity best defines you personally: orphan, slave, or child? Pray for a revelation of your sonship/daughterhood and the breaking of the strongholds of being an orphan or slave. (You will also have an opportunity to read about this in more detail in the next chapter.)

Question #2: How well do you, your team, and your church family understand, live out, and pass on the centrality of the Father's desire to celebrate family? How could you better differentiate between the Father sending Jesus to "save" us (which is true) to the Father sending Him to ransom us from orphanhood to redeemed children? (The distinction is massive in its effect on the health and fruitfulness of our churches.)

> **Exercise:** Read and discuss these fabulous texts:
> Galatians 4:4-7
> 2 Corinthians 6:16-18
> Ephesians 3:14-15

ADOPTED!

*For he chose us in him before the creation of the world
to be holy and blameless in his sight. In love he predestined us
for adoption to sonship through Jesus Christ,
in accordance with his pleasure and will—to the praise
of his glorious grace, which he has freely given us
in the One he loves.*

—EPHESIANS 1:4-6

In the fall of 2003, as their newest expression of "Plan A," the BCC friends had taken the leadership of a small discipleship school called "Transit." At best, their efforts were limping along.

Near the eight-month mark of the school—and knowing all but a few of the students were considering leaving the program—they decided, "Well, nothing we are doing is working well, but we can't get Pete's idea about opening prayer spaces out of our thoughts. So, what if we put one of these prayer spaces in the middle of the University of Missouri, Kansas City (UMKC) campus?" They knew that many of the students lived in the dorms on campus and most didn't know Jesus. If prayer could have an effect on the unsaved, then there wasn't a better place in Kansas City to see how it might work.

So they put a "sacred space" in a spare room on the first floor of the international dormitory. Within one week they saw the Lord move profoundly in the middle of this un-prayed-for space. Word had spread that some "Christians" were in the dorm praying and befriending anyone who wanted to "hang out." Throughout the week a steady stream of students showed up for prayer, all sanctioned by a key administrator in the school who the Lord had planted in the university as a "woman of peace." She was thrilled that the team was available to bring the love and compassion of Jesus to their students.

By the spring of 2004, the principle of initiating prayer where people usually don't pray became a cornerstone that all the friends would cling to moving forward. "Jesus moved into our neighborhood, becoming flesh, through us and our prayers," Adam told me. "He loves to dwell where we don't think He's going to be; prayer takes us where He wants to go."

Around that same time, they started to understand the Lord's purposes for them more clearly. Their controlling question became, "If the Church is Plan A—and that's how the Father wants to meet and transform the world—how can we partner with Him in this endeavor?" They knew the ingredients included living together in that season and being friends that prayed and dreamed, but they didn't know how to "bake the cake" that would transfer what they were experiencing together into the lives of others. "Okay, this is the foundation, but what are we building?"

As things would happen, it was in the midst of that season that Pete and Samie Greig moved from England to Kansas City so Sammy could rehabilitate from a near-fatal brain tumor. The Greigs had not only launched 24-7 Prayer five years earlier, but were also overseeing the birth of the first "Boiler Room"—a "neo-monastic" community in Reading, England—with their mate

Andy Freeman. It was the first "church plant" of the 24-7 Prayer Movement.

Why "Boiler Room"? In the late 1800s, a group of American ministers visited the church of Pastor Charles Spurgeon. In giving them a tour of the facilities, he asked if they would like to see the power source of his ministry. Thinking he was going to take them to some kind of utility closet to see the furnace, they politely declined, but he insisted. He led them into the basement, down a hallway, and up to a closed door. The Americans were ready to be unimpressed. Then he swung the door open. There, spread across the floor of the room, face down, were several individuals praying.

"This," Pastor Spurgeon said with a twinkle in his eye, "is my boiler room."

Over the years of his ministry, whenever Charles Spurgeon was asked the secret of his success, he simply answered, "My people pray for me."

I was in Kansas City meeting with Adam, David, and Nathan again. In the course of our conversations, I asked them a question regarding a new prayer community we had been observing in Reading, England: "What do you think about the 24-7 Prayer community in Reading?" I had ulterior motives (of course) and was fishing for a response. I felt it was time for them to plant a church, but, wanted the instructions to come into their own hearts from Jesus, not from me.

Not having anything but guesses, one of them finally said, "You don't think we should plant a church, do you?" I remember grinning, saying nothing, until they looked at each other a little freaked out. Taking this "bombshell" to prayer they clearly heard the instruction from the Father, "It is time for you to step out and use the last year of Transit to plant a church."

Though they were scared silly, the Lord was faithful to confirm this new adventure for them. The first seed of the Kansas City Boiler Room (which later became Navah Church in 2015) was firmly planted in fertile soil.

THE FATHER—WHO WE ARE: A FAMILY OF SONS AND DAUGHTERS

We are all familiar with the passage that is often called "The Parable of the Prodigal Son." The Father had two very different sons and loved them both. There is ample imagery in this parable of Israel and the Gentiles that proved to be a shocking revelation to the Jewish culture who heard Jesus tell this story. I think Jesus was preparing His disciples for the grafting in of the Gentiles, though I'm not sure they understood that nuance at the time. The firstborn son (Israel) was jealous of the returning, wayward son (the Gentiles), and did not understand what the father meant when he said, "Did you not know that all I had was yours all along?" The eldest son was too busy working in the father's house to enjoy what he had. It was the father's deep desire that the eldest join the younger son in the party. He probably wondered how any proper Jewish father could honor a second son. Why would he kiss his wayward son and lavish him with a party? Because that is the nature of our heavenly Father and His attitude toward His alienated Family. Every one who comes home is worth celebrating.

It's often hard for us today to realize how radical the concept of God as a loving Father was when Jesus first introduced it.

> Jesus said to them, "My Father is always at his work to this very day, and I too am working." For this reason they

tried all the more to kill him; not only was he breaking the Sabbath, but he was even calling God his own Father, making himself equal with God.

—JOHN 5:18

When we begin the Lord's Prayer by saying, *"Our Father in heaven"* (Matthew 6:9), we are unleashing a spiritual and psychological revolution. We are saying that the Entity that created the universe is not only good, but also loves us (and in that loving makes us worthy of that love). He wants to relate with us as a father does to his child—and not just a *father*, but as intimately as a *daddy* or *papa*. As Paul tells us,

> You can tell for sure that you are now fully adopted as his own children because God sent the Spirit of his Son into our lives crying out, "Papa! Father!" Doesn't that privilege of intimate conversation with God make it plain that you are not a slave, but a child?
>
> —GALATIANS 4:6-7 MSG

As a rule, fathers don't have a great reputation in our current society, but our Father in heaven is a good Father, and we see that in His relationship with His Son. Take the best father you can imagine, and then take that up a notch on the goodness and lovingness scale by a power of ten. This is God *our* Father.

In "The Parable of the Prodigal Son," despite the ingratitude and drivenness of his elder son and the sorry state of his younger son, the father chose them *both*. Why? Because they genetically belonged to him. They were his children, nothing would change that. In the same way, God the Father chose us because we are in His Son (in Christ). As Paul wrote:

For he chose us in him [genetics] *before the creation of the world to be holy and blameless in his sight.*

—EPHESIANS 1:4

This type of love comes from a deep love in the Father's heart that is rooted not in behavior, but from a deep sense of ownership. He told Israel that in all of their imperfection and rebellion, *"Do not fear, for I have redeemed you; I have summoned you by name; you are mine"* (Isaiah 43:1, emphasis added). Never doubt that we are *"God's possession"* (Ephesians 1:14)—chosen, wanted, and relentlessly pursued by the Father to win our hearts. He is the Father who throws a party on our behalf just as the "waiting father" did for his sons in the parable.

In Ephesians 1, Paul elaborates on all the Father has laid out for His children. In just ten verses, Paul explains the Father's party for the Gentiles and the six things He has prepared for His sons and daughters by virtue of this grand celebration:

1. He chose us – 1:3

2. He adopted us as children – 1:5

3. He forgave and redeemed us – 1:7-8

4. He revealed His secrets to us – 1:9

5. He made out His will to include us in His inheritance – 1:11-12

6. This "will and testament" was notarized by the Holy Spirit – 1:13-14

This is how the work of Jesus brought us into the Father's Family—we've been fully adopted!

This is the Gospel!

KICKING THE SLAVE MENTALITY

We have not only been chosen, but we are also wanted by the God of the cosmos. Many who come to Christ think of themselves as the "servants of God," but that moniker can bring unwanted baggage with it. We like to say "servant" rather than "slave" because it sounds a little better, but they are quite similar in essence. They both express a mentality of lowliness that we think is humble, but it is not. Slaves are chosen to get a job done and servants never feel valued, but we have been adopted by God to be *His children*. God doesn't need workers, He wants kids.

This is not just semantics; it is a covenant matter that Jesus paid for with His own blood. This adoption changes our identity for eternity, it gives us the family name *"above every name"* (Philippians 2:9), a banner of love over us, and proclaims us heirs to all the riches of the Father. Our adoption into His family negates the malevolent power of any human ancestry and the brokenness we have known in our earthly lives.

So who are we and what is our identity in the Father now that He has sent His Son to save and redeem us? We are His adopted sons and daughters; we are His eternal, squeaky clean Family!

> The Spirit you received does not make you slaves, so that you live in fear again; rather, the Spirit you received brought about your adoption to sonship. And by him we cry, "Abba, Father." The Spirit himself testifies with our spirit that we are God's children. Now if we are children, then we are heirs—heirs of God and co-heirs with Christ, if indeed we share in his sufferings in order that we may also share in his glory.
>
> **—ROMANS 8:15-17**

Jesus, as He was giving His last discourse to His disciples in John 14, made this amazing statement, *"I will not leave you as orphans; I will come to you"* (John 14:18). Now, those of us who had dysfunctional families, or no family at all, have been included in the ultimate Family. We are forgiven of our "pigsty" ways, no longer unwanted, not alone, not guilt and shame ridden, nor need we suffer from the loss of our true identity. There is to be no more "Who am I?" We are now family members and have access to the Father's full inheritance. And just to make sure we get the point, He reiterates the obliteration of our old identities:

> But when the set time had fully come, God sent his Son, born of a woman, born under the law, to redeem those under the law, that we might receive adoption to sonship. Because you are his sons, God sent the Spirit of his Son into our hearts, the Spirit who calls out, "Abba, Father." So you are no longer a slave, but God's child; and since you are his child, God has made you also an heir.
>
> —GALATIANS 4:4-7

There is a significant difference between human adoption and our heavenly adoption. When a couple adopts an orphan child, they are getting a precious little human with different genes than their own. The "biological" parents forego the rights to be parents of the child and the new family receives the baby with all the rights and privileges of that family.

In our heavenly adoption, however, an amazing thing occurs. He first takes us out of the clutches of our kidnapper, brings us home, and then *changes* our genetics back to the original birth family—of the Father, Son, and Holy Spirit. We are ransomed and reborn into His family, not only with all heavenly rights and privileges, but with *His* DNA, the image of the Son of God. Adam's fallen genetics are replaced, and we become "new creations." Simply fantastic!

It would be fair to say that the summation of these incredible verses is that we are now bloodline children of God's Family. Yet church constructs in so many settings have not fully embraced the sonship and daughterhood of all believers in a manner that it alters their organizational structures, their ministry philosophies, or their behaviors toward one another. Too often, rather, we find an epidemic of guilt, shame, and drivenness. Despite their adoption, the orphan spirit of born-again believers still holds sway over them. The only way we can change that is by "being formed in the family." To come to the Father is one thing, but to be turned into a son or daughter only happens within a family atmosphere filled with His love. He didn't come to make us moral beings, or even "Christians," but to give us the power to become sons and daughters of the Father. A stunning promise!

This is the Gospel!

THE SHEPHERD'S CENTER

About three months after first recognizing the call to plant a Boiler Room in Kansas City, David and Adam stumbled across the Shepherd's Center. During one of their 24-7 Prayer weeks at UMKC, David and Adam were out on a prayer walk of the campus. They saw a large house they assumed to be a frat house. David, being his "Chicago, bold self," went right up to the door and knocked. When an older lady answered, they were both surprised. She told them it was a ministry center for the elderly—a ministry outreach center of a local church in the neighborhood. She invited them in.

Within twenty minutes of conversing with the hostess, she ended up saying, "I don't know why I'm telling you this, but we're moving our ministries out of the Shepherd's Center." So, David boldly relayed the vision for the Boiler Room and their hearts' desire to have a place where they could conduct regular prayer and host an art studio for reaching out to students. She asked them to come back and meet with her again.

When they did, without any preamble, she offered them keys to the building, saying they could take possession of two of the floors immediately. Adam recalled, "All of a sudden, the meeting we'd had with Jon became a scary reality. Maybe we were actually going to do this 'church-plant' thing."

New Transit students had just arrived, so the team told them, "It looks like we've got a house on campus and you're here for more than a training program. You're here to plant a church with us."

Although they were quite clueless, they felt they had the "experts," Pete and Samie Greig, to help. Pete and Samie pitched in to clean out the basement and prepare the first prayer room for the incoming students and budding community. The seeds of the Kansas City Boiler Room now had a place to sprout.

It would only be a matter of months, however, before God started planting an even greater vision in their hearts.

NOW WHAT?

Question #1: What does your church or ministry resemble the most—an orphanage, a corporation, or a family? What are some of the descriptors of the identity you have selected, and how is the Lord instructing and encouraging you to embrace the Family DNA instead?

Question #2: How do you, your family, and your "team" members relate to God—as Father or in some other way? (How one relates to the Father reveals much about their own identity: orphan, slave, or son.)

> **Exercise:** Meditate on Romans 8:15-17 and reflect on your own journey toward relating to God as "Abba, Father."

Question #3: How central to your ministry and teaching is the topic of being "child of God"? How do you and those around you celebrate "the every blessing in Christ" party thrown by the Father according to Ephesians 1:1-14?

> **Exercise:** Contemplate the Father's party favors in Ephesians 1:2-14 (see the list below). Go through each of the six "spiritual blessings" in the text, meditate on them, and then celebrate all the Father has provided His Church. (You'll become intimately familiar with these "blessings" as we'll be looking at them more closely in the next few chapters.)

Receive them and refute all differing mindsets!

1. He chose us – 1:3-4
2. He adopted us as His children – 1:5
3. He redeemed and forgave us – 1:7-8
4. He revealed His secrets to us – 1:9
5. He made out His will to include us in His inheritance – 1:11-12
6. He gifted us His Spirit as a guarantee of that inheritance – 1:13-14

> **Exercise:** Out of this text consider developing a teaching series on combatting the orphan and slave spirit and solidifying people's rootedness in their adoption by God. Plan for "trickledown" into your small groups, ministry times, and follow-up counselling.

FORMED IN THE FAMILY

Dear friends, let us love one another, for love comes from God.
Everyone who loves has been born of God and knows God. . . .
This is how God showed his love among us: He sent his one
and only Son into the world that we might live through him.
This is love: not that we loved God, but that he loved us and
sent his Son as an atoning sacrifice for our sins. Dear friends,
since God so loved us, we also ought to love one another.
No one has ever seen God; but if we love one another,
God lives in us and his love is made complete in us.

—1 JOHN 4:7, 9–12

ust after the New Year of 2005, Adam received a set of very clear
dreams from the Lord. In the first dream, he saw the lady who
managed the Shepherd's Center hand him three envelopes. One
was addressed to him and the other two to David and Nathan. He
could see that his envelope was the thickest and had a sense that
the contents were going to hit him the hardest. It simply said, "I
regret to inform you but you're being voted out of the Shepherd's
Center and will soon be asked to leave."

Adam told me that, "in the dream I started to weep, then the
scene changed. I was still weeping, but in a warehouse space where
David was saying to me, 'I don't know why you are weeping. It's
going to be all right, because where we're going is so much better.'"

Adam woke up from the dream to find actual tears in his eyes. Again, he heard to Lord ask him, "Why are you weeping? The Church is a people, not a building." He replied shakily, "Okay, okay God, the Church is the people not a building, *but please don't take the building away.*" But the Lord was insistent, "No, the Church is the people not a building."

This first encounter with the Lord on this issue was before they were even officially calling their gathering a Boiler Room. The message was clear, "I want you to know that the Church is a people, not a building."

When he shared this with the rest of the team, Nathan voiced what everyone else was wondering, "If we lose the Shepherd's Center, will we survive? Or maybe we will thrive and losing the building will be a catalyst to becoming the people of God? Isn't that what Adam's dream is telling us?"

There were a lot of nodding heads in response. They were beginning to get the idea.

As Adam finished relaying the story of his first dream and saw how it was received, he seemed excited to relay the second dream.

In this dream, he was sitting in the Shepherd's Center in a circle and was sitting next to a friend from South Africa. While they were praying, the friend turned, looked at Adam, and said, "You're a shepherd like in Ezekiel 34." Adam wasn't aware of the content of Ezekiel 34, so when he woke up, he read the text.

It was a rebuke towards the shepherds of Israel essentially saying, "Why did you not go after the stray, heal the sick, bind up the broken? Instead you use the resources on yourself. Therefore, I will be the Shepherd and my arm will save." He had a sense that the Father was warning him about being a shepherd that used people to get "the work of the ministry" done, instead of a shepherd who loved the people and went after those who are broken in order to bring them home.

Adam felt this whisper in his heart that they would lose the Shepherd's Center building, but that God would rather make the community into a "Shepherd's Center people" for the city, like in Ezekiel 34, than have it become just another local church. He sensed the Lord asking him, "Would you be willing to live that kind of life? Would you be a people, a shepherding people like the Chief Shepherd, who went after those who were hurting whether you have a building or not?"

THE FATHER—WHAT WE DO:
Love "The Family" and the Least Among Us

Adam had now been asked the same question and given the same invitation Peter had received in the last chapter of John: *"Do you love me?"* Then *"Feed my sheep."* When we love the Father, Son, and Holy Spirit, God asks us to become shepherds of His love to His lost and found "sheep." We are asked to take the love we have received from the Father and poor it out on others, so much so that it becomes the trademark of who we are as the Family of God:

> "A new commandment I give to you, that you love one another: just as I have loved you, you also are to love one another. By this all people will know that you are my disciples, if you have love for one another."
>
> —JOHN 13:34-35

Loving unconditionally, like God does, is impossible within our natural human capacities. It is only when the Gospel is deeply imbedded in our spirits by his Spirit, and we dump that failed Adamic fellow at the cross, that we find the capacity to love one another. When we are overwhelmed by all that the Father has done for us personally, it would be ludicrous not to pass His patient love on to those in the Family of faith—it is the only agenda!

Family is the place where we grow up—parents and children alike. It's where our identities are formed. It's a safe place where we have room to try on various expressions of who we'd like to be and suffer only minor consequences for mistakes. Yes, it is a place of correction and teaching, but most importantly it is a place where we remind one another constantly that "I love you." It is where we teach reconciliation. A child disobeys, is chastised, and then immediately embraced back into the family: "We all mess up, and there are things we shouldn't do, but we love you. You are my child. Let's remember this lesson together and do better tomorrow." We need such an environment to form our identities. Without family, the world is too dangerous a place to make mistakes.

As image-bearers of Jesus, we choose each other as He chose us, we adopt one another into our hearts as we have been adopted, we see each other through redemptive lenses, without trying to conform each other's behavior to our own standards. We forgive each other from betrayal, abandonment, harsh words, and misunderstandings because that's what God did for us. Because we are "joint heirs" of His grace, we see each other as Family members who have been given a secret that we are meant to fulfill together as His "household." As sons and daughters, we inherit what the family will and testament specifies.

> In Him also we have obtained an inheritance, being pre-destined according to the purpose of Him who works all

things according to the counsel of His will, that we who first trusted in Christ should be to the praise of His glory.

—EPHESIANS 1:11-12 NKJV

An inheritance is the legal assignment of a person's assets, an allotment to the heirs of all that is owned. Our Father's wealth is available to us as His children. In the Parable of the Prodigal Son, the older brother was jealous of what the father was lavishing on his wayward brother, but the father told him, "Why are you chafing at this? Everything here is already yours."

The whole *raison d'etre* of this inheritance is that we *"should be to the praise of his glory."* (See also Ephesians 1:6, 14.) That's what subjects do in the presence of their sovereign. They worship! Everything they do reflects back on Him to whom they have pledged fealty.

Our inheritance from Him is to make Him look good, for Him to have preeminence in our lives and all that we touch! The result is that we live as legitimate overseers of the estate and dispense its wealth and establish His desires within our circles of influence. Everywhere we go, we should be gushing over upon others from all that He has bestowed upon us.

This is the Gospel!

Though we are a weird and wonderful assortment of creatures, this is the Father's agenda for us and the source of our love for others. We love each other because He loved us first. If we have "churchy" agendas and anemic sermons echoing in our hearts that don't conform with the Father's declaration of our covenant adoption into His family, our love will be conditional, and we will end up with some disastrous deformity at our proverbial feet.

We were not marked with deformity, however, but with something far more glorious.

When you believed, you were marked in him with a seal,
the promised Holy Spirit, who is a deposit guaranteeing our
inheritance until the redemption of those who are God's pos-
session—to the praise of his glory.

—EPHESIANS 1:13-14

For an inheritance to be consummated, the owner of the estate has to die. This is God's "Last Will and Testament": a contract that has deeded us equity in the eternal estate through the death of His Son. In human affairs, every will has a guarantor and is signed by the owner of the estate. The recipient must consummate the owner's wishes with a signature of their own.

It is with the "pen of faith" that we sign the "heavenly document" that says we agree that the inheritance from the Father is legally ours. In the case of our heavenly inheritance, this will is then notarized and stamped by the Holy Spirit as an absolute guarantee that everything the Father has and all that He has promised to make available to us for eternity is final. He put His Spirit, His signet ring, into the hot wax of our born-again spirits, as it were, and sealed the contract. Done deal—the inheritance is ours!

This is the Gospel!

These then, are the spiritual blessings that we have as sons and daughters by what the Father has done through His Son. Notice the language of this covenant is all "family" language: sons, daughters, adoption, inheritances, wills. The whole of God's blessing is lavished on the sons and daughters of the house. Throughout the first three chapters of Ephesians, Paul lays out God's plan for His household followed by a magnificent charge: *"As a prisoner for the Lord, then, I urge you to live a life worthy of the calling you have received"* (Ephesians 4:1).

When we go a little deeper into Paul's construction here, it becomes very fascinating. He begs us, based on this magnificent treatise on the work of the Father through Jesus, to *live a life worthy of the calling."* The *King James Version* says it a little differently: to *"walk worthy of the vocation."*

Vocation is an interesting word, as it is often used to sum up both one's life's work and one's life's calling—which were really seen as one in the same. The word translated *vocation* in the text above is *klesis,* and refers not to a vocational calling as such, but to an invitation. (Remember the Father's invite to the party?) Paul then indicates that we were *"called"* to this invitation at the end of the verse. Its root—*kaleo*—indicates that this invitation is being called out or shouted to us by name.

So if we put it together, Paul has just presented this amazing treatise on all that God has made available to His sons and daughters through the Father, Son and Spirit (Eph. 1-3). He admonishes us by saying, "I'm begging you, walk worthy of this *invitation that is being shouted out and is calling you* by name." Father is giving a boisterous invitation to the sons and daughters to accept His inheritance and all His blessings in His beloved Son.

That sounds like a party, doesn't it?

This too is the Gospel!

JUST FOR EMPHASIS

Years later Adam was sitting in the prayer room, just hanging out with the Lord, and God spoke to his heart: "Adam, I didn't die for all your big ideas or your visions or your strategies. Do you want to know why I gave My life?"

Adam said, "Yeah Jesus, I want to know!"

He said, "I gave My life for the Father to have a family. Young men have ministries, but fathers have families. What do you want to be? Do you want to be a young man who uses people for his vision and strategies or do you want to be a father who has a family? I want you to lay your life down for the same reason I laid My life down—so My Father could have His Family."

This thread goes all the way through the tapestry of the KC Boiler Room/Navah story and culminates in the Lord repetitively reminding the Navah leadership, "The Church is a people, not a building." Adam didn't understand at the time that the Father was saying that there was a reformation, a redefinition of Church coming and that they would no longer be people who merely "attended church," but that they would *be the Church—His Family.*

About a month after Adam's dreams (February 2005), they ended up losing the building just as God had shown them. They got a call from the Center Supervisor and she read them the letter refusing their right to continue in the space.

That was that!

So, they decided if the Church is not a building, then their "church" would start meeting in homes as friends, praying and dreaming the Father's dreams together. Just when they had resigned themselves to this new direction, the Father opened up a fantastic new meeting option for their little nomadic community.

NOW WHAT?

Question #1: As the Lord whispered to Adam that "the Church is not a building but a people," how does that play out in your context? If the Church is not a place to go, but a people to become, what mindsets need to be challenged and what practices embraced to truly make the Church of Jesus people-centric?

Question #2: Does your church or ministry operate on the premise that "adopting people into your hearts as He adopted you" is an imperative in Scripture and a thoroughly non-negotiable tenet in the Family of God? If not, how can you better align yourself with God's adopting heart and pursuit of His Family?

Question #3: In what ways could you invite the Lord to help yourself and your team extend more unconditional, unbiased love to the people who will come to Christ through your witness?

Question #4: What work in your own heart(s) is necessary to see the love levels go up in your church family? (Instead of frustration, impatience, keeping track of offences, fear of confrontation, lack of communication, displeasure, religious stubbornness, indifference, anger, etc.)

THE INVERTED KINGDOM

They formed a mob, set the city in an uproar,
*and attacked the house of Jason [**looking for Paul and Silas**],*
seeking to bring them out to the crowd. And when they
could not find them, they dragged Jason and some of the brothers
*before the city authorities, shouting, "**These men who***
*****have turned the world upside down have come here also,*****
and Jason has received them, and they are all acting against
the decrees of Caesar, saying that there is another king, Jesus."

—ACTS 17:5-7 **ESV** (emphasis added)

The Kansas City Boiler Room held its first meeting in the loft of the Monarch Building on September 5th, 2005. (That was only four days after Adam's first date with Juli, who he would marry a little over a year later on October 1, 2006.) In those early days, they had about thirty or so people attending each service.

As they were setting up for that first meeting, they recognized a small problem with their new space: There were these huge pillars standing throughout the center of the meeting room. Right where they were set up to teach was a pillar strategically placed to disrupt almost all natural sight lines. Being that said pillar was immoveable, they decided to jokingly name it the "Jesus Pillar"— that would remind everyone Jesus was the main thing one should see, not whoever was teaching. That was important because they got a strong, challenging word from two different people before they started at the Monarch building. Both effectively said, "Adam, you are a gifted teacher. Do *not* build this church around your gift." That was such wisdom because to this day, they have made sure not to build around any one person's personality or gifting. This shaped a resolve in them to help various people develop their particular gifts and not build around one person. This has created a healthy culture that celebrated their unity in Christ and honored each leader's unique differences. They were a team of friends. It was kind of the Father to prepare them ahead of time and warn them of the pitfalls that come with building on unique personalities and the gifts of one person apart from Jesus.

Despite the accomplishment of being a handful of twenty-somethings starting a wobbly "church family," what Adam and the others didn't know was that they were still on God's operating table undergoing reconstructive surgery. Our twenties are all about finding out who we are—forming our identities as capable, independent, remarkable adults. (I like to tease twenty-somethings that they are still a bit "iffy" since their brains haven't yet fully formed. That doesn't usually go over very well.) As a result, the KC Boiler Room team felt the challenge of God's dealings with them personally in addition to the pressures of planting the church and leading a whole group of other twenty-somethings. Thankfully, they didn't get a pass on any of the spiritual formation and transformation process of their growing up journey.

Adam and the team discovered that pursuing Jesus had to be more central than prayer itself. The Jesus Pillar became more of an important symbol to the community than they realized. Regularly they gathered around the pillar and prayed, "Jesus we want you to be the center of this church. Please tell us whenever we move You out of the center." Every person had to contribute so they could mature in Christ, and that maturity came only from their own sincere pursuit of Jesus Himself.

In their initial years, the KC Boiler Room community saw people of various backgrounds come to Jesus, hurting people come to faith, and many deeply engage with their new extended family. At the same time, they saw some leave or get hurt because they weren't getting what they needed. There was another dimension they needed to add, but they didn't know what it was yet.

CREATIVELY CONSTIPATED

The Monarch building was in midtown and the loft space with the Jesus Pillar was where they were first officially dubbed themselves the Kansas City Boiler Room. It lived up to its name by the first summer as there was no air conditioning to push back the 100-degree July heat.

Adjoining the loft was another room they decided to use as an artist studio in order to reach out to local artists in the community. Before the Boiler Room was launched, Adam had a prayer time with the Lord where God indicated that the Church was "creatively constipated." Adam had no idea at the time what the Lord was talking about, but later came to realize that all the creativity was locked up in the bowels of the Church—there was nowhere for creatives to express what God was inspiring in them. He felt the Lord warning him to "release the mess; don't control this."

In another prayer time, Adam saw a picture of the two sides of the brain. The Lord made it clear to Adam, "The Church is giving away one side of the brain and you need to retrieve the creative and the non-logical and the non-reasoning aspects of it." Having an artist in the Boiler Room was so much more than just having an artist in an art studio; it was a reconciliation of something, an opening up of what worship is, and more widely of who God is. It was powerful. The first person to use the art space was Linnea Spransy. She was a Yale art graduate, a stunning artist, and the epitome of a creative soul who had a heart for Jesus. She used the loft to create beautiful pieces that were garnering her recognition from all over and resulted in a number of Kansas City Art Institute students starting to come to the Boiler Room because of her connection to it.

Adam recalls the first times he went and sat with the artists, "I felt prompted in my heart to say, 'Welcome to the Church.' I would rarely use that language, but I clearly felt it to say, 'Welcome to the Church!' When I did, I saw a few of them starting to cry." He realized that many of them had never believed that the Church and artists could coexist, let alone reconcile. That sentence was a reality, "Welcome to the Church." It was like saying it was okay for them to come home. "They'd experienced church as institution or church as rules. . . . Some of them had had almost no experience with the Church growing up in family backgrounds that were different. They never really had a vision that their heart as a creative and as an artist could coexist with a word like 'church.'"

These budding artists lived in a world where what they created was being so constantly critiqued and criticized that they'd come to tie their identities to what was said about them at the Art Institute. When they started showing up at the KC Boiler Room and learning about who they were in Christ and how God saw them as His Family, it was a radical shift for them. The more of this they absorbed, the more they grew. As Adam described it, "Linnea and her friend Kristen Montgomery started meeting weekly with other artists, basing their activities together on Acts 2. They began to learn a rhythm of communal prayer, worship, and family. Linnea and others hosted movie nights and created loft spaces to share their art. Then they began to turn their art studios into sacred spaces. It grew to somewhere around sixty or seventy artists and then began to connect to the wider KC artistic community."

It was a privilege for the Boiler Room community to walk with these students. They felt the Father leading them into a journey of helping these artists see that they were not what they could produce, but something much, much more *in Christ*. They were loved by the Father and wanted in His Family—it was their birthright; their identity was in Him, the ultimate Artist, not in whatever they could do or create.

As part of the effort to help people see this, the KC Boiler Room held weekend gatherings for the art students called "Identity Weekends." They started seeing people come into freedom in Christ because they weren't being accepted simply for what they could produce or perform anymore. You could feel the layers peeling back, a foretaste of how the Father wanted to reveal their adoption and identity to all spheres of society. These little, local lessons with the artists—just one group of people—was actually going to become the very heart and core of all that the KC Boiler Room was to become. They just didn't know it yet.

THE SON—WHAT HE HAS DONE:
Established His Kingdom as Servant King

Jesus came in low. The appointed King and Deliverer the Scriptures promised was born in a barn and laid to sleep in a feed trough because His earthly parents didn't have enough clout to warrant space anywhere inside. He grew up in the streets as a carpenter's son, likely learning the trade from His father as was the norm of the day. He didn't go to university nor was He a disciple to a great Jewish theologian as Paul was. When Jesus started his ministry, He picked a gaggle of misfits to follow Him, washed their smelly feet (of all things), loved them soundly, then promptly died a criminal's death. In order to establish His rule over His creation again, He gained the right to retrieve the keys to the earth that Adam had surrendered to Satan and established His supremacy over all things. (See Ephesians 1:19-23.) As Paul described His mission and how He accomplished it, Jesus

> Who, being in very nature God, did not consider equality with God something to be used to hisown advantage; rather, he made himself nothing by taking the very nature of a servant, being made in human likeness. And being found in appearance as a man, he humbled himself by becoming obedient to death—even death on a cross!
>
> *Therefore God exalted him to the highest place and gave him the name that is above every name, that at the name of Jesus every knee should bow, in heaven and on earth and under the earth, and every tongue acknowledge that Jesus Christ is Lord, to the glory of God the Father.*
>
> —PHILIPPIANS 2:6-11

Jesus was a King—the King of kings—but also unlike any king we have ever seen before—a King with a heavenly approach to earth's rule. His Kingdom was already given to Him and it couldn't be taken away—not even by His own death. So, with His place in the Father's heart secure, He "made Himself nothing" by society's standards. He didn't need to impress any human and didn't need their approval. He was loved by His Father and knew that He would never be outside of His care. He was free to be the ultimate counter-revolutionary.

I'm not really impressed with feet. Although a necessity, they are truly strange creations when you think about it. They're encased in socks much of the time, subject to unfriendly encounters with *terra firma*, tend to emit unfriendly odors, and are just best ignored. I'm in the minority, I think. Paul called feet "blessed" while Jesus had the audacity to feature the filthy things as an example of the nature of His kingdom. As He washed their feet, He told the disciples, *"I have set you an example that you should do as I have done for you"* (John 13:15).

Jesus was not proposing that we form a tradition around washing people's feet, but that we show the ultimate hospitality and honor of a dirty job normally done by servants. That was the point, "I am a servant, therefore, serve one another!" it is the ultimate strategy for puncturing power structures. Most all cultures and religions are built on pyramidal, hierarchical power structures. Jesus was having none of it. It was to become the *modus operandi* for all those that followed Him.

His death was the ultimate show of servanthood: serving the Father's wishes at the expense of the contamination, rejection, and humiliation of all creation.

The pattern of heaven's Tapestry is Jesus, the consummate servant. His Kingship is over a Kingdom that works from the bottom up—it's not about places of position that other's serve according to a hierarchy, but a rotating honoring of one another towards growth: *"Submit to one another out of reverence for Christ"* (Ephesians 5:21). It's a place where the "leader" puts aside authority over others for the sake of seeing others flourish. It's where humility is taught primarily by example. The strength of this Kingdom is not defined by the grandeur of its King, but by its weakest links—only when the "least among us" become strengthened does the Kingdom advance.

This is the Gospel!

GROWING TOO BIG TO BE ONE FAMILY ANYMORE

The Boiler Room grew spiritually and numerically that first year. Having started at about thirty or so, they grew to averaging around fifty, and then as more artists and others connected with them, they started having about seventy-five show up at their Wednesday night gatherings. The team was determined to get their pattern from studying the Scriptures to see what it said regarding the nature and practices of the early church, and they knew that would be hard to do with so many starting to show up at the gatherings. When Floyd encouraged Adam to reconsider Acts 2:42-47, it was like throwing a stone in a pond—it began to ripple, the effects and impact of which are still being seen today. In talking about it, David Blackwell summed up what they needed to do: "The only way to live this text out in practice is in homes." So they launched home groups devoted to *"the apostles' teaching and to fellowship, to the breaking of bread and to prayer"* (Acts 2:42) and called them "collectives."

In the coming year, the collectives—which they now call "missional communities" and still bear the same DNA as prayerful families on mission—began to grow in number and maturity. Collectives formed from the artists that were coming to the church, but eventually the team figured out it was better to have people of various backgrounds and interests. The diversity made the groups more relevant and healthy, and they stayed together longer. Shared proximity seemed to be a better way to form groups than shared interests. As the church grew and the demand for new collectives grew, there was a temptation to find a few willing souls to start groups in their homes and let them take off, but the Lord interrupted that logical train of thought. He indicated that the leaders had to live being family on mission before they could teach it.

Fighting the malaise of Western culture's aversion to sacrifice and to carefully guard our personal space and schedules, a couple of friends hit on an idea to break this tendency toward inward thinking. Two of the young team members, Joel Bryce and Nathan Chud, began frequenting a downtown eatery called John's Big Deck. They would take a number of "bros" from their collective, watch Monday night football, eat burgers, and get into conversations with the men at the bar. One of those who often came with them, Justin Andrews, was a runner. Over time Justin attracted a number of other runners from John's to begin hanging out with their wider collective—a good example of "we reproduce after our own kind."

Actually, this little weekly bar escapade was the result of a commitment on the part of various collectives to "adopt a business." This only solidified a value that would later become imbedded in the beliefs and practices of the entire church—identifying a focused mission brought them health. The church of Jesus, they were learning, exists to be "missional" and serve the "least among us."

The team recognized that the Holy Spirit had been working with the KC Boiler Room to bring them into their identities as sons and daughters of God from the very beginning. Surrounded by a fatherless society with broken families, dysfunction in education, government, and business, they realized that if they didn't rediscover God as Father for themselves, how could they possibly give good news to the world around them?

They began to use the phrase, "A prayerful family on mission." They broke this down to mean focusing on

- » all of life in God's presence: prayerfulness,
- » all of life with God's people: family,
- » all of life with God's passion: mission.

How would they equip everyday believers in *every* place they were living to reach *every* person? This was the intriguing invitation. So, they drilled down deeper into the idea of becoming a missional community.

It would be nice to say this led to steady growth over the next five years of the church, but the truth was growth came in fits and starts—and mostly fits. They found that God tended to want to go deeper in each of them before He allowed them to go broader into the Kansas City region. "We were still looking to see friends praying and dreaming," Adam told me. It was still evolving, but it always seemed to start there—that was the foundation for everything they did. As they strove to become a "prayerful family on mission," they started seeing people building their lives together and "even moving homes to be in proximity so that they could adopt neighborhoods together and make disciples." Because prayer remained a primal discipline and the team remained constantly open to the leadership of the Holy Spirit, each time something threatened to become a program with its own agenda, they drew back to Jesus as the center and retooled to make sure they didn't take off with "community" or something else at their core rather than Christ. That kind of constant navigational course correction doesn't always make for the smoothest of sailing.

Of course, over time, churches full of young married couples don't just grow by making friends in the outside community, they grow because the families in them reproduce—they make babies! One big challenge with young couples is they have babies and *babies change everything.* As their families grew, the twenty-some-things were getting a dose of reality that began to transform the shape of the missional communities in those homes.

They experimented with family groups with and without kids—more trial and error, more prayer and stumbling. A major hurdle was the over-scheduled lives that people tend to create just by living with kids in the USA and the "inconvenience" of including children in any meetings, let alone having enough energy to stay awake through the meetings after long days at work. The KC Boiler Room leaders decided not to push it, but to let life and the conviction of the Holy Spirit have its effect over time.

Then about five years into the church, the Bryces and Chuds were called to start a community in Boston, and the gene pool of trusted leaders was suddenly severely drained. In a huddle of the leaders' team, despite the discouragement of the depleted and wobbly groups, they declared to the Lord and each other, "God hasn't changed His mind and we have to keep going."

Help was soon to come.

NOW WHAT?

Question #1: Who or what is the equivalent to a "Jesus Pillar" in your church or ministry? What is your constant reminder to keep Him in the center of all that you do? What mechanisms, symbols, or commitments are in place to help keep each other focused on Jesus as your primary calling?

Question #2: Since Jesus is the Servant King, how do you allow Him to wash your feet, that is, serve you? How comfortable are you in allowing the Son of God to bless you unashamedly, be your Source in weakness, and the One to forgive you when you derail?

Question #3: How would you "wash each other's feet" (metaphorically speaking) like Jesus, in your church family? How will you prevent the "pastor(s)" being seen as above the others in importance? Are young leaders learning the beauty of "serving in another man's vineyard," or are they trying to be noticed by their "amazing deeds and exploits" in order to climb the ministry ladder?

Question #4: How diverse is your church family? Do you cater to both right and left brain types (artists & scientists, feelers and thinkers)? What principles did you learn from the KC Boiler Room team adopting the "artists' community" that you would want to pray that God would do in your midst?

APPOINTED HIS EMISSARIES

Now that I, your Lord and Teacher,
have washed your feet,
you also should wash one another's feet.
I have set you an example that you should do
as I have done for you. Very truly I tell you,
no servant is greater than his master, nor is a
messenger greater than the one who sent him.
Now that you know these things,
you will be blessed if you do them.

—JOHN 13:14-17

Sometimes, wanting to be biblical, by doing something like appointing elders, and wanting to avoid a disaster by not appointing them too early, can create a cosmic conundrum. With barely anyone over thirty, the team was anxious to align themselves with the biblical pattern in all aspects of church life. They had started as a small circle of friends and they were all loaded with leadership potential. (So much so, in fact that today, the Lord has flung a number of them out of Kansas City and into the wilds of Africa, Asia, and the Middle East.)

Around the second year after their formation, they were each still struggling to identify their particular giftings, much less lead a church. The Lord was faithful to give them counsel not to build around one person's gift. This was difficult due to Adam's amazing teaching gift. As they stayed with this commitment though, various gifts and abilities began to emerge in others on the team.

In the initial years of the KC Boiler Room, a loose leadership team of about eight had come together: Adam, Juli, David, Molly, Nathan, Marisa, Wendy Andrews, and Mary Arndt. Juli's prophetic and practical gifts become a perfect complement to Adam's role as teacher, and she and the others in the group all contributed to defining their strategic direction as the church grew. As Adam described it, "Honestly, very little would have ever actually come to pass without God working through Juli each step of the way." Around this "core team," there were about thirty people who they would consult in one way or another regarding important decisions. This configuration led the church for a number of years. Since they were still so young, myself and other of my more "marinated" colleagues would come in regularly to meet with them, teach, and give pastoral as well as marital and child-raising advice—each time I visited I fell in love with them all over again. They were so hungry for the Lord and really knew His voice in a spectacular fashion.

In 2012, the church had grown significantly and was in need of more shepherds to oversee the affairs of the church. A group of "non-vocational" people were selected to sit on the first formal eldership team alongside the "vocationally-situated" core team. These thirteen elders soon found themselves in turbulent waters. Decisions were proving hard to make and internal wrangling's began to rise to an eventual crescendo. Each person they selected was there for a reason and because everyone on the core team respected them greatly, but the combination of personalities showed they were still young and unseasoned.

First of all, as young as they were—all still twenty-some-things—meant a high level of idealism, a tendency to think in absolutes, and only a scant amount of "seasoned" wisdom to share amongst themselves. They tended to either think too alike or too differently and were not very good at separating principle from preference. Very few of them had enough life experience and maturity yet to fulfil the scriptural requirements for elders found in 2 Timothy and Titus, let alone a clear enough sense of who they were in Christ to trust themselves or each other. It's tough to come to a consensus if the team is still on the journey of forming their identity in Christ. (A must for an elder!) How can you give in to a different way when your identity is still tied up in doing it your own way? That demands maturity.

Secondly, some members of the team had imported unresolved relational issues into the eldership. Residual pain and broken patterns in any leader will come to the surface as soon as there is any pressure applied and will only be exacerbated by the burden of leadership. Even with just the pressure to be godly, wise, and lead their peers, the cracks in some characters were too much and "stuff" oozed out. It is nearly impossible to be a servant of Jesus to others while the self-protection meter is running on red.

Thirdly, there was an insufficient biblical foundation for understanding what elders are and are not meant to be and do. Neither did they have a strong grasp on the Scriptural blueprint for church. These shortcomings often meant they were debating opinions more than biblical principles, which always makes it difficult to come to any kind of agreement.

Fourthly, our 24-7 Prayer USA oversight team felt that couples should not be invited to the eldership simply because they are married to each other. We felt that eldership was both a character and gifting issue and should be evaluated person by person, not simply on the merits of one of the spouses. In some cases, both of the partners did meet the requirements of eldership, but not because they were married. This issue seemed to produce the most confusion. There were "elders" who were truly elders and some that were not: a burden too big to bear on any one person if the calling and anointing is not there, much less on a couple.

So, the 24-7 Prayer USA oversight team was invited to get involved more deeply. After many conflabs to sort out the issues and soothe the pain, we felt it best to disband the current configuration of elders. We left the "core team" in place as elders (as they were mature and qualified), created a year-long training on the biblical requirements of eldership, and invited any of the Missional Community leaders who aspired to eldership to go through the training.

THE SON—WHO WE ARE:
Sibling Servants of the Upside-down King

Now that Jesus is our life, we carry His image as sibling servants of the Servant King. We become His emissaries on the earth, but we don't do it alone. The end of the days of "solo," entitled leaders as a norm should summon loud applause and great relief from those seeking to be disciples of Jesus. We weren't designed to be heroes or have self-initiated visions of grandeur. The whole basis of our lives and ministries is the result of being called to be servants in His footsteps. To come into this calling, we must learn to be recipients of His grace and mercy as Paul did, and be just as void of any arrogant feelings of entitlement. Once again, leadership in this Kingdom does not teach humility by tenet, but by example. It is caught rather than taught.

We are servant-heirs with Jesus, the younger siblings of the King who rules through grace, peace, and love rather than power. We have the power of God on our side, but it is not to wield as we see fit, only has He does. We become vessels of His grace (see 2 Timothy 2:20-21), to be used for His purposes, but share in the joy of the transformations His purposes bring (see Matthew 25:21, 23). That means every personal ambition, every dream, every skill, every triumph, and every defeat, has to be surrendered and exchanged for a far better purpose: to serve Him unconditionally as we have been instructed, *"Whatever you do, do it all for the glory of God"* (1 Corinthians 10:31). That means we don't need to take credit, it all belongs to Him. In fact, the less credit we take, the better, as well as the more glory He gets.

But this doesn't mean we are sent as lambs to the slaughter either, though Jesus did say *"I am sending you out like sheep among wolves"* (Matthew 10:16a). Too many in the Church have made the mistake of equating "servant of God" with "doormat." Jesus wasn't! Neither do we serve from a place of defeatism, hoping someday God will redeem our suffering on the other side of the pearly gates, but we serve from the place of an empowered child of God, emissary of the King. There are certainly times we will lay down our rights and even suffer for the throne, but more often than not we should *"be as shrewd as snakes and as innocent as doves"* (Matthew 10:16b) relying with confidence on His grace and wisdom to see us through. (We'll look at this process in more detail in Part Three.) We are not ill-equipped, and we do not lack godly imagination—for *"we have the mind of Christ"* (1 Corinthians 2:6) after all—God has not left us helpless or unable to hear from heaven.

Why is that? Because He has established an entirely new relationship with us as His friends.

"I no longer call you servants, because a servant does not know his master's business. Instead, I have called you friends, for everything that I learned from my Father I have made known to you."

—JOHN 15:15

Jesus uses the word *servants (doulos)* here to describe their past status as slaves. This word means "bond-slave" and in this context, is talking about "involuntary" subservience to a master. Paul tells us that we were once involuntary slaves *(doulos)* to sin. (See Romans 6:17, 20). Sin had us bound.

There were, in Rome, those sold as slaves, those that were indentured (slaves for a preset number of years), and those who had their ears pierced to show they had given their lives to their masters to be bondservants. Adapting this cultural practice in terms the Church could understand, Paul calls himself a *"servant* [bondservant] *of Jesus Christ"* (Romans 1:1, insert added)—remarkably using the same word *(doulos)* that is used for a born or indentured *slave.* Now, however, he is using it to describe his *voluntary* choice to put himself in bonds under the love of the Servant King. It was in this framework as a voluntary slave to Jesus that he experienced Christ's words, *"for everything that I learned from my Father I have made known to you"* (John 15:15) as we noted before. Paul, in putting himself fully under the authority of Christ, became His friend and was entrusted with revelation from Him, the *"mystery . . . which was not made known to men in other generations as it has now been revealed by the Spirit to God's holy apostles and prophets"* (Ephesians 3:4, 5).

The Father always intended to free us from the involuntary (born or indentured) slavery *(doulos)* so we would voluntarily choose to subject ourselves to becoming bondservants *(doulos* again, strangely enough), thus entitling us to be given access to the secrets of the Master. (Funny how one word can have such diverse meaning depending on which side of the cross it is employed.)

Perhaps the best way to illustrate this is to use an example from a book called *The Numbers Game* by Chris Anderson and David Sally.[19] In the book they ask about what makes a great professional soccer (*football* for my friends "across the pond") team and contrasts it with what makes a great professional basketball, baseball, or (American) football team. If you have a Michael Jordan, a Kobe Bryant, or a LeBron James, your NBA team is going to be in the playoffs year after year. The right pitcher or quarterback can turn a decent team into a world champion. In such cases, it's worth spending big money to get a star, because that will make your team a winner.

But soccer is different. Soccer has more players for one and plays on a much bigger field. Because of this, one star player is great to have, but ineffective if you can't get him or her the ball. In basketball, the star can drive the court and score, but that's nearly impossible in soccer. A pitcher can control an entire game defensively, and a clutch QB can snatch victory from the jaws of defeat time and again. In soccer, however, it usually takes ten to twelve good passes to set up a goal, and failure on any one of those will mean going on defense until you can get control of the ball again to set up another ten to twelve passes. Because of these, basketball, baseball, and (American) football could be considered a "strong link" sport—meaning the success of the team is defined by its strongest player(s)—while soccer is a "weak link" sport—wins and losses are more defined by the weakest players on the "pitch" and not the stars.

In building organizations, people too often take the strong-link approach and almost never the weak-link approach, especially in the West. We like our stars, after all. We like to go see them and if possible be seen with them. That's what a lot of people build their identities around. A star can draw a crowd and build up a megachurch that is a mile wide and an inch deep, but is this what we are after? Is the Church a weak-link or strong-link game? Is the Kingdom of God about only the heroes of faith, or the people in the pews going out into the world to be salt and light?

I don't believe the Kingdom of God is about stars or how big a crowd we can draw; I think it's about its "position players"—how effective the body of the church is being in interacting with their neighbors, coworkers, and the person behind the checkout counter at the grocery store. While many churches build their congregations on great platform presence, the Kingdom of God is about the lowest on the totem pole. Jesus calls us again and again not to gather about great leaders and personalities, but go to the "least among us" and raise them up. Kingdom (and church) success is a "weak link" sport. This is what reconstruction is all about. Our churches aren't to be defined by the Gospel Identity formed among the leaders, but among the youngest in the faith among us. Kingdom success is defined by how well we are growing them up. Successful parenting isn't about the performance of the parent, it's about the confidence and competence of the child to care for themselves and others. (And of course, immature parents don't very often help form mature children, either.)

I think this is why Jesus didn't say, "Okay, everybody, I've gotta go. I'm leaving Peter is in charge. Do what he says—I'll tell him what to tell you—and you will all be all right." No. Instead Jesus says that they are all His "friends" and each has the responsibility to come to Him on their own. It was His intent we would reveal His Kingdom *together*, each playing our part as directed by the Head of the Church. This is one of the great mysteries of what "church" actually is.

> In all wisdom and insight **He made known to us the mystery of His will,** according to His kind intention which He purposed in Him with a view to an administration suitable to the fullness of the times, that is, the summing up of all things in Christ, things in the heavens and things on the earth.
>
> —EPHESIANS 1:8-10 NASB (emphasis added)

So what is the "big secret"—"the mystery"—that is ours to know as His friends? In this passage, the word *administration*—or "dispensation" in the KJV—is the Greek word *oikonomia*. This beautiful word refers to the "the management of a household or of household affairs,"[20] especially a religious one. God has established a suitable household that will administrate and oversee the process of everything coming into alignment under the kingship of Jesus, manifesting His Kingdom in our midst. God's redemptive plan has always been that heaven and earth will be restored back to creation's original purpose and we sons and daughters, the Church, will be the household—the tribe or "nation" of God—to see it to fulfillment. He is assuring us that the mandate to have dominion over the earth will be accomplished under the authority of Christ *through each of His Family members.*

That's quite a mystery He revealed to us, one that most of the old covenant Jews never dreamed of. We get a peek at the future fulfillment of this promise when John writes that,

> "The kingdom of the world has become the kingdom of our Lord and of his Messiah, and he will reign for ever and ever."
>
> —REVELATION 11:15

This should reveal "church" in a very different light. To move forward after the deconstruction of ideas and structures we saw in the last section, we are urged to be reconstructed to see, like Adam and the team at the KC Boiler Room, that the Father wants His Family, a household of faith, one that is suitably and fully equipped to usher in the full revelation of Christ on the earth. (And you thought we were just supposed to hang on until He returns—bah!)

This is the Gospel!

THE FAMILY GROWS DEEPER AND BROADER

During this same season, a new emphasis grew within the KC Boiler Room leadership team. As Adam described it, "Personally, and for many of our leaders, we realized we had never received anyone older than us as anything more than mentors or strategists. God started to challenge us from the New Testament with Paul's words about 'My son Timothy, in the faith.' That begs the question, *Do I have a father in the faith? Do I know what it feels like to be spiritually fathered and mothered?*"

This line of thinking led Adam to a realization. He confessed to me, "Hey, I have a real need for you, but I don't have a *felt* need. In fact, I've spent my whole life not needing anybody and I've leveraged that to basically plant a church for my own identity as opposed to starting the church as a family." But Adam never forgot what God had spoken to him about his call to plant the KC Boiler Room: "Young men have ministries, but fathers have families. Which do you want to have?" In order to do that, Adam knew he and the team needed to receive older moms and dads in the faith and do it vulnerably. They had to be willing to sincerely invite them into their lives.

It was after nearly eight years of loving Adam and walking with him that his attitude of "I have no felt need for you" was confronted by the Father. We were in a 24-7 Prayer Gathering at Believers Church in Tulsa, when we felt led to invite those present to receive a "father's blessing" if they had never been or felt blessed by their earthly fathers or father figures. It was almost a perfunctory and haphazard invitation. After we gave the invitation, Adam came sauntering up to Roger Nix and I lackadaisically and said, "I suppose I should ask you guys for a father's blessing since things aren't going very well with my own dad." In fact, Adam had not had a full breakthrough in his relationship with his earthly father since the time we'd met.

Roger and I laid hands on him, searching for some profound prayer to pray over him when, "Boom," he fell to the ground and started groaning. He lay there for a very long time while the Father visited his fractured heart. That was a pivotal point in Adam's journey with the heavenly Father and a new season in our relationship together as "old guy" and "young buck." The Father graced us with a new affection and trust that follows us to this day. Thank you, Father!

People who are all the same age don't do a very good job of being fathers and mothers to each other. It takes multiple generations to be a family. "So,' Adams states, "we started desperately praying for older moms and dads in the faith," Adam later told me. "It took us a few years and then Jesus started answering that prayer."

The first thing God did in answer to these prayers was to take the KC Boiler Room leaders on a "heart journey" to become reconciled to the idea of spiritual parents. Adam explains that, "We started realizing that the big words of the Kingdom weren't *transformation* or *justice* or *revival*, but *mom, dad, brother, sister, son,* and *daughter*. Even the word *community* had to change. It was a stepping stone to family, but too broad a concept. Because many who joined us every week had been hurt by their families and were now being healed by the Father's love, their theological grid needed to change.

"It was incredible to watch as a few brave over-fifties began joining us for worship. They must have felt very out of place among all of these twenty-somethings; they kind of just held the space there. Over time, they began to attract more and more moms and dads in the faith, which started changing the entire complexion of our church." The gene-pool seemed to be expanding. The wisdom of age was coming into view and hopes for a broader, healthier, and more successful eldership lay ahead.

Near that same time, what the KC Boiler Room team had learned in opening up and inviting in the artists' community was replicated in hosting events for urban hip-hop dancers after someone in the church led a cousin—who was a prominent hip-hop dancer in the area—to Christ through one of the Collectives. His girlfriend then followed, and then others. One of the women who had come out of a lesbian relationship to date one of the guys that started attending had "a radical encounter with Jesus and we ended up marrying the two of them and baptizing them in a bathtub at one of the houses." Despite lives being changed, a mistrust among the group arose and what had looked at first as a promising movement of the Gospel just as quickly died out. The church leaders were left to pick up what pieces they could. It was painfully disappointing!

Then, through the relationships of a guy by the name of Ian Flowers, who slept in the Boiler Room because they had invited him off of the streets, the church got on the map for the "train hopper" culture. Many of these had the desire to live the Jesus life, but apart from any establishment or institution. "They started showing up at our building and staying for extended periods of time. It was an opportunity for us to get to learn from them and serve them. We ended up having loads of these kind of nomadic kids with their joy, wild stories, and dogs coming through regularly for three, four, five years."

These things really deepened the questions the team had already been asking, namely "What does it mean to see the Gospel flourish in the lives of people who are commonly ostracized from the Church? And how do you foster family in cultures that are effectively made up entirely of orphans?"

These were questions that would lay the groundwork for what God was going to do next for this group of praying and dreaming friends.

NOW WHAT?

Question #1: Do women, youth, seniors, minorities, and the poor feel that they are heard, championed, and seen as *equal in value* in your church or ministry? If there is a sectarian power structure in your church (hostility between various groups), what does the Lord want you to do to make Jesus the centerpiece of church life that every person and every group sees as their unifying factor? (Instead of complaints of unfairness, victimhood, inequality, etc.)

Question #2: What is your qualification for your leadership calling and ministry assignment? What was Paul's?

> **Scripture:** Meditate and reflect on 1 Timothy 1:12-17. What was the criteria for God calling Paul? (vs. 15.) What was the reason God chose the worst guy possible? (vs. 16.)

> **Scripture:** Consider this companion scripture: 2 Cor 5:11-15. How does Paul's singular motivation (vs. 14) for serving the Church compare to your own motivation for what God has called you to?

KINGDOM DREAMING

Therefore do not be ashamed of the testimony about our Lord, . . .
but share in suffering for the gospel by the power of God,
who saved us and called us to a holy calling, not because
of our works but because of his own purpose and grace,
which he gave us in Christ Jesus before the ages began.

—2 TIMOTHY 1:8-9 **ESV**

The gatherings at KC Boiler Room were now in the hundreds and having enough collectives to keep up with the need for them was falling behind. As the leadership become concerned that the pendulum was swinging away from the "table" to the "meeting," the Lord began speaking to them about more intentional leadership training for both the collective and church leaders. Impressed that they were in need of knowing "who has been this way before," the Lord supplied ample and able "recruits" in the form of Jeff Vanderstelt and Joe Steinke.

Jeff, a fabulous teacher and practitioner in "street level" Jesus-living, had developed a biblical practice of "saturating" neighborhoods with the love of Jesus in community with his friends. Soma Church* in Tacoma, Washington experienced first-century church in a twenty-first century context under his leadership. Jeff and the

---

* As I mentioned before, Jeff has since moved on to be the pastor of Doxa Church in Belleview, on the other side of Lake Washington from Tacoma.

Soma team became a tremendous boost to hungry leaders at the KC Boiler Room.

Then there was Joe Steinke. Joe, originally a Madisonian Wisconsonite, had recently moved to Kansas City with his wife, Angie, and their kids, to establish 24-7 Prayer's "Academy." Already a leader on the 24-7 Prayer USA national team (along with yours truly) and a friend to the Boiler Room church family, Joe (who just happens to be an avatar of Bono) brought a father's touch to biblical leadership training. With a certification from the Biblical Institute for Leadership Development (BILD.org), he began to partner with Adam and the 24-7 Prayer USA team to lay foundations for ongoing, onsite, Socratic group learning from the Scriptures. What was birthed were the Antioch courses, and their subsequent babied-down "First Principles" classes designed for house groups. This was water to a thirsty land.

Within the next couple of years, the team's DNA became clearer. Spiritual maturity in the leaders was on the increase thanks to the intentional, systematic diet of biblical instruction for the Church of Jesus. (It was in this season the team from Believers in Tulsa started regularly connecting with the KC crew to learn from each other and experiment with putting what they were learning into action.) These relationships and the subsequent creation of deeper biblical roots led to growth in spiritual passion and new levels of maturity and capability in the leadership.

This kind of discipling process is more than book learning; it is a cocktail of group reflection, character development, and daily practice in the context of respective and diverse home groups. They were learning to *make disciples . . . teaching them to observe* (Matthew 28:19-20) everything Jesus taught. And as they did, these disciples were equipped to make new disciples, and the results were stretching them even further.

As Adam described it to me, "We were trying to build missionally and build life in the Kingdom towards those who aren't presently in the Church. So that's really been our passion and our focus over the years. I would say, because of the age we were when we started the Boiler Room, most of the first decade was weaning us off of earning and performing for God's favor and feeling the pain of our rejected hearts and orphan stories. It was about God finally bringing us into the spirit of adoption, and, helping us get ahold of what it means to be 'beloved' and in *the* Family.

"We started to realize that many of us, because we have broken homes or families, we were trying to be 'found in the family' or 'found in community' and very quickly started to turn *community* into an idol when we did that. We needed to be found in the Father, in His love, in His voice, to find an identity in Him to be safe in. That lead to a deepening of our quiet times, a greater confidence in who God created each of us to be, and a beautiful journey into a 360-relational orientation that the Kingdom is a family—and that that's where personal transformation happens.

"We just kept rehearsing the Gospel. Anything that looked like fruit—like our initial success with the artist and hip-hop communities—was continually cut off, and that brought us back to the depths of our identity in Christ and deep rootedness in His love and being loved and valued as Family."

THE SON—WHAT WE DO:
Serve One Another and the "Least Among Us"

Historically, we have mangled this beautiful word, *ministry*, in the Church. "Ministry," or "the ministry," has been used to demarcate between the clergy and laity. Regrettably, we have come to use the word *ministry* and *minister* to refer only to those that serve church or missionary organizations vocationally. One of the primary words used for *ministry* comes from the Greek word, *diakonia*—from which we get the word "deacon"—and means primarily "service, ministering; especially of those who execute the commands of others."[21] The word is straightforward enough, and the problem isn't so much in the word itself, but in how we aim it.

Ephesians 4 is one of the most thorough passages in the New Testament on the Church and its purpose—as well as the function of *ministers*. Let's take a look at it in full context, and then dive into different parts to focus on what Paul is teaching us here:

> It was he who gave some to be apostles, some to be prophets, some to be evangelists, and some to be pastors and teachers, to prepare God's people for works of service, so that the body of Christ may be built up until we all reach unity in the faith and in the knowledge of the Son of God and become mature, attaining to the whole measure of the fullness of Christ.
>
> —EPHESIANS 4:11-13

We generally focus on verse 11 in this passage, which delineates what has classically been called the "five-fold ministry": apostles, prophets, evangelists, pastors, and teachers. Regardless of the fact that we are much more comfortable with the last three today than the first two, we tend to call people who have these gifts *ministers* and consider them as "those who do the work of the ministry." They indeed do *ministry* as "bond-slaves" of the Gospel, but are *not the only* ministers the Lord has provided in His Church (as many seem to think of "ministers" today).

So what is this passage saying?

Look at the passage again. Verse seven tells us: *"But unto every*

one of us is given grace according to the measure of the gift of Christ"
(Ephesians 4:7 KJV). Everyone has been given grace (*charis*) from
Jesus. There is no article before *charis*, which means it is one grace
that He dispenses in various portions—"measures"—from the ultimate gift which is Christ Himself. He is the "gift" and gives "measures" of His own various abilities, dispensing His grace in such a
way as to make up His dimensions—His *size and shape*, as it were.
To realize His dimensions, to make up one Body with one Head,
our goal is to come into a *"unity in the faith and in the knowledge of
the Son of God and become mature, attaining to the whole measure of
the fullness of Christ"* (Ephesians 4:13). How big is that *"measure"*?
Big enough to *"fill the whole universe"* (Ephesians 4:10).

How then, do these small measures of the one grace become a
unified representation of the Body of Jesus Himself? Well, we all
draw from one grace, but it is dispensed in many ways. Some, *not
all*, have been chosen by Jesus to be apostles, prophets, evangelists, pastors, and teachers. Remember, Jesus is the "Apostle of our
souls," the "Prophet" of prophets, the great Evangelist, the "Chief
Shepherd," and the Master "Teacher." Paul emphatically tells us
that out of Christ's own character and being, "it was He that gave"
these particular giftings to the Church.

How were they, these "five-fold" gifts from Jesus, meant to
engage the Church? By doing exactly what Jesus always did: come
as servants to His creation—in this instance, to the Church itself.
And what was the goal? *"To equip his people for works of service,
so that the body of Christ may be built up"* (Ephesians 4:12). This
"equipping" of God's people comes from a Greek word referring to
the refitting of a ship or the resetting of a broken bone. This is their
"ministry" then, to perfect or mend God's people until they are
returned to God's original design for them—viable body parts operating in unity to make up the full dimensions of Christ Himself.

And what is the purpose of all this mending and perfecting? To prepare them for "works of service" as "servant-ministers" of the Servant King. (Just like Him!) Here the word *diakonia* is used to speak of the servant nature of the "ministry" of God's people. So, out of the one grace *all* are ministers and all with different functions, all committed to growing up into maturity to form the very Body of Jesus in their communities. (The body is a perfect example of a weak link organization, after all. Great eyesight does little good when the kidneys or liver is failing.) Here is another way to put it:

> The apostles, prophets, evangelists, pastors, and teachers furnish and equip the believers to do the work of the ministry, which results in building *up the church.* The Church builds itself in the faith as the members care for one another, show love, and generally manifest the other gifts God gives (as mentioned in Romans 12 and 1 Corinthians 12). Yet the Church also builds itself as it reaches out to its surrounding community with the love of Christ, drawing others into the fold. God has given His Church an enormous responsibility—to make disciples in every nation (Matthew 28:18-20). This involves preaching, teaching, healing, nurturing, giving, administering, building, and many other tasks. Fulfilling this command solo would be impossible. But God calls us as members of His Body. No one should be a bystander, an observer.[22]

Paul summarizes the nature and purpose of this body of "ministers" all connected to Jesus, the Head:

> Then we will no longer be infants, tossed back and forth by the waves, and blown here and there by every wind of teaching and by the cunning and craftiness of people in

their deceitful scheming. Instead, speaking the truth in love, we will grow to become in every respect the mature body of him who is the head, that is, Christ. From him the whole body, joined and held together by every supporting ligament, grows and builds itself up in love, as each part does its work.

—EPHESIANS 4:14-16

In other words, in a typical church service, the ones on the stage and speaking from behind the pulpit *are not* the only ministers, the people in the pews are as well! (This idea has been around and given ascent for a few decades, but the old pattern still seems entrenched in far too many of our churches—we have basketball instead of soccer thinking.)

It is our task as leaders in the Church to help God's people see that they are ministers in life and that they have a viable "ministry" by virtue of being recipients of His grace. Unfortunately, many of God's people have still not gotten this memo, nor have the leaders shed themselves of the error of denying people inclusion into "the ministry" and their high calling in God.

So who are disciples of the "Servant King"? They are *ministers*. To whom? First, one another, to build each other up in Christ; then to make disciples of others until the formation of all of these "parts" together in unity form a representation of Christ—His Body, the *"fullness of Him who fills all in all."*

Remember that Paul began this exposition with *"I urge you to live a life worthy of the calling you have received"* (Ephesians 4:1). We discovered that this isn't a "ministry calling" *per se*, but an invitation being shouted at you to fulfill all that Jesus did to make the Church His dwelling place and a people through whom *"the manifold wisdom of God should be made known to powers and authorities in heavenly realms"* (Ephesians 3:10). Who is *"you"* in Ephesians 4:1? *"You"* is the reader, not just *"you"* in the office of pastor, teacher, evangelist, etc. So, *you*, in the pew, what is *your* gifting? What is *your* slice of God's grace that can only come through *you*? What is *your* ministry? What dream has God put on *your* heart to make the world a better place around you and please the heart of your Father? What ministry of reconciling the creation of God has He called *you* to and gifted *you* for? And how does that gifting and servant's heart function as part of your local church family and out into your community?

And how about us leaders? Are we committed to minister to the "ministers," to see them come into their gifts and release them into their fields "that are ripe for harvest"?

Remember, we're not in this alone—yes, God has called us individually, but He has also called us together. That is what it means to be a missional family. We each have our part, and that part is to champion the giftings and callings of each other: *"From him the whole body, joined and held together by every supporting ligament, grows and builds itself up in love, as each part does its work"* (Ephesians 4:16).

The making of ministers isn't primarily for "church work"—in other words, "serving the church" and making sure the church organization continues as an organization and can sustain itself and its programs—but for building up the Father's sons and daughters to be formed in the image of Jesus, His *"whole measure of fullness."* His whole Body, the Church is to look like Him, be like Him, and serve like Him. All of our young leaders need to recognize the difference between two different motivations, service and authority, and recognize that they are servants under the authority of the Sovereign King called to equip His people for the work of their ministries.

I have talked to scores of young leaders who are focused on climbing the ministry ladder—which, of course, is a contradiction of terms: climbing a ladder of success is diametrically opposed to the joy of becoming a servant to those we lead. Any ministry that is focused on "ministry activities" and not on equipping people is something other than what Jesus modeled for the sons and daughters of God. And of course, that equipping isn't just about people *doing* the work God has called them to, but *becoming* the people God says they are—forming within each of us the Gospel Identity we have as the children of God, the siblings of Jesus, the co-heirs of Christ.

According to Paul, we are in a race to see who can "outdo one another" in love, not succumbing to the illusion of climbing to a place of notoriety over God's people. Jesus gives His Spirit to servants, not idolaters—to lovers, not to experts or Christian "gurus." Peter confirmed this truth when he wrote,

> Now that you have purified yourselves by obeying the truth so that you have sincere love for each other, love one another deeply, from the heart.
>
> —1 PETER 1:22

This is the Gospel!

DEVELOPING THE RHYTHMS OF THE CHURCH GATHERED AND THE CHURCH SCATTERED

As the KC Boiler Room continued to grow both in numbers and in depth, the team found themselves expressing the Church in two forms: the Church gathered—Sunday morning and other meetings where all or most of the church was invited; and the Church scattered throughout homes and neighborhoods around Kansas City. The Church gathered was a weekly rhythm of family reunion—the larger family of smaller families gathered together to worship and connect over common ground. The language of the church even changed to the point that they didn't like to talk about *community*, but instead *family*. Adam described it to me this way: "For a generation broken in family, we realized community was like a stone in the middle of the river that was safe enough to get you off the bank, but you were left in the middle of the river. It gave you a place to stop and rest, but, didn't get you to the other side." Getting to the other side took being formed in the Family of which God is the Father. Community left you high and dry, but still stranded. "If you're going to be adopted, it's all about Father and Family. That's what the Kingdom of heaven is."

The Church scattered found expression in the Missional Communities (MCs) and the rhythms they created for walking with God on mission in life outside of "big church." This was a process that evolved over time into diverse representations of being family on mission in different neighborhoods. As I mentioned before, from its foundations, the KC Boiler Room was deeply imprinted by "neo-monastic" groups elsewhere in the world. They provided traditions that created context for prayer, family, and missional activity as well as practices for remembering to plug into the presence of God throughout the day. It wasn't unusual to set smart phone alarms at strange times based on verse numbers in order to pray for certain things: at 10:02 (Luke 10:2) to pray for laborers for the harvest; at 1:43 (Acts 14:3) to pray for the release of signs and wonders; or to say the Lord's prayer at noon; etc. They called it "remembering Jesus on the road."

Many of the Missional Communities would have family nights where they gathered and ate together and then would dig into discussions about Scriptures—very Acts 2:42. Sometimes they would have nights where the Bible time centered around *lectio divina*, a practice of reading over the same Scripture passages several times, each with a different emphasis, and turning these passages into prayers. Each group was allowed to find its own path. As Adam described it, "For our missional communities, the rhythm is prayer, family, and mission, but again, we don't mandate them, but we do serve and coach and train into those and really pastor people's journeys."

These groups are founded first on human relational plain, and then being formed in the identity of the Father and finally, cultivating mission in the hearts of those gathered. "They're learning to not only be family with one another, but then welcome their neighbors or whomever is on the heart missionally into the same family—or the MCs—they're a part of. Depending on if you're adopting a neighborhood or a network of relationships, you begin to walk in a rhythm of life that includes those you want to love in a way you want to love them. The idea is to just put Jesus on display in their everyday lives."

In Legacy East, an underserved neighborhood on the east side of Kansas City, where both the Coxs and Blackwells lived and led a Missional Community, they came together with their neighbors every Friday night. "Neighborhood night," as they called it, was a mixture of ages and cultures where they shared a meal, expressed thankfulness, and played all kinds of games, including the all too wild "kickball madness." The relationships formed on those nights spread beyond the weekly get together into sharing life's joys and pains, celebrating birthdays, attending local football games, and helping each other in a crisis. Legacy

East slowly changed lives through simply loving neighbors like family.

Just as the seeds of the KC Boiler Room were planted through two friends doing life together, the church continued to grow using the same emphasis on relationship first, loving people where they are, and putting the Family of God on display in the day to day. It was still prayer and stumbling and moving at the speed of relationship, but they also knew the foundation they were building upon was solid, and it was making a difference.

NOW WHAT?

Question #1: How do you define and use the word "minister" or "ministry" in your church context? Do your people grasp the beauty of their own ministries or do they hope to be free of their "secular" job so that they can someday become "ministers" or "missionaries" for God?

Question #2: Have you established a culture of "loving the least" in your church family? The poor? Accusers? Betrayers? "Time suckers"? Jobless folks? Ask the Lord to show you who He wants to give you a heart for or if you carry a bias toward one group of people over another.

Question #3: After reading the section on church "gathered and scattered," which "delivery system" is the most biblical and most effective in "making disciples?" Without throwing large gatherings or small groups out the window, how can they be better prioritized and synchronized to create a seamless framework that equips people to be missional disciples and a blessing to the city in which they live?

THE SPIRIT OF TRANSFORMATION

*"But very truly I tell you, it is for your good that I am
going away. Unless I go away, the Advocate will not come
to you; but if I go, I will send him to you. . . .
"When he, the Spirit of truth, comes, he will guide you into
all the truth. He will not speak on his own; he will speak only
what he hears, and he will tell you what is yet to come.
He will glorify me because it is from me that he will receive
what he will make known to you. All that belongs to the Father
is mine. That is why I said the Spirit will receive from me
what he will make known to you."*

—JOHN 16:7, 13-15

An interesting thing happens in many churches as they start to grow. Because we're reaching far and wide into our communities, we don't want things to be weird or uncomfortable for newcomers. We want our services or house meetings to be places where they feel at home. Whether we realize it or not, we start to want to keep things within our control rather than leave them open for the Spirit of God to move as He sees fit. As a result, we start to act a little like the Holy Spirit is the "crazy Uncle Albert" of the family and begin putting subtle constraints on Him—especially when someone steps out of line saying they are speaking for the

Spirit when they are really just trying to get attention. This can often stifle the presence of the very Person—the Holy Spirit—people need the most.

While the KC Boiler Room leaders loved the ministry of the Holy Spirit and let Him have free reign in their meetings together, a few misuses in the local church culture in general and, to a small extent, in the KC Boiler Room itself caused the leadership to think it might not be safe for newcomers to see displays of the Holy Spirit if they came to a larger gathering. (Such leanings are always of dubious origins.) In response, since the team remained open to God's guidance, He gave Juli a dream that began to sort the church out regarding the Holy Spirit.

In the dream, many Missional Community leaders were gathered telling amazing testimonies of what Jesus was doing in Kansas City. We all began to sing, returning praise for what He was doing through the community. In the middle of it, people started grabbing different boxes, utensils, and instruments around the room and started worshipping under the power of God. They were playing on anything they could find, any instrument. The worship was beautiful, some of the most beautiful sounds I'd ever heard being played. Then the power of the Holy Spirit fell on the room and I had a vision inside of the dream.

In this vision, I was walking along the shoreline holding hands with Adam and having fun, but we seemed to be looking for something in the sand. I knew immediately that we were looking for two objects: a piece of fruit with a bite missing out of it, and a missing piece of a shell. We finally found the missing piece of the shell. When we put it together, Adam looked up and said, "We will never leave this piece again—it's the power of God; it's the power of love."

A few months later, the team was at a retreat with the wider leadership of the church and the Holy Spirit started to move. Adam began to weep. He heard the Spirit say to him, "You think you're a better pastor than I am. You think you're safer than I am, but the Kingdom is in me, the Holy Spirit, and I don't want you to ever change the subject again. I want you to stand up and apologize to the church for thinking you're a better pastor and that you're more safe than I am." Adam was grieved. He realized that he'd spent the last four years sheltering people from the one Person who could change them and love them and bring them joy. Before he could even get out the words, "I'm sorry," the Holy Spirit said, "Okay, we're good."

He couldn't believe he could grieve the Holy Spirit to such an extent and be forgiven before he could even get out his repentance. However, all the Holy Spirit wanted was Adam's heart and the hearts of the church. Adam thought from that point on they would start to see manifestations of power, miracles, and healing as they had seen in various instances when the church was very young, but that didn't happen. However, the Father seemed to hold back those manifestations for a season in order give them a greater revelation of the Spirit. What he didn't realize at the time was that the Holy Spirit is a person and that the Church is called to be Trinitarian in the fullest sense. It couldn't just receive the Father and the Son and be complete, it must also receive the person of the Holy Spirit as well.

This is a massive lesson for this generation—that the Holy Spirit is not just a mystical source of spiritual gifts and occasional manifestations, and He is certainly not irrelevant. He is a full person that reveals the Father and gives testimony of the Son. He is the means through which we experience the Presence of God. Too often the Church wants His fruit and His power, but is afraid, if we let Him in completely, He will do some crazy thing that will embarrass us and chase people away—like we know better than God does how to reach out to His creation.

We need to realize that in our orphan culture, it's impossible for people to be adopted into the Family if we don't welcome the Spirit of adoption. As we've already looked at in Romans 8:15, it is by the Holy Spirit we are able to cry out, "Abba, Father!" The goal of being forgiven, of being born again "of the Spirit," is to reunite us with our Father in heaven. The Spirit is asking, "How can you give what you don't have?" It is not up to us to bring people into His Family, we don't have the power to do that. The Holy Spirit is the Spirit of adoption, not us. We have nothing to give others until the Spirit of God has formed it in us anyway—how can we ever think we can be the Church without Him?

When Adam apologized to the congregation, every moment of his transformation was the Holy Spirit already working in their midst. When Adam invited the Holy Spirit back to lead the KC Boiler Room, he didn't know how he would unearth his own identity and become more rooted and grounded in the full love of the Son of God. Adam declared with passion, "I will never apologize for the Holy Spirit again." And from that time on, he said, "He [the Holy Spirit] began to move me out of rejection, loneliness, and perfectionism." It wasn't about sign and wonders or great worship, the Holy Spirit was anchor Adam in the bedrock of the Son.

As the Holy Spirit did this work in Adam, it affected every person on the team as well. Through it, they continued their journey—to be found in the father and formed in the family—into the deepest part of their hearts.

THE SPIRIT—WHAT HE HAS DONE:
Sent to Manifest the Kingdom of God on the Earth and Fill It with His Presence

Adam's confession is attractive and very simple. I often ask a room of leaders if they have a fear of the Holy Spirit or if they have been offended by believers mishandling spiritual gifts. The stories vary. They often say, "It is a turn off when a person breaks out in prophecy that is loaded with their own agenda." True, nonetheless, it is important that we don't derive our pneumatology on the basis of weird Christians and personal, painful experiences. If we have theological differences, that's to be expected—as long as we don't relegate the Spirit of God to *our* framework and fail to invite Him to trash our "religiously correct" and safe castles. There is no ultimate downside to surrendering our fears and control and inviting the Spirit to take His rightful place—while we also have a responsibility to discern true expressions of the Spirit from the false. Knowing that, we should be able to confidently and simply extend the invitation, "come Holy Spirit"—and then, watch out!

> Now the Lord is the Spirit, and where the Spirit of the Lord is, there is freedom. And we all, who with unveiled faces contemplate the Lord's glory, are being transformed into his image with ever-increasing glory, which comes from the Lord, who is the Spirit.
>
> —2 CORINTHIANS 3:17-18

In Christ, there is no veil over our face as Moses experienced. Instead, the liberating Spirit of God is enabling us to see Him as no one ever did before the day of Pentecost. I find it interesting that in the Old Covenant, if they saw Him, they would die, and in the

New Covenant, if they didn't see Him, someone dies (spiritually at least, if not naturally).

It is as we gaze upon Jesus with spiritual eyes that we begin to be transformed into His image as sons and daughters. All this is the work of the Spirit sent to deliver us from our mere natural cerebral abilities and teach us to see into the mysteries of the spiritual realm. The Spirit causes the pattern of the tapestry to come into view as He empowers us to see the plan Jesus is orchestrating from His place at the right hand of His Father's throne in heaven. I believe it is fair to say t that the presence of God is not an end in itself, but the gateway to transforming us into His image!

The Spirit of the Lord has come and His work is to relay messages from the throne room of heaven to the battlefronts of earth. If you are wondering what the Word of God teaches about the nature and function of His Church, it is the Spirit that will reveal it to you. If you are wondering what lies in the future of the Church, it is the Spirit who will inform you of upcoming Kingdom strategies. He will teach you all Jesus spoke of and is still speaking regarding His present and future Kingdom:

> If ye have heard of the dispensation of the grace of God which is given me to you-ward: How that by revelation he made known unto me the mystery; (as I wrote afore in few words, Whereby, when ye read, ye may understand my knowledge in the mystery of Christ) Which in other ages was not made known unto the sons of men, as it is now revealed unto his holy apostles and prophets by the Spirit.
>
> —EPHESIANS 3:2-5 KJV (emphasis added)

There are some who think that all that Jesus said and did is contained in the Gospels alone. And yes, thank God for the *kerygma*—the proclamation of the work and life of Jesus in those same Gospels. Fortunately for all of us, however, Jesus didn't stop speaking, healing, teaching, prophesying, building His church, or relaying His plans to us after His ascension into heaven. In reality, He continued to lay the foundations of "the way, the truth, and the life" through the apostles and prophets who were dispatched as mouthpieces from His position on the throne. This was the *didache*: "the teaching," "the faith," or "the instruction"—that we discussed back in Part One. He proved to the disciples that He was as alive on His throne after His ascension as He was when He walked Israel's dusty roads with them. The Spirit that was sent to them was *"the Spirit of Jesus"* (Acts 16:7; Philippians 1:19). Jesus's body left, but His presence was still with them through His Holy Spirit.

The story of Jesus isn't contained in the Gospels alone. It courses through all of the Scriptures and still jumps out of the pages into our generation. The same Jesus of Matthew, Mark, Luke, and John keeps speaking and ruling His creation for eternity. Jesus spoke to the apostles, prophets, and other men and women through the Holy Spirit from the throne of God about His ongoing governance and plans for creation. These were His instructions given to the leaders of the Church concerning the "household order."

In the verses above, Paul reiterates the ongoing word of Jesus to him in regard to the *"mystery of Christ"* (Ephesians 3:4). (We had a glimpse into this mystery in Ephesians 1 when Paul was relating to us the summing up of all things in Christ. [See Ephesians 1:9,10.] In Ephesians 3, he tells us that the relaying of this Kingdom mystery to the Church comes from Christ by the Spirit, the one who *"will speak only what he hears"* [John 16:13].)

The Spirit of God is the intermediary between heaven and earth and speaks directly to the human spirits of those that are listening and hungry to get heaven's mandates. Just as Jesus was "made flesh" incarnating Himself in His creation, the Spirit in us is active for us to incarnate Christ and to become "flesh" to the world around us. It is through the Spirit we are transformed into His image, and as a result can transform the culture around us as well. This too is the Gospel!

SOCIAL ADVENTURING

The KC Boiler Room team had another very significant experience around the same time they invited the Holy Spirit back into their midst. I was there with our "Oversight Team" that was tasked to gather with the KC Boiler Room team once a year. A word was given in the middle of this meeting stating that the Boiler Room was going to be given the "Family crest of Saint Patrick." The person who saw the picture saw this crest as a four-leaf clover. We didn't quite understand it. (Maybe because I was "resting in the Lord" on the couch at the time? Okay, I was asleep—it was a long meeting and I was exercising my "old guy" rights.)

As the Oversight Team began to pray about this word, we heard the phrase, "You're going to be planted at the crossroads of society and will be planting the church in the spheres of society. Just as in Saint Patrick's day, there will be a reformation of the spheres of society." We were encouraged, but no one quite knew what it meant.

As we contemplated this further in prayer, a knock came at the door. Being closest, I went to answer it. As I opened it, there stood a rather bewildered looking fellow. He handed me a book. "It's for Adam," he said, turned, and walked away quickly. As he disappeared into his car, I looked at what he had handed me. On the front of the book there were four four-leaf clovers. I closed the door and brought the book to the rest of the group. For some reason, it seemed worth interrupting our prayers to take a look at.

The title was *Christianity and Social Adventuring* written by a man named Jerome Davis. It had been published in 1927. The book was a treatise on what it would look like for the Kingdom of God to be as leaven through all of society, to fill and transform nations through active discipleship in all the spheres of life. It was dedicated to a family who "loves the fun of social adventuring for international friendship."

We thought, "What better description of 24/7 Prayer and the Boiler Room Network could you possibly have?" As we looked at the name that was on it, we saw it was dedicated to a woman working in China and others in South Africa and Alaska. We realized all the people in the circle in the living room that day were strategically connected to those same regions of the world.

This was one of those supernatural moments that made us stop and reflect again on, "What would it look like for us to not only make disciples or plant churches, but for the Church to be God's family, His people, filling every place with His presence in all of culture? How do we shape our thinking and lives to ride that wave within the four walls of the Church?"

It looked like we suddenly had a new incentive for finding out.

NOW WHAT?

Question #1: Have you behaved as though you (we) are a better leader than the Holy Spirit? Do you consult and invite Him to reveal His will on *every* issue in your life and ministry?

Question #2: Does the Holy Spirit have free reign in your life, or do past painful experiences and fear of the unknown cause you to be fearful of the Holy Spirit's free reign?

Response: Invite the Holy Spirit to identify those fears and blockages. Then repent and receive new instructions for moving forward under His leadership.

THE ULTIMATE GRASS-ROOTS
MOVEMENT

Therefore, if anyone is in Christ, the new creation has come:
The old has gone, the new is here! All this is from God,
who reconciled us to himself through Christ and gave us
the ministry of reconciliation. . . . We are therefore Christ's
ambassadors, as though God were making his appeal through us.
We implore you on Christ's behalf: Be reconciled to God.

—2 CORINTHIANS 5:17-18, 20

In the light of their ongoing biblical training—and the realization that everything the Church ought to be about was growing up sons and daughters who could take the Kingdom into the world around them—the KC Boiler Room team began "frontloading" the missional communities (MCs). The team was beginning to see that the best expressions of the MCs were not those who gathered to just become a family, but those who became a "prayerful family on mission"—who also formed some kind of focus for giving back to or helping others. The question was asked of all group leaders, "Who are you called to love and how are you called to love them?"

This was a filter for those wanting to be MC leaders who may not have made the values shift from an inward to an outward focus yet. As Adam described it, "Yes, the Father had called us back to the Family, the Son had welcomed us into the Kingdom and appointed us as His servant-friends, but now the Holy Spirit was standing by and whispering into our ears that there were things we needed to be doing in the greater Kansas City area.

"What was He telling each of our leaders?"

The core team felt God "pressuring" them to expand their MC leaders' visions by plugging them into the Holy Spirit afresh to receive their "missional assignments." David explained, "We had to first believe this was God leading us, then wait for Him to work in the hearts of the leaders. We waited for six to nine months before some of them could answer the question 'Where and how are you called to love?' So, slow is okay."

As this was happening, new MC leaders were identified and plugged into the established training regime. In addition to the ongoing training, six "MC coaches" were provided to be on call and facilitated monthly events with all group leaders. As new leaders and their friends slowly became MCs, it was observed that many new people coming into the KC Boiler Room orbit were not ready to make that level of commitment. They still needed to be oriented to the KC Boiler Room's values as well as helped through personal issues from their pasts. So stepping-stone groups were formed called "Connect Communities." They were more like the original Collectives, created to focus on bringing people into the Family, but not on being missional yet. This made room for those coming from other orientations, different mindsets, and still a little too beat up to develop friendships yet. The CCs created a save environment in which to learn to pray together, study the Word, or get established in the Family.

THE SPIRIT—WHO WE ARE:
Spirit-empowered Ambassadors or "Missionaries"

It was the Holy Spirit that turned Adam and Eve from mere physical creations to reflecting the very image of God. After the Fall in the garden, that image was altered. Although it was the Spirit of God whose presence rested on the Ark of the Covenant in the Tabernacle, the image of God could not yet be transferred to the people of God. There had not yet been a perfect sacrifice for Eden's infractions. It was the Spirit of God who again came to Solomon's temple made with human hands, although the people of Israel remained fundamentally unchanged (even though the priests occasionally fell over from the power of His Presence). The priests kept the law, but it couldn't yet be *"written on their hearts"* (Romans 2:15). Under the law the presence of the Spirit could not yet bring the image of the Creator back to His creation.

Then Jesus changed everything!

The Spirit came to a virgin and the infant that was conceived carried the DNA of the living God. The child, Jesus, was the "exact representation of the Father" (see Hebrews 1:3)—and grew up to become God's Ambassador to establish the Kingdom of heaven by the power of His Spirit. It was that same Spirit that made a mid-course correction (metaphorically speaking), missed the temple made of stones, and landed on a bewildered huddle of disciples waiting in an upper room according the Jesus's instructions. The Holy Spirit inaugurated them by His presence, imbedded the image of God in them, and released them as Kingdom emissaries to the chaotic world of their day. We moved from the covenant of His Presence *with* the people of God, to a covenant of His permanent habitation *within and upon* His people.

Viva la revolucion!

The Holy Spirit is the ultimate "Missionary," the first fruit of Jesus's sending heaven to earth to reclaim it by divine right. Jesus instructed the disciples to stay put until they received this same Spirit. His rationale? *"But you will receive power when the Holy Spirit comes on you; and you will be my witnesses in Jerusalem, and in all Judea and Samaria, and to the ends of the earth"* (Acts 1:8). To be an emissary of the risen Christ, one must have delegated authority outside one's own resources—and be willing to see from God's perspective in order to become a viable "witness." The word in Greek for *witness* is *martys*, from which we get the word "martyr." This is indeed a life and death matter, not an option for disciples.

In retelling his testimony in Acts 26, Paul clearly understood this relationship between revelation and witnessing for Jesus, *"Now get up and stand on your feet. I have appeared to you to appoint you as a servant and as a witness of what you have seen of me and will see of me"* (Acts 26:16, emphasis added).

Jesus knew exactly what He was conveying when He said to His disciples, *"Apart from me you can do nothing"* (John 15:5). Paul, the servant-witness and ambassador of Christ, echoes this sentiment when he declares, *"For those who are led by the Spirit of God are the children of God"* (Romans 8:14).

Because we are helpless without Him, He sends His Spirit. But He sends His Spirit for power to witness to those who are willing to be led by Him—sons and daughters! Being in a parent-child relationship with the Father is the prerequisite of all Kingdom activity. Being a "convert" or a "Christian" is not enough. Until one has a revelation of their adoption by the Father, the Spirit's power cannot fully manifest. We have to "see" it by revelation, not merely "know" it by instruction. The amount of biblical knowledge and the anemic nature of our corresponding revelation of that knowledge has left us broken and needy in the Church of God.

Orphans and slaves simply cannot carry out the instructions of the Spirit of God. That is precisely why the Father sends the Spirit of adoption to us with joy—He is the precursor and prerequisite to being sons and daughters who are ambassadors in the Kingdom. If we don't have a revelation of this "work," we won't have the power to "witness" to the Father's magnificence. We might do "Christian work," but we won't be seeing the "signs accompanying those who believe." (See Mark 16:17.) That is reserved for those with a true revelation of their adoption!

Earlier, we celebrated the nature of being reconciled to the Father and being given the "ministry of reconciliation" as our life goal. God befriends us, turns us facing outward, and says, "Now, there are a lot of prodigals and lost sheep out there—I want them! So kindly go and befriend them as you've been befriended by Me." This call to reconcile the world is now to be our life's mission.

Paul punctuates the theme of reconciliation—of restoring friendship with a fallen world—by saying, *"We are therefore Christ's ambassadors, as though God were making his appeal through us. We implore you on Christ's behalf: Be reconciled to God"* (2 Corinthians 5:20).

The whole book of Acts celebrates the expansion of the Church across the Roman Empire. To challenge this global power structure, God raised up children through Christ, sent His Spirit to lead them, and terrorized darkness with a revelation the witnesses had received through the power of the ascended Christ. These were martyrs in spirit, and sometimes in body, willing to lay down their lives for the One who died for them because they had recognized that they were a people in transit—pilgrims that boisterously declared,

> *Our citizenship is in heaven. And we eagerly await a Savior from there, the Lord Jesus Christ, who, by the power that enables him to bring everything under his control,*

*will transform our lowly bodies so that they will be like his
glorious body.*
—PHILIPPIANS 3:20-21

It is hard to be led as a son or daughter, empowered as an ambassador, and move out in the authority of heaven if you are still rooted to this earth: seduced by temporal things, hopeful in political ideologies, committed to a "comfortable" life, and walking in the fear of human opinion. As Paul wrote elsewhere:

Therefore, if anyone is in Christ, the new creation has come: The old has gone, the new is here! All this is from God, who reconciled us to himself through Christ and gave us the ministry of reconciliation: that God was reconciling the world to himself in Christ, not counting people's sins against them. And he has committed to us the message of reconciliation. We are therefore Christ's ambassadors, as though God were making his appeal through us.

—2 CORINTHIANS 5:17-20

As the children of God, we became "new creations" and were "made beautiful" through the agency of new birth, but we've also been called into being like Him, to become change agents, restorers of His rhythms, and reconcilers of the corruption all around us back into God's original intentions for beauty, truth, and life. The Church isn't a waiting room where we bide our time until we can get into heaven. Instead, God's saying, "Since you're now a new creation and are reconciled, get up and start reconciling the world around you. You are My ambassadors and I'm making My appeal to My broken creation through you. And, so that you know you are able, I will send me Spirit to live in you and empower you."

The conclusion? We are His earthly representatives and God is using us to "bring those out in the world home from every sphere of life and make them beautiful." Will it be hard at times? Yes. But we are not alone in the endeavor. The Holy Spirit is with us to lead us into success in our calling. *"We know that in all things God works for the good of those who love him, who have been called according to his purpose"* (Romans 8:28) and *"in all these things we are more than conquerors through him who loved us"* (Romans 8:37). The key is to follow as we are led.

This is the Gospel!

"I WILL CHANGE YOUR NAME..."

As the Spirit was leading the KC Boiler Room forward into becoming a family that desired to embrace those who did not yet know that adoption was available to them, they began to feel the name "Kansas City Boiler Room" no longer told the story of who they were. The Boiler Room name spoke of a certain pressure and productivity, while the Spirit was addressing them continually as sons and daughters asked to enjoy the fruitfulness that comes from resting in Him. They loved their old name because of the people associated with it, but they felt there was a new name that would become evident if they were open to the Spirit's leading.

As they asked their church family, "What are the words that represent us the most?" The word that kept coming up over and over again was "home." People would come in the doors and say, "I feel like I'm home." Others would come to faith and the first thing they would say after they received the Jesus was, "I am home."

On a Sunday morning before Adam was going to share a vision with the church of Jesus transforming hearts, homes, neighborhoods, and nations through their "family on mission" initiative, a visiting friend had an interesting conversation with him. Adam told me:

My friend began to tell me that he had been studying words on worship. "There's a word I've come across that I can't get over, and it means 'home.'"

At that, he had my full attention. He didn't know I'd been thinking about new names for the church.

He said, "Yeah it's not just *home* like a noun, it is actually a verb."

I thought immediately, "If *Church* can be both a noun and a verb. . ."

He went on, "It actually means 'to find rest, to bring home, and to make beautiful.'" He continued, "There were no vowels in the ancient Hebrew text and so every letter was connected to a picture."

I was getting antsy because he still hadn't spoken the word itself.

He said the first letter "N" is the picture of a seed with a sprout and it stands for the generational legacy of a father and a son. The second letter "V" is a picture of a tent peg anchoring the Hebrew home and from which we get the word for "home."

"The last letter is incredible, it's where God added 'ham' to Abram to get Abraham. That extension is a picture of breath, like the Holy Spirit."

My first thought when I heard this was "Gospel"—a father sent his son, "N," to bring us home, "V," by the power of the Spirit, "H."

Adam remembered the "missing piece" from Juli's dream that they would "not be able to live without." Now he was desperate to know what the word was.

He didn't sate my curiosity, but went on to explain, "The first use of it was when the children of Israel crossed over the Red Sea into their deliverance. There, standing on the banks of promise, they watched all their slavery swallowed in the sea as the Egyptian Army followed them in and was consumed. In that moment, as they began to worship God for His deliverance and adoption. Moses cries out and says, "God you are my strength, God, you are my song, and I *navah* you God."

The word was *navah*! Moses was saying, "I bring you to rest; I adorn you with beauty; I bring you home."

That was when Adam knew that the Father was renaming them, not for a website, or for slick branding purposes, or a sign on the building, but across their hearts. For ten years God had been bringing them home. To "bring home" is the story of salvation from sin and adoption into His Family. To "make beautiful" is that once we come home, He restores our lives, and our whole worlds. This is the brand or signet ring seal of the Spirit that closes the contract between heaven and earth, God and man—a rather superior form of marketing to the manmade attempts to attract people to "our" churches.

In this one word we find adoption, redemption, salvation, and restoration—the "God Story" which is the Gospel. What if the Church could "bring home and make beautiful" all across the world? What if what He was doing in the newly renamed Navah Church—and throughout their homes and neighborhoods—flowed into all spheres of society?

NOW WHAT?

Question #1: Do you view yourself as a "missionary" in your neighborhood and workplace? If not, what teaching have your received to cause you to believe you have not been sent into your geographical assignments? How will you respond to the Lord's invitation to see yourself as his servant to your "world?"

Question #2: Have you, your team, and your church manifested your ambassadorial bona fides in your locale—dispatching messages from the throne and revealing His heart to the citizenry you are assigned to? Are you joyful in persecution? Are you witnesses of Him in every testimony?

> **Exercise:** Read, meditate, and respond to 2 Corinthians 5:17-20. Does this text describe beliefs and practices of your church family?

A PRAYERFUL FAMILY ON MISSION

*Since we live by the Spirit, let us keep
in step with the Spirit.*

—GALATIANS 5:25

Through the discipline of asking questions, Navah Church began to wonder how a "prayerful family on mission" would empower everyone, every day, to carry God's story everywhere. How could they reimagine "Church" imbedded in all the spheres of society? They sensed that God was inviting them to reimagine the Church even as society was reimagining work—such as the emergence of co-working spaces and the millennial model of collaborative ecosystems where everyone contributes toward a greater good. They started to dream of what it would look like for these same co-working spaces and the Church to collaborate for the common good of the city. What would it look like for them to love the city as humble servants and to work together to reveal Immanuel: "Christ with us"?

Around the time when we had all received that St Patrick "social adventuring" word, Adam had another dream. The day he woke up from that dream was the same day Kansas City closed down thirty of their sixty schools. He started thinking what would happen if the church acquired one of those school buildings. So, they started to pray as a team. Adam recalls, "I can't think of another three-hour period in the history of our leadership team where we sat under such a clear spotlight on our future. I wrote as fast as I could as the Spirit began unfolding an understanding of this dream." Through the content of the dream, he realized that the Father was inviting them to move into one of these schools. He saw a place for artists and entrepreneurs to be with the family of God together in one facility. There would be non-profits and for-profits, land for gardens and . . . so much! The dream was bigger than he could get his mind around.

Adam wrote this whole vision down and then offered a simple prayer: "Father, I still don't know that I'm a son, what can You do in my heart in the next five years?" He knew this vision was too big for a slave or an orphan and was anticipating the Father's work of sonship in his life in order to grow a vision of this size and nature. It would be in those five years that the Spirit would do the work of adoption in Adam's heart.

Adam had written this vision down in his prayer journal in 2010. In 2016, the year they renamed themselves "Navah Church," they began revisiting the dream about creating co-working spaces and the church collaborating with businesses and nonprofits. However, all the deals for buildings they had been looking into acquiring had fallen through. All the while, the dream kept getting stronger and stronger in their hearts. They had the sense they were to keep pursuing Jesus' guidance even though each different option they explored ultimately proved a dead end. They told the church they were going to move out of the Monarch building in the near future because they were outgrowing the space, but they had no idea where they would go. Every year it was the same question, "Should we move out?" And then, "Okay, but where to?"

In 2016, the Lord corrected them, "You see your small building as a limitation, but I'm using it as leverage to drive your roots deeper into Me."

"Okay," they thought again, "We'll keep digging in with what we have."

With Kansas City closing half of their inner-city schools, a number of churches in the city decided to offer help to the remaining schools. Led by Gary Schmitz, a force in the city-wide unity movement and a 24-7 Prayer walking advertisement, the "Adopt A School" program was initiated. It would turn out to be something that would teach Navah a whole new way of being missional.

In 2016, Navah Church adopted a school of mostly inner-city minority children, Attucks Elementary, and began tutoring them in math and English. Major events were held at the school each year where the whole Navah community pitched in to create the menu and provide the food. That Thanksgiving, as the children's families gathered, the Navah team served eight turkeys and 300 pounds of mashed potatoes. Out of these celebrations, and the tutoring the children were receiving, a number of families began attending some of the MCs. This blend of the Great Commandment (to love) and the Great Commission (to make disciples) was at full sail in downtown Kansas City.

THE SPIRIT—WHAT WE DO:
Going Missional: Demonstrating and Proclaiming the Kingdom

The command to receive the Holy Spirit, be witnesses, and go local, regional, and international, speaks of going where the Gospel has not yet penetrated. The pattern of Paul and his band of apostles was to *"not be building on someone else's foundation"* (Romans 15:20). The whole rationale for the mission of the Church was given to all believers and was one of dispossessing and possessing hearts and cultures that had not yet heard the Gospel proclaimed or seen it fleshed out in human lives. There were apostles and other church leaders that did a great deal of travel, but the bulk of God's people never travelled outside their city limits, but made their homes missional lighthouses. The *whole* Church was engaged in demonstrating and proclaiming the Gospel.

As we discussed in Part One, it was the *kerygma*—the proclamation—of the Kingdom Gospel that first penetrated human hearts for the early church, then defined each person's identity in the Godhead, resulting in the family "doing the works of Jesus." Everything the Church did was to spread the good news and love of Jesus. There was no huddling, no sense of being a subset of Roman or Jewish culture—they were the "hair on fire" brothers and sisters of the ruling King.

God is calling leaders today to do more than send and support missionaries. He is asking them to train all of God's people to be "on mission" in their own missional spaces in their communities. We do this in the context of being a family of families in love with God and each other, which provides the foundation for loving the world. It is impossible to juggle discipleship, missions, training, and various gender and generational groups in the church without something falling through the cracks. An organizational or departmental approach to biblical injunctions will not be able to keep all the balls in the air. It is being founded as a family, led by the Spirit, and rooted in our Gospel Identity that will make each of us into functioning "parts of His Body" to fulfill all of God's plans for His Church and our world.

If we are to be those body parts, however, and manifest what God has planted into each of us as His sons and daughters, then we are going to have to walk more fully in step with the leading of the Holy Spirit. This is not an option. No matter how strong our family ties or personal identities in Christ are, it is the leadership of the Holy Spirit that makes us sons and daughters. He is the Spirit of adoption as well as the Spirit of manifestation. He is the Counselor, our Advocate, our Comforter, Helper, Intercessor, Strengthener, and Backup. He is the Muscle and Brains of our operations. He has access to all of the resources. He knows what to pray for when we don't. He knows all the right people to which to introduce us. He's got all the right connections. He knows all the right vendors for us to work with. He's got the master business plan, the correct organizational chart, and He knows the ropes for getting things done in the halls of government. He is the ultimate spokesperson for truth, justice, and equality. He just flat out knows how to get stuff done and revitalize every person we come into contact with in the process.

So why on earth wouldn't we want to be in contact with Him every second of every day? Especially when He is so much closer than a text message or a cell phone call. I mean, we check our smart phones every few minutes, how often in a day do we check in with the Holy Spirit who has the keys to all these things that we want to accomplish in our lives?

At Navah, prayer became a similar way of life, "the air we breathe," as Adam put it.

If you are trying to pray or do family or do mission without the "Gift" the Father promised, in my experience, you might as well forget about it, because it won't work. Without freedom in the Spirit, you're never gonna pray, because it will just be another hollow ritual. The Holy Spirit is the greatest Pray-*er* in the universe traversing between the throne in heaven and our spirits on earth. The Spirit knows and delights in the Son and the Father and shares the intimate details of God with us through Him—He knows the well-worn path from the heart of God. We don't start teaching people how to pray with form, we start with freedom in the Spirit. We start with a revolution in the heart of every believer. When I bring someone to pray with me, I get right into "How do you see the Father? What's your relationship like with the Holy Spirit? *Listen.* Can you hear the Holy Spirit?"

In the book of Acts, *"They joined together constantly in prayer"* (Acts 1:14). It became a way of life for the early church that was to be the pattern in the ages to come. Prayer is simply the communication interface between heaven and earth that gives instruction from and transmits our ambassadorial reports to the throne of God. For the early church, they took full advantage of this open channel to the Jesus—who was now in heaven *"at the right hand of God . . . interceding for us"* (Romans 8:34). Filled with the Spirit, they prayed in the Spirit, because

> The Spirit helps us in our weakness. We do not know what we ought to pray for, but the Spirit himself intercedes for us through wordless groans. And he who searches our hearts knows the mind of the Spirit, because the Spirit intercedes for God's people in accordance with the will of God.
>
> —ROMANS 8:26-27

Just tracking the prayers in the books of Acts shows us how pervasive this interchange was:

» 1:14 – They were steadfast in prayer as they gathered to wait.

» 1:24 – They prayed before they chose the replacement apostle for Judas.

» 3:1 – They prayed in the temple.

» 4:24-31 – Their prayer of praise after Peter and John's release from prison resulted in an earthquake.

» 6:4 – The leaders deferred to others to deal with disgruntled widows so they could give their attention to *"prayer and the ministry of the word."*

» 7:59 – They commissioned the "table servers" with prayer.

» 8:15 – They prayed for the new Samarian believers.

» 9:11 – God told Ananias to find Paul because *"he is praying."*

» 9:40 – Paul's prayer raised Tabitha from the dead.

» 10:9; 11:15 – Peter went onto a roof to pray (and see a vision: *"Do not call anything impure that God has made clean"* [Acts 10:15]).

» 12:5, 12 – The church was praying when Peter was miraculously released from prison.

» 13:3 – The leaders at Antioch were *"fasting and praying"* when the Spirit spoke to send Paul and Barnabas on their first missionary journey.

» 14:23 – Paul and Barnabas *"appointed elders for them in each church and, with prayer and fasting, committed them to the Lord."*

» 16:13, 16 – Paul went to find a place to pray.

» 16:25 – Paul and Silas were in jail *"praying and singing."*

» 20:36 – Paul knelt and prayed with the Ephesian elders on the beach.

» 21:5 – Paul knelt and prayed with the disciples, their wives, and children, in Tyre.

» 22:17 – Paul is found praying in the temple in Jerusalem.

» 26:29 – Paul prayed for Agrippa (he was *almost persuaded"*).

» 28:8 – Paul prayed for Publius' (leader of Malta) father and he was healed.

It is interesting to note how directly the Spirit's activity and the prayers of the Church were linked—an example for the Church today. Here is the great promise!

> Do not be anxious about anything, but in everything, by prayer and petition, with thanksgiving, present your requests to God. And the peace of God, which transcends all understanding, will guard your hearts and your minds in Christ Jesus.
>
> —PHILIPPIANS 4:6-7

This too is the Gospel!

A NEW SPACE TO STRETCH THEIR LEGS

Near the end of 2015, after many failed attempts to find the right building for their lofty dreams, a man name Gerald called Adam and said he'd like to meet with the team from Navah. Adam knew of Gerald through a mutual friend who was running his coffee business in a co-working space in which Gerald was the CEO just outside the city—it was called Plexpod. So the core team from

Navah went down to tour the facility.

It was 25,000 square feet of incredible co-working space with nonprofits, startups, and established businesses within a beautiful shared environment. And it was at full capacity! The team was deeply impressed. It was a quality enterprise that exuded excellence.

After their "oohing" and "ahhing" over the facility, Gerald sat the team down and explained, "Well, we're planning on putting a 'mothership' of Plexpod down in the middle of the city."

Okay. Adam's mind was whirling.

Gerald continued, "We're thinking of having around 300 to 400 members representing fifty to seventy organizations—many of them small teams and individuals—housed in 160,000 square feet to start, and we've also set aside twelve acres around the building for a number of things, including urban gardens. We already have a growing group of entrepreneurs and nonprofits signing up to get on the waitlist." After naming some of the businesses and organizations, he firmly had the team's attention. He said that their coffee business was going to franchise and move over to the new facility as well.

Then, as the team sat there bleary-eyed at the magnitude of the endeavor, Gerald popped the question: "We would like Navah Church to move into our new facility in Westport. Are you familiar with the co-working space concept?"

He had no idea they'd been exploring the concept in light of reimagining the way they functioned as the family of God in the city. Adam shared, "Wow, you don't even know how crazy it is that you would ask."

He said, "Well, we've heard about you guys and have trust in you and are aware that this new facility is in your current neighborhood."

"You really got me interested," Adam confided. "Okay, well, where is it?"

Gerald said, "It's Westport Middle School."

Adam almost fell out of his chair! The journal entry Adam had recorded five years before was about a location that God would lead them to so artists and entrepreneurs and nonprofits could all move in together. He saw room for gardening as well as communal space for people to follow whatever dreams God had planted in their hearts. Westport Middle School just happened to be the only building you can see out of the tiny window of the prayer room in the Monarch building. So whenever someone in the room happened to look out the window, they had prayed and dreamed over Westport Middle School—for five years—without even realizing that would one day be the place they would call "home."

When Adam got back to his house, he ran into his office and started searching through years of journals for the appropriate entry. As he began to read the entries from 2010, it was as though he had written it *after* the conversation he had just had with Gerald. Every detail was there, including the name of the school.

Adam, full of amazement, told me, "It would have been incredible if God so sovereign, so wise, had told me ahead of time, but the part that touched my heart as I began to weep was to read my heartfelt prayer at the end of the entry, 'I need to know that I'm a son and what You can do in my heart in the next five years.'"

It was easy for God to do the miracle of providing a building, but who would be the people that inhabited that new facility? The real miracle was the journey to prepare a people to walk in the promise of what God wanted to do all along. That is the journey of the Church—the journey of *becoming* sons and daughters, of *demonstrating* the Kingdom, of *manifesting* the God's ways into the culture. They longed to be children whose identities were not wrapped up in church growth or their successes in their missional outreaches or in how well they could pray or anything else they could point to. The journey of their hearts was that God Himself would become their exceedingly great reward.

God once told Moses, "I'm going to give you the promise, but I can't go with you."

Moses looked back at God and said, "No deal—You are my reward."

Adam realized that through those years, just like Moses, they had actually become content with being His family, loved by Him, and doing life with Him as their reward. Yet the Lord had dreams for them to come to a place of collaboration and contribution for the good of the city, a context that was much larger than they thought their church could be—a fulfillment of the word given through the book with the four-leaf clovers to become God's social adventuring family.

Becoming Navah had been a wonderful God adventure none of them would trade for anything, but at the same time God, with a twinkle in His eye, seemed to be saying, "Kids, you haven't seen anything yet."

NOW WHAT?

Question #1: What is the place of personal and corporate prayer in your life and with the church family? How can you move from the "meeting" to the "table," a relational journey with God and each other to find peace and get instructions from the throne for your "footstool" issues?

Question #2: How do you and your church demonstrate and proclaim the Gospel to the people around you? Is the Lord leading you to inculcate a "missional" gene in all that you endeavor to do, and if so, what steps will you take to make this paradigm shift?

Question #3: What are some of the barriers you have encountered in helping God's people receive His burden for the "lost?" What mindsets seem to block the free flow of speaking and living the Gospel in your neighborhoods and workplaces?

> **Exercise:** This is a major issue in Western cultures: Preconceptions about "evangelism" and "sharing our faith" seem to have doused the fire in our bones. Transactional methodologies and guilt-ridden teachings haven't helped. Ask the Holy Spirit to "clean the pipes," reveal the source of the blockage, and prepare you to follow His lead. This takes some time in most churches (for it to be a natural and not a forced passion) and could prove to be the fight of your lives. Push through!

KINGDOM MISCHIEF—
CONTINUED

"The one who is victorious I will make a pillar in the
temple of my God. Never again will they leave it.
I will write on them the name of my God and the name
of the city of my God, the new Jerusalem,
which is coming down out of heaven from my God;
and I will also write on them my new name."

—REVELATION 3:12

I spoke with Adam in Kansas City in the summer of 2017 and he told me, "We've only been in the new space now about six months. We ended up moving in seven years to the week of that first journal entry in 2010. (God has a funny thing about sevens, I guess). We set money aside to help renovate space within the complex and the first thing they asked us to do was to create a quiet space. We said, 'Well, what about a prayer space?' They said, 'What do you mean?' We were like, 'Well, here's what it looks like.' They responded, 'Yeah, absolutely.'

"That 'prayer space' was open on September 11th, 2017, not long after they had opened. The building is now at about thirty percent capacity and it will be at ninety percent—so it will be several hundred-people working there—within the next two months. I think prayer spaces and co-working places wed together is a completely new concept for pretty much everyone. I don't know very many places anywhere doing it.

"Before we were even completely finished with it, people were sneaking into the prayer room to use it. I was having coffee the other day down there and someone overheard me talking Sabbatical; he then started talking about the need for rest and reformation and work rhythms. I told him, 'Well, that's why we're starting a prayer space at Plexpod.' He was like, 'I know. We've already been coming down and sneaking in here for a couple of weeks now.' These guys were following Jesus!"

Adam went on, "Now that we've officially opened the prayer room, we've had some of the workers coming in to receive prayer. Some are believers, some from different streams of the faith, but they are coming in and praying. We just do a simple, liturgical process—*lectio divina*—at different hours of the day like the monastic rhythm we've learned from the other Boiler Rooms and other Christian communities. We invite them to give their work day to the Lord and invite His presence into their day. We create a written prayer guide for each day. People from any of the organizations in the building can come at any point and pray through the guide in about fifteen minutes. Then we facilitate that process together at noon. It's a few weeks old now, so it's hard to say what the complete fruit is, but we're already seeing that it's an encouragement to the people who show up. People know there's a place they can go and step into God's grace, even if just for a few minutes."

"Our heart is to be faithful in this rhythm and be there so when people do go through a crisis—one of those times when everybody becomes a pray-er—we'll be there to share God's love. We plan on seeing the co-working space grow and evolve—who knows where we will be with it next year at this time—it's a brand-new experiment. The possibilities are really endless."

I think it's easy to look at where Navah Church is now and think of them as innovators and hold them up as a model of what an expression of church can become if we refuse to move forward without the Spirit of God leading us. At the same time, it would be a mistake to look at where they are now and emulate it without acknowledging the seventeen-year process that led them here.

The Blackwells, the Chuds, the Coxes, and the others would be the first to tell you, "Don't do what we are doing and think it's 'what the Spirit is doing in the Church today.' We're not cutting edge. It's about being found in the Father and formed in the Family. It's not about what we do, but who we've become—and who we are becoming through what He is leading us into now. Don't follow what we do, if anything, follow how we've been formed. It all begins with knowing who we are in the Gospel, in the Family, and walking in step with the Spirit from there."

FOUND AND FORMED

Restoring God's Kingdom starts with restoring each of us in the divine Family. It means creating within us an identity established through the Gospel—extrapolated from the tenets of who God is, what He has done, what that means about who we are and what we do from there. It's not an overnight process. Not many of us get the famous "come to Jesus," road-to-Damascus experience of instant change. There's work to do—work on ourselves, work to help others with, and work to step into.

While I can tell you it's not easy, I can also tell you it's worth it. In fact, nothing else on this earth is worth as much. It's a journey and an adventure you won't trade for anything else. And it all starts with being found in the Father, established in that Gospel Identity, formed into the children of God we are called to be in His Family, and then released as groups to be Kingdom emissaries. We were never, ever intended to go about mission alone.

It is from that point that we learn to dream again—that we learn to revive the desires of our hearts, the one's God put there, and start to step into the unique plan and purpose He has for each of us. But what does becoming a transformational people look like? That's what we're going to celebrate in Ken Janke's amazing journey that we'll discuss in the next section.

IN CHRIST WITH THE FAMILY

Before we go on to Part Three, I think it would be worth taking one more look at the chart I adapted from Jeff Vanderstelt's teachings on Gospel Identity and to explore the gist of each of them one more time. We need to remember that accepting the Gospel is not a one-time decision that saves us, but a lifetime journey in becoming. It is not about "point of sale" Christianity—a one-time purchase with guarantees of our success—but about joining into a miraculous partnership with each aspect of the Godhead, as well as each other, to bring about the fulfillment of God's marvelous redemptive plan for the earth. There is seriously no other adventure like it—or as fulfilling.

For reference, here is the chart we looked at in Chapter Nine:

Our Gospel Identity

Who God is	What He Has Done	Who We Are	What We Do
FATHER	Sent His Son to adopt us into His family.	Sons and daughters in the Father's family.	Love one another as a holy family under the authority of the Father. (A heart issue.)
SON	Established His Kingdom on earth as a Servant King.	Servant-heir subjects of the King—princes and princesses (the younger siblings of the King).	Serve the least among us and one another in the name of the King. (A matter of practice.)
HOLY SPIRIT	Sent to manifest the Kingdom on earth and fill it with the presence of God.	Spirit-equipped and empowered ambassadors/ missionaries/ emissaries of the Kingdom.	Proclaim and demonstrate the Kingdom for all to see.

This chart not only establishes important characteristics about who we are in Christ, but also the journey of being found in the Father and having our Gospel Identity formed in the Family. My suggestion? Take these following issues to the Lord with your friends, team, and family—let God speak to you about His reconstructive agenda for you within the context of each area. Taking the boxes left to right, then row by row, we learn:

1.   **The Father sent His Son to call us back to the Family.**

God is a father and can't help himself—He wants His creation back, starting with us. He was willing to sacrifice His only Child to get you and I back into the Family fold. The Father initiated the call for us to come home.

It's what He's done!

2. The adoption papers have been signed, sealed, and delivered.

The Spirit of Adoption is on call and standing by for whatever needs to be done to help us take our place in the Royal Household—this is our new nature. Too often, once the ink dries on the adoption certificate and the paperwork has been filed away, we still don't quite believe we're really in the Family and that it's where we belong. There's no quick fix to that. Once we are found in the Father, it then takes time to be formed in the Family—and it often means going back to the Father again and again.

Why?

Because too often we mistakenly substitute being in the Family for having a relationship with the Father. The Father wants His kids to know how to climb up into His lap and receive His full attention—it's a prerequisite to all He wants to do with and through us. Unfortunately, however, too many go entire lifetimes without ever realizing they have a right to that place with their divine Dad. Regardless, the invite stands! We are His adopted kids! He picked each one of us out individually!

It's who we are!

3. Learning the Family language: Love.

Every family, whether intentionally or not, picks up the spirit of the parents and has a "flavor" all its own. In our heavenly Father's Family, we are able to love others because the Father first loved us. We love with His love, or we don't *really* love at all.

"Do you love me?" Jesus asked. "Then love my sheep."

It is because the Father loves us that we love our brothers and sisters in the Family. It is because of the love of the Father that we are able to go into a world that is as likely to spit on us as they are to embrace us. It's how we are able to love others no matter what they do to us. And it is by that love that everyone around us is able to tell which Family we are part of.

It's what we do!

4. The Son reset the power structures.

"Jesus called them together and said, "You know that the rulers of the Gentiles lord it over them, and their high officials exercise authority over them. Not so with you" (Matthew 20:25-26). Human power structures are focused on "lording over" or "exercising authority over" others. Some nations call their governmental leaders "ministers," but have fallen prey to the seduction of power, thus negating the true meaning of the title—being a "servant" to the people. Not so with Jesus: *"The Son of Man did not come to be served, but to serve, and to give his life as a ransom for many"* (Matthew 20:28).

The call for leaders in the Family of God is to realize that Christ's Kingship and His government operate perfectly, because He knew He was loved by His Father and had nothing to prove. There is nothing weak about being a supreme servant, it was Jesus's power source and should be emulated. Be known for it!

This is what He did!

5. Sibling-heirs of the Servant King.

Now that we've received the Father's inheritance and our identity is no longer as slaves, we are free to manage His household as servant-sons and daughters—it is who we are!

Sincere serving is impossible without an identity overhaul. No one has the capacity to be selfless without a life transfer from the Servant King. It means we own nothing, have nothing to defend, nothing to protect, and nothing to advance except His heart and desires. To be a true servant, one has to have a master and be radically committed to extending the desires, wishes, and commands of that master. We cannot serve two masters of any ilk—we will love one and hate the other. Without a revelation and major heart surgery, we will always end up being our own masters.

Servant-heirs! It's who we are.

6. It's time to dream again.

Remember those dreams you had as a kid? That thing within your heart that you felt you were put on this earth to accomplish? Jesus said, *"The Kingdom of God is within you"* (Luke 17:21 KJV). Within our dreams, talents, and desires, there is a divine mission to reconcile this world back to the Father. It's time to pull those dreams out again and see what the Father wants to do with them. But wait, there is a caveat! You can't want to be great for your own ends, and you can't realize your dreams by focusing on fulfilling them in your own strength. It's like everything else in the Kingdom—it's upside-down!

> Instead, whoever wants to become great among you must be your servant, and whoever wants to be first must be your slave.
>
> —MATTHEW 20:26-27

Just as Jesus's own dream for a Family was realized by laying His life down and eschewing greatness, He served His creation and allowed the Father to validate His Kingship. Paul reminds us, *"Let each of you look out not only for his own interests, but also for the interests of others"* (Philippians 2:4 NKJV). Loving and serving others is a counter-intuitive art form that we learn by walking openly with those God has put beside us in the journey. You want to be great? Follow the leader!

It's what we do!

7. The Spirit is still brooding over chaos to birth Christ's Kingdom.

Nothing has changed since the dawn of creation. The Holy Spirit is still being dispatched to bring life to earth's "chaos." Just as He birthed Jesus—the "Seed" of the Kingdom—into an earthly womb, He birthed the Church in Jerusalem's hostile religious environment and continues to birth "heaven on earth." Just as Paul was determined to confront Caesar with the new King, the Spirit is seeking only to promote Christ's supremacy through His Church to every heart and every domain of society. As He came in power at Pentecost to instigate a revolution, His power is no less needed today to cleanse the temple and recruit legitimate witnesses who will penetrate earth's darkest shadows with terrifying light.

It's what the Spirit does!

8. From the Throne to the footstool: "Not your will but Mine be done."

Jesus's good Jewish boys went from believing Him to denying Him, doubting Him, and even hiding behind walls in fear to becoming a highly unified band of revolutionaries, *virtually overnight*. What happened? They received the cosmic hookup between the Throne Room of heaven and the foot stool of earth by none other than the Spirit that brought identity to Adam and Eve. Now the Spirit has brought identity to this new creation: the image of Christ! The Spirit not only gave the disciples a new identity and power to bear witness to the ascended Christ, they became the link between heaven and earth, the King's ambassadorial entourage.

Our whole bent of life should now be one of hearing Him and observing to do everything He has commanded us to do. Aligning our lives, as any emissary would, to the desires of our Potentate is our birthright and the essence of our new nature. The Spirit was sent to bring His Kingdom so that we would choose to lay aside all personal agendas and fulfill the desires of the One we represent—it's our new nature as ambassadors of the King and our "ministry" to the inhabitants of His Kingdom.

The only possible way we can take up this high calling is to be radically committed to hear the Father say to us, "not your will, but Mine be done." That's our cue to say back to Him, "Amen, Father, not my will, but Yours be done."

It's who we are!

9. **We walk in step with the Spirit, in partnership with God, living the adventure of a lifetime.**

Now that we are ambassadors—representatives of God in our own backyards—He doesn't see us as slaves to do His bidding, but as *His partners*. Jesus didn't call us "friends" frivolously. He meant for us to consider the secrets of heaven as part of our inheritance as members of the Family. We can no longer contemplate the "easy life," but revel in His promise to fill us with His "peace that passes understanding" and be invited into His joy. Then we head out into the "fog" by His command.

It's what we do!

LET LOOSE ON THE EARTH

Peace is the currency of Kingdom envoys; joy is the fruit they bring. Now empowered by His Spirit, and our nature changed from slaves to sons and daughters, we are free to bring change to our neighborhoods, workplaces, and cities. The Spirit of the Lord has been made available to deliver our instructions, empower us to do them, and protect us from the fallout of people's resistance to His great love through us.

NOW WHAT?

Question: Now that we are at the end of this section, let's ask again: "Are you and your church community more familiar with isolated Christian topics or the unified truths found in the Word concerning your Gospel Identity?

> **Exercise:** Consider a study of Gospel Identity until you, your team, and your people are fluent in it. Teach it on hot days, cold days, and while standing on your head (if it helps) and so on. Do whatever it takes to imbed it in hearts!

> **Exercise:** Take the review of the Gospel Identity on page 222 and pray over the contents of the chart. Ask the Spirit of the Lord to guide you in an evaluation of your Gospel Identity intelligence and revelation quotient.

PART THREE:
TRANSFORMATION

THE GROVE STORY
The Anatomy of a Transformed Neighborhood

The essential task of the Church

is to work for its society's shalom,

to work for the full and total

transformation of all the people,

forces, and structures

with the love of God.

—ROBERT LINTHICUM,
Transforming Power

GOD'S KID

"All authority in heaven and on earth has been given to me.
Therefore go and make disciples of all nations."

—MATTHEW 28:18-19

Ken remembers the shock on Lori's face when she first saw the house he'd bought for their family in Fair Haven. It wasn't a look of pleasant surprise. Despite being relatively near Yale University, Fair Haven was a "pretty rough" neighborhood that had no shortage of challenges. In fact, the state of Connecticut had designated it an "empowerment zone." What did that mean? It meant Connecticut would really like to "empower" someone to figure out how to fix the area, because they had no idea.

It wasn't just the condition of the house, either. Their new home stood just three blocks from "the projects." "The projects" was the name of a neighborhood that had the feel and "cared-for" qualities of bombed out Beirut. Half the windows were blown out and there was no grass growing anywhere—not even between the cracks in the sidewalks. Prostitutes stood openly on the corner of the park, and it wasn't surprising to hear gunshots echoing down the streets. It was far from what typical American families would consider the ideal place to raise their kids.

But, then again, the Jankes weren't a typical American family.

If there is an "American dream" lifestyle for a pastor and his family, it wouldn't be much different than what the Jankes had just left. Ken had been the pastor of a large, prominent church in the North Dallas area—a wealthy neighborhood in a lovely, mostly middle-class community. It was the type of church most pastors hope theirs would someday become—and yet the questions on Ken's heart weren't about megachurch success, or even where to take such a church next. Instead, he couldn't get the words Jesus spoke at the end of the book of Matthew out of his head. "If Jesus told us to disciple nations," he told me, "how *do* you 'disciple nations'? What does that look like? In fact, what does it look like to simply disciple a city or a neighborhood?"

Ken knew how to run an established church in a Bible-friendly part of the country, and while he understood that this was an important calling, it wouldn't help him answer his questions. He wanted to experiment—to be a practitioner of something he longed to see and hoped would have transformational results. He had to go somewhere the Gospel wasn't so well received. He had to go someplace that really needed the Gospel from the ground up, someplace he'd never been before, someplace as different from where he'd grown up as he could find.

As he and Lori considered various options and prayed over them, they settled on New Haven, Connecticut. They had friends there who invited them to come and see if there was a place for the Jankes in their ministry orbit. They were beginning to feel something for New Haven itself and wanted to go somewhere where they felt an open door into the city. So Ken resigned his pastorate and they moved.

The open door with their friends wasn't what they had expected it to be, however, and it didn't pan out. All the same, it wasn't long before Ken's heart led him further into Fair Haven, one of New Haven's predominantly minority neighborhood. He'd bought the house he was now showing Lori in a fit of impulse and out of a sense of calling to the place. Within just a few months, Ken had taken his family from a beautiful home in a white, low-crime suburb to the inner-city "empowerment zone" of Fair Haven where there were no churches—let alone mega-churches—in site.

Moving the family into Fair Haven was a big shocker to Ken's whole family. They found themselves dealing with a lot of cultural disconnect and transitional trauma as a family. Despite this, Ken knew they were in the right place to search for answers to the questions God had put on his heart.

After moving in and getting his family relatively settled, it was time for Ken to go to work. The trouble was, he didn't have a place to show up every day like he'd had back in Texas. So what was he going to do? What was it going to look like to plant a church in this new place? He could sit around wondering, but rather than doing that, he decided to start roaming the streets of the neighborhood, get to know the place, and try to figure out what his contribution could be.

As he did this, he remembered praying, "Lord you know who the people are that I'm supposed to pastor. You put a pastoral grace on my life, but I'm struggling to know how to put it into practice."

He later told me the answer he got to that prayer was one of the clearest he's ever gotten from the Lord, which was important, because at first it didn't seem like an answer at all. Rather than give Ken clarity on his mission in Fair Haven or tell him what he was supposed to do next, God spoke five words that would change Ken and his trajectory forever.

God simply replied, *"You know you're my son."*

"YOU KNOW YOU'RE MY SON"

So often we focus on what we are supposed to do for God—what our "calling" and "purpose" are—and very little on who God has called us *to be*. When I say that, I'm not talking about personal integrity, character, or being "a good person"—though all of those are wonderful things. I'm talking about what I've seen to be an initial foundation piece in so many different people and ministries I've worked with—and not having such a foundation hurt me in my younger years. So often we want a purpose and mission to be the driving force behind our lives and expect they are what will lead us to greater fulfillment. Yes, it is fulfilling to have tangible accomplishments and see the fruit of our labors in the lives of others, but that's not where God wants to begin with us—nor was it where He began with Jesus.

Jesus certainly had an important purpose and mission when He came to the earth—and one that would not be without tremendous challenge. But of all the different things God could have told Jesus as He was beginning His ministry, the only thing we know God told Him for sure was, *"This is my Son, whom I love; with him I am well pleased"* (Matthew 3:17).

Looking back over the leadership formation that transpired at both Believers Church and Navah, you see God doing the same in them: before He gave them a mission or led them into what they were supposed to do, God insisted they first know who they were in Christ. The first thing the Father did was meld them together into His Family. The first characteristic of the Church of God on the earth is that it is *relational*—and that starts with our relationship with Him.

Think again of the pattern we explored in the previous section as we looked at our Gospel Identities: Knowing who God is leads to understanding what God does and then to discovering who we are as a result—all before ever learning what it is we are supposed *to do*. People before place; being before doing; adoption before assignment.

Jesus didn't come to the earth to die for your sins because there was something He wanted you to do while you are here, He did that so that you would be returned to the embrace of the Family. The stuff we do—our purposes and calling—isn't really about getting stuff done, it's about God liking to do stuff with His kids. We're not doing it so that He will be pleased with us, we're supposed to do it knowing He's already pleased with us. Imagine it like a dad laying down on the floor with his child and saying, "Okay, what are we going to build with these Legos®?" Or asking, "Where does Ms. Bunny sit for the tea party again?" Then, as we mature, He wants to give us a place in the Family business: a workplace that's all about making dreams come true. Is that because He cares so much about those dreams coming true? He does, but only because He cares so much about you first.

That's why Jesus called His disciples *friends*. *Friend* is a term of relationship—partnership really. It's about being joined at the heart and then doing things together.

In a recent conversation I had with Adam in Kansas City, he said something about prayer that really echoes this formation: "Everything changes in prayer when you know who you're coming to and who you are when you come." Everything changes in prayer when you know you are coming to a loving Father. This is why, when the disciples asked Jesus to teach them to pray, He started by teaching them, *"When you pray, say: 'Father . . .'"* (Luke 11:2).

And it changes even further when we realize we are as sons and daughters—princes and princesses—coming to our Father King. As Adam described it when we spoke: "If we're praying to a

distant distracted Dad—or authoritarian Father—and we come as
a beggar pleading with him, how does that align with Scripture?
When you look at Jesus's teaching on prayer, the main thing He is
trying to get across—especially, when He is teaching about *asking*
prayer—is that we have a devoted, delighted, attentive, listening
Father who has called us "beloved" and established us as a co-heir
with Christ. As confidence begins to change in the heart—which
again, is connected to that heart journey of the Holy Spirit bringing adoption—we find that every activity has to be run through the
transformation of adoption or else it ends up being an orphan/slave
activity. Jesus always talked about the Kingdom from the inside.
Prayer changes when the inside of someone begins to change."

Whenever Ken shares about what happened in New Haven,
he always shares the story of God telling him those five words:
"You know you're my son." Ken smiles when he speaks that phrase.
"I always like to share that because that's a good starting point
when you hear the Father say, 'You're my son.' That's important
in my story, because I'm fully aware of what it's like to pastor *not*
knowing what it means to be a son. I had come from the place of
being a slave with an orphan spirit." That was exactly what needed
to change first for Ken. Part of his journey was a necessary deconstruction of an orphan/slave mentality and formation into living
as a son.

The genesis of prayer is when a child of God comes under the
canopy of a loving Father, not the religious requirements of being
a "good Christian." Prayer is not merely a mental exercise, nor a
litany of reading down a "grocery list" of prayer requests—nor is it
a religious discipline to be tucked into our busy schedules. Rather,
it is surrender to the Spirit who will teach us all things, speaks of
Jesus, and works through our sonship and daughterhood in God's
Family:

But when he, the Spirit of truth, comes, he will guide you into all truth. He will not speak on his own; he will speak only what he hears, and he will tell you what is yet to come. He will glorify me because it is from me that he will receive what he will make known to you. All that belongs to the Father is mine. That is why I said the Spirit will receive from me what he will make known to you.

—JOHN 16:13-15

No wonder he is always trying to lead us into "lifestyle" prayer: to *"Pray without ceasing"* (1 Thessalonians 5:17 KJV).

THE CORNERSTONE OF PRAYER

I was in a season of relearning and deepening my understanding of this principle of "lifestyle prayer" while living in Sacramento in the mid 1990s. I was rushing to a citywide pastor's prayer gathering and realized my breath was borderline offensive. So, I swerved into a 7-Eleven market to mitigate the horror. As I was walking to the door I remember asking the Lord, "How I should pray for this business?" I immediately sensed the Lord's love for the proprietor and began praying for whoever might be revealed behind the doors. As I walked in the door to get my breath mints, I heard a booming voice say, "Why are you here?" (What shop owner or employee—in the US anyway—greets customers with something like that?)

Turning, I saw a fabulously regal Sikh gentleman, all be-turbaned with the requisite beard and dark penetrating eyes.

"Help!" I said to the Lord.

And I immediately got a response. "I have come to bless your business, sir," says I.

Waggling his fingers to invite me closer, as though we were long lost friends, he launched into a story of how his sons had let him down and were not willing to take the store so he could retire. No one came into the store the entire time I pronounced the "blessing of the Father God" upon him. With tears in his eyes, he asked me if I would continue to pray for his troubled heart and recalcitrant sons. I did and was invited back to talk more about the love of Jesus and the God that blesses people. I arrived at the prayer meeting with a grateful heart . . . and minty breath!

Most of us have benefited from prayer movements like the International House of Prayer, 24-7 Prayer, Burn, and others. They are powerful catalysts to encourage God's people to pray. These, however, were never birthed by God to champion particular prayer methodologies over others, set up a special group of pray-*ers*, or solely relegate prayer to certain places.

It is in the nature of us humans to erect memorials and traditions around methodologies and systems that may at times actually inoculate God's people against a simple, daily, focused conversation with God about every issue orbiting our lives. Being in the presence of the Lord in "prayer rooms" and "houses of prayer" should inspire us to take His presence outside those walls and into the traffic of our daily activities. We all have access to the throne and are all invited to carry out His will in our geographically assigned areas. There is much to learn from various approaches to prayer, but Jesus is inviting every disciple to say, "Teach me to pray."

As city transformation was capturing the minds of God's people around the same time I encountered that Sikh gentleman, a particular phrase became popular, "make your city a 'prayed-for' city." For a city to be "prayed for," it takes every believer in the city, deployed as an intercessor, into every domain that they engage in every day. At first, we thought citywide prayer meetings might be the answer. We soon came to realize that God was calling all of His people to engage their world in prayer in their everyday schedules—a grassroots movement of "lifestyle pray-*ers*" being the norm, and gatherings being the exception. So ministries like Harvest Evangelism and Mission America launched the "Lighthouses of Prayer" initiative in the 1990s. This was an early attempt to encourage people to be alert to the Spirit's presence wherever they went and make that home, that office, that restaurant, that school, a "prayed-for" location.

Despite this, it is rare to find a Sunday service where the whole community is called to pray for an issue, let alone interrupting a service to do so. In many church business meetings, prayer is cursory at best, while corporate prayer meetings are often sparsely attended and have the aura of a "duty performed" rather than a vibrant journey to partner with heaven's power and beauty.

How is it we have come to believe we can do the work of God without "prayer and supplication"? Perhaps our corporate impotence is a reflection of the lack of conviction at the individual level to the efficacy of prayer in the hearts of each disciple—a conversion to "lifestyle prayer" rather than leaving it for "In case of emergency." Perhaps it is, in addition, not yet something that emanates out of sonship and daughterhood? It's hard to pray as a child coming to a Father when we don't fully believe that's who you are to our Father or that He doesn't want to withhold anything from us.

Many feel they had to become "intercessors" or pray "night and day" to be of value in the Kingdom. Not so. Certainly, there are those called by God to sequester themselves in prayer closets, and they have been a tremendous blessing to the Church, but at the same time, they may have inadvertently sent the message that everyday folks were lesser creatures, less spiritual, or not nearly as committed. (I have had numerous conversations to this end.) Most of us are not called to long periods of time in "prayer rooms"—instead, we are called to pray as we walk the pathway of our lives (what, in many neo-monastic circles refer to as "prayer on the road"). Both deep personal alone time and praying as we go are expressions of prayer equally valuable to the Father. Prayer at its root is simply communication between God and His people.

If there is one things I can say about Ken Janke, it's that he is a pray-*er*; he is a man who has built his life on moment-by-moment, two-way communication with the Father. No wonder God selected him as His vessel for bringing transformation to New Haven. One of the four "lifestyle" practices of the early church in Acts 2:42—"*They devoted themselves to the apostles' teaching and to fellowship, to the breaking of bread and to prayer*"—was prayer. The early church met from "house to house" *to pray*. Many continued rhythms of prayer in the temple courts. Upon Peter's imprisonment, the believers gathered for corporate prayer and Peter got sprung! The greatest mission movement in history got started in Antioch with a circle of "*prophets and teachers . . . worshiping the Lord and fasting*" (Acts 13:1, 2).

Every believer has a direct line to the throne and has authority to dispense the answer of his/her prayers upon the precious targets of God's affection.

Frustrated that your boss won't give you a much-deserved raise? Go to the Provider of your life. Turn walking the dog into a reason beyond poop-scooping: pray for your neighbors, the Housing Association, the cantankerous lady on the corner in the purple house, the jobless, the divorcees, single mothers, or just anyone who happens to cross your path. God is moving His people to adopt a lifestyle of talking to the Son of God, the great Intercessor, about the encounters of our daily lives. Without a relational prayer life with the Father through Jesus, we will be left with a transactional "work-oriented ministry" and perfunctory prayers that are impotent to transform any aspect of our lives and the world around us.

STEP TWO

Notice in Ken's story how the nature of his relationship with God allowed him to simply ask questions in prayer and wait for instructions. In this same manner, Ken continued to walk the streets of Fair Haven, drilling down into the truth of his sonship more and more each day.

Ken remembered one day confessing to God, "You know, all I've ever done is pastor in a building standing behind a pulpit." Now he had no pulpit, no building, and his new "congregation" were the broken inhabitants of a wild neighborhood. But rather than focus on that, as he came across people, he'd introduce himself, and then start asking them about their families, why they lived there, and where they'd come from. Slowly he started to get a feel for the place and its people.

It was while doing that, God finally gave Ken instructions for what He wanted him to do: *"I want you to steward the dreams of the people in your community."*

NOW WHAT?

Question #1: Do you walk in the assurance of your sonship in Christ, or are you driven by expectations, goals, budgets, and other "keep you up at night" nuisances? Is your life built on rest and dependency, or busyness and crisis management? Ask the Father for His perspective on the way you "do" life and community. Seek His instruction on how to live out of a paradigm of rest and surrender

Question #2: Is prayer "the air you breathe" in your ministry, or a duty and a constant struggle?

> **Response:** Ask the Lord to reveal the source of the frustration and to show you His instructions for making it come from the genetic of Jesus within you, not an external "plug in" appendage. (Think "human," not "robot.")

STEWARDING DREAMS

Take delight in the Lord,
and he will give you the desires of your heart.

—PSALM 37:4

K en had no idea what God meant by "stewarding people's dreams," but he figured the best way to find out was to ask. So as he walked, prayed, and chatted with his neighbors, he began inquiring after their dreams. He stood on front porches and sat with folks in their yards asking "What do you dream about for your family? What's your big dream for the neighborhood? Do you have a dream for this city?"

He learned three things. The first was that *everyone has a dream*. No one balked when he asked them about their dreams. Even if they were resistant at first, everyone understood what he meant and were eventually willing to tell him what they dreamed about.

The second thing he learned was that often—quite often, in fact—*people abort their dreams*. They do this for several reasons, which he also learned. One reason is people feel alone in their dream. Ken commented to me, "I've never seen a dream realized in isolation. We were built for community, and it's in the context of the Trinitarian design of our identities as sons and daughters that we flush out the dreams God has bestowed upon us, *together*."

Another reason is people don't feel validated, which can look a lot like fear of failure. As he scratched the surface of this a little more, he began to see the scars and wounds left from words spoken by a parent or someone close. Things like, "You can't do that! Who do you think you are?" Or "That's never been done before!" Or "What's the point of trying?" Ken noticed, "People take on those criticisms like ragged garments they wrap around themselves, obscuring the beauty of their own stories."

And finally, he learned where there is lack of access to resources or information, people will never get started. Access is critical. People need to have within their reach the resources and tools necessary for them to move forward with their dreams. Ken would hear people say, "Look around you. Who dreams in a place like this?"

The lesson Ken learned that impacted him the most was that *people are always dreaming*—even if it's in fits and starts. Whether they're dreaming of starting a new business or they have an idea for something they want to see realized in their neighborhood or there's something they want to be able to do with their family, or within the community, or out in the world, *they're always dreaming*.

So, Ken began telling people if they were willing to take the first step, he would be willing to come alongside to help them pursue their dream. This started a series of adventures he would never forget. Like Alice following the White Rabbit, you never really know where you will end up when you begin dreaming with people.

SERVING OR BEING SERVED?

Ken's whole posture concerning his neighborhood is a refreshing change from current mindsets towards church planting and ministry. Leaders can too often be focused on finding the right people to fulfill their own "callings," hopes, and dreams—a vision-first scenario that employs God's people to help leaders fulfill their own dreams and missions. Instead "Pastor" Ken devoted himself to the discovery and pursuit of the dreams of his neighbors. Rather than going out and "building a church" to serve, he went out and tried to establish the God-given dreams of those God was calling to be a church. It was in serving others like this that Ken discovered his own destiny. This is in the line of *"Anyone who wants to be first must be the very last, and the servant of all"* (Mark 9:35), and *"whoever loses their life for my sake will find it"* (Matthew 10:39). There is our up-side-down Kingdom again! It's going to demand turning some of our thinking around.

For example, I've always been slightly mystified by the religious tradition I and others grew up with of praying over our food in restaurants. The waiter or waitress is standing right there in need of a benediction, and we're blessing the food. *Huh?*

I flipped the script on this one time, and boy, I was glad I did—even though, initially, it got me in some hot water. I was meeting with a group of church and ministry leaders in a Mexican restaurant in California. Tucked away in our little side room, our waitress would come swooping in all cheerful and swinging food around with great skill, generating a slight breeze. When the food was finally served my fellow "burrito eaters" looked at me expectantly—time to "say grace." *Groan.* Avoiding eye contact with my brethren, I said to the waitress, "We're a bunch of

'Jesus freaks' and are about to pray for our food, but we'd much rather pray for you—is there anything you need God to do for you today?"

She beamed immediately and said, "Oh yes, today my boyfriend and I are moving in together and we have no furniture. Could you pray that we get some furniture?"

A perfect moral dilemma! I could see the blood drain from the faces of my colleagues and almost read their minds, "He wants us to pray for two fornicators to get blessed by God? They're about to 'live in sin' for Pete's sake." Yup! Fornicators need blessing too. So, I thanked her for her request and promptly asked the Lord to provide furniture for this beautiful young ("fornicator!") woman.

Two hours later, food devoured, agenda completed, bill paid, waitress finished with her shift and long gone (or so we thought), we headed to the parking lot. A car came careening around the corner, stopped dead in front of me, and out jumps Miss "I need furniture." She stormed up me. "You'll never believe it! We just got furniture for our new apartment!" When she'd gotten home from work to meet her boyfriend, a truck was waiting at the curbside loaded with furniture—source unknown.

"Okay!" she shouted. "Who is this guy you prayed to?"

Happy to oblige, we introduced her to Jesus, the "furniture provider," and hooked her and her boyfriend up with a great church in the city to continue her journey into Jesus.

Everyone needs to be accepted and blessed whether we approve of their behavior or not. Everyone has a dream and the Father stands ready to fulfill it—through us! After all, it's not like Jesus can't handle such things.

I certainly I found it even harder to pray for food alone after that!

"THEREFORE GO . . ."

On Oct 4, 1992, a Boeing 747 cargo plane crashed into the Bijlmermeer high-rise apartment complex on the outskirts of Amsterdam, Netherlands. We were there as missionaries when it happened. There were forty-three known fatalities and perhaps hundreds of undocumented workers and their unidentified families horribly incinerated in the crash. It devastated the neighborhood.

In the months prior to that, our team in Amsterdam had been sensing from the Lord that we were to deemphasize our ministry centers in the city and begin to encourage our staff to establish their homes as "lighthouses" of prayer and ministry in their respective communities. Chris and Brian Clarke, a British couple, and their two boys, had taken this to heart and begun visiting their neighbors in the Bijlmermeer apartment complex. I remember the immense dedication they made to prayer, walking their massive complex, and praying that the Father would give them an open door to the hearts of the residents. People seemed to be reluctant to come to their apartment, although a few began coming around for drinks and conversation. Chris and Brian had no agenda for their little gathering; they were just ready to serve any needs that rose to the surface in the goings on of this interracial neighborhood.

It wasn't too long after this period of time when Chris was standing at her kitchen window, watching in horror, as the El Al Cargo plane came hurdling into the neighboring building; a fully fueled bomb that left fire, smoke, ash, and debris throughout the entire neighborhood. Chris and Brian were amongst the first to respond. Because they had been where God pulled on their heartstrings to be, the Lord was able to bring much needed comfort, healing, and redemption to this shell-shocked neighborhood through them.

An African man was in one of the buildings at the time of impact, crawled out onto a railing, and jumped three floors to the ground to escape the flames. Rushed to the medical relief tent with multiple broken bones, he was visited by the Clarkes and a small team of YWAMers deputized by the rescue authorities to comfort the victims. Upon recovery, this man and many others impacted by the tragedy were drawn by the love of Chris and Brian and were frequent visitors to their home.

Chris and Brian started as grief counselors, then became disciplers, and finally "dream weavers" (like Ken) of these traumatized new friends, many of whom had come to Christ in the time they'd known the Clarkes. This family owned their neighborhood in prayer, started a house group awaiting instructions on how to serve, and were deployed as His "emissaries" into the midst of this terrible tragedy. They became a "house of refuge" to restore people physically and spiritually, and then walked with them into the beauty of daring to dream again.

See what can happen when we open ourselves to serve as the Lord directs?

This kind of "church planting" and "dream weaving" is a shift in thinking for most in Christian circles today. We are often afraid that we will lose our own dreams if we invest in the seemingly trivial or insignificant dreams of others. However, Jesus, speaking of His own nature, said, *"Greater love has no one than this, to lay down one's life for one's friends"* (John 15:13). He also said, *"If you have not been faithful in that which is another's, who will give you that which is your own?"* (Luke 16:12). Such is the nature of the inverted Kingdom; the way up is usually down.

As we saw in Part Two, Jesus our Servant-King set the template for His followers—*lay your life down to make others great.* We must recalibrate our mindsets to serve and not be served. That is the power and essence of the Kingdom of God. In our self-serving generations of today, this shift in thinking and practice by the disciples of Christ is the only thing that has the potential to turn our cities and nations around.

As leaders, it is imperative to discern the motives of our ministries as well as that of our team members. Are we dedicated to creating a "servant culture" and follow in the footsteps of our Servant-King? He *"did not come to be served, but to serve"* (Matthew 20:28); He came to surrender His life knowing His future rule was in the Father's hands.

Notice how many times in the Gospels Jesus asked questions or made statements of those inquiring of Him in order to ascertain what their dreams were before He ministered to them. The dream of blind Bartimaeus: *"What do you want me to do for you?"* (Mark 10:51), food for the multitudes: *"Gather up the leftover fragments, that nothing may be lost"* (John 6:12); fishless fishermen: *"Friends, haven't you any fish?"* . . . *"Throw your net on the right side of the boat and you will find some"* (John 21:5, 6), greedy young rulers: *"Go, sell your possessions and give to the poor, and you will have treasure in heaven"* (Matthew 19:21), dead relatives: *"Lazarus, come out!"* . . . *"Take off the grave clothes and let him go"* (John 11:43, 44)—impossible dreams were coming true! It's not like Jesus didn't know what they needed, but He still wanted to hear what they were dreaming before He helped make it real.

I could go on with all the examples of Jesus fulfilling the dreams of people despite adversity, poverty, sickness, political oppression, and even death, but I think these examples suffice. The ultimate dream Jesus served was to deliver His creation from itself and to fulfill the longing in every heart to be free of the shackles of sin and bondage. He didn't bring this freedom by fiat or governmental edict, He did it by laying down His life to make other's dreams come true. Paul understood the beauty of a fulfilled dream!

> What a wretched man I am! Who will rescue me from this body of death? Thanks be to God, who delivers me through Jesus Christ our Lord!
>
> —ROMANS 7:24-25

FINDING THE BOTTOM OF THE "RABBIT HOLE"

As he began to gather a few "dreamers" in the community, Ken soon realized that neither he nor they had what it was going to take to see their dream fully realized. Dreams can never be realized in isolation—it takes a community bringing their contributions. Ken came to see that dreams are realized when we are committed to steward the contribution we hold, and we're willing to share that contribution in helping others. It echoes another one of those principles of the upside-down Kingdom: *"Whoever sows generously will also reap generously"* (2 Corinthians 9:6).

At the same time, Ken realized that, quite often, once someone recognized their need, there was usually someone close by with surplus or skill in that area to meet that need—if they would only ask. And then there was usually something the asker could give back. So Ken started networking people in his neighborhood with each other to match needs with training, skills, or resources others could provide. He would find people who cared about similar things and have them share their dreams with each other. As he did, he inadvertently became a neighborhood organizer, bringing his community together around projects and things that people wanted to see realized for their children and neighbors.

One of the first dreams Ken helped address was from a young mother: "Kids in these projects need to be more healthy," she declared. A lot of kids were sick a lot of the time. Ken soon learned that when you set out to address something that is a concern, it is often the symptom of something else. It was indeed like Alice's proverbial rabbit hole—once you dove in, the bottom is always much deeper than you originally thought. Addressing one problem always seemed to expose a deeper root cause, and then addressing that root cause revealed one that was deeper yet. There were always many systemic issues beneath the initial issue that led you to wonder "Just how deep does this thing go?"

What started out as a simple desire to see the kids become healthier soon led to uncovering the problems of hunger and malnutrition that were rampant within the confines of their impoverished neighborhoods. If the kids did eat, it was junk food, because it was cheap and accessible at the bodegas (convenience stores) around the projects. So, the first thing they decided to do was to educate local families about nutrition and the importance of eating fresh fruits and vegetables. When they started, if they showed the kids a carrot or a potato, the kids had no idea what it was—the rabbit hole got deeper. How were they going to introduce kids to basic fruits and vegetables if they'd never even seen them before, let alone had them available where they shopped the most?

So Ken and his neighborhood of dreamers worked with an organizations like "City Seed" and others to bring a farmers' market to the local park. Once the farmers' market had gotten underway, they realized that just having access to fresh fruits and vegetables wasn't going to be enough if the families didn't have the money to buy them. So again, they had to get out their shovels and dig down deeper.

They investigated the possibility of using their food stamps at the farmers' market. The city seemed agreeable to that idea, but this provision didn't serve all of their neighbors. There were a lot of undocumented citizens and because of their status, they didn't have access to food stamps. So they talked to the local free health clinic and asked if they would write prescriptions for fresh fruits and vegetables. They agreed. So now, many of the undocumented citizens could go to the free health clinic, get a prescription for fresh fruits and vegetables, and then come to the farmers market with their prescriptions. Ken's network then raised money so that anybody with a prescription could receive so many dollars of fresh fruits and vegetables each visit for free.

Now that they had a supply of fruits and vegetables coming to the community, they felt they could to go back to the kids and teach those lessons about how to eat well. They noticed one of the schools had some land that wasn't being used, so they approached the school leadership to see if they would allow Ken and his neighbors to use that land for planting gardens. After they agreed, they began growing vegetables on the school grounds with the help of the students and others in the community. The school let the kids to come in and work the ground until the kids began to see a full cycle of fruits and vegetables grow from *their own* gardens.

And so, problem solved, right? Hardly! Once these vegetables started arriving in their homes, few families seemed to know how to cook them. Like their kids, they'd never seen fresh vegetables before! So, next step? Cooking classes!

Meanwhile, the local bodegas where kids spent their pocket money still sold nothing but junk food. Addressing this challenge required a little more ingenuity. You have to show businesses a benefit if you are going to convince them to change their offering.

Ken's network put their heads together and came up with a plan. They instituted a program to do a makeover of the bodega with paint, a thorough cleaning, and a cash register instead of the tackle boxes under the counter—*if* they would be willing to supplement the junk food they sold with healthy snack alternatives. In exchange for the makeovers, store owners agreed to sell fruits, nuts, and vegetable snacks. These healthier snacks completed the cycle of making healthier food choices possible for kids.

Slowly but surely, they filled that pesky "rabbit hole," and as they did, they discovered something else: solving one problem gave them momentum towards solving the next.

Ken and his crew were only getting started.

NOW WHAT?

Question #1: Are you "building a church" or "weaving the dreams" of your people and those they do life with? Again, is your church "institution and leadership vision centric" or "people and their divine dreams centric"?

> **Scripture:** Consider if you and your church family are aligned with these two verses: Galatians 6:10 and Romans 12:10.

Question #2: If the Lord invited you or your church family to follow Him into the worst sections of your city, what would be your emotional and spiritual response? What would keep you from saying "yes"? Is He, perhaps, asking you to strategically target a neighborhood in your city even now?

THE CHURCH WITH NO BUILDING

*They broke bread in their homes and ate together
with glad and sincere hearts, praising God and enjoying the favor
of all the people. And the Lord added to their number daily
those who were being saved.*

—ACTS 2:46-47

As dreams started to be realized in Fair Haven, Ken had some friends move to the neighborhood to help with the church Ken and family thought they had come to plant. Since they didn't have a building or location and didn't feel moved to find one yet, they started gathering together in each other's homes. The longer they did this, the more they wondered what it would look like if they just were a church minus the building.

Ken had been doing a lot of reading and had friends that were experimenting with new communities and "neo-monasticism," as well as the way the Celts (Irish) had spread the Gospel throughout Europe after being converted to Christianity by Patrick. While the church of Rome had the habit of following the paths of the conquering Roman armies and setting up their cathedrals in the towns the Romans dubbed capitals, the Celts set up their mission stations at the crossroads and in the marketplaces, where people gathered the most. The Roman Church expected people to come to the basilicas for the sacraments and to attend services, while the Celtic tradition was to pray and then go out among the masses and serve whatever needs they found, from helping feed the poor to getting businesses up on their feet. One of the most common duties of the Celtic monks was to become scribes and reproduce whatever books and written documentation were needed.* The more Ken read, the more he identified with these Celtic monks in relation to his calling to New Haven.

But the Celts didn't call themselves "monks"—because monks were those who built monasteries to seclude themselves away from the outside world. Instead the Celts called themselves "friars." This title came from mashing together the Latin, *frater*, and Old French, *frere*—both words for "brother." Instead of staying behind walls like monks, friars went out into the community. Instead of being "cloistered," friars had an apostolic, entrepreneurial bent— they went out into the communities around them and basically, like Ken and his crew, stewarded the dreams of others. (For example, think of Friar Tuck in the Robin Hood tales—out in the world on mission and fighting for justice—and being a little ornery and per- haps rough around the edges as he did it, though always lovable at the same time.) Their robes and traditionally odd haircuts (the top of the head shaved with a "halo" of hair left around the outside) were evidence of the Gospel in action in the community wherever they went and whatever they did.

To Ken, that sounded a lot like what they were doing (without the weird haircuts): being "a family on mission" in their commu- nity, they started calling their gatherings "The Friary" and talked

---

* In fact, in his book, *How the Irish Saved Civilization*, Thomas Cahill argues that theses Celtic practices saved almost all of the classic Greek and Roman literature precisely because they recorded these works outside of the Roman capitals that were plundered and burned to the ground when Rome fell.

about the shared principles of community, commitment, and contribution that the friars held as their central values. They committed to one another and to helping fan each other's contributions in the context of realized community within their neighborhood. Unlike the friars of old, the members of The Friary didn't all live under the same roof, but gathered together regularly in one another's homes.

THE THREE PROTOCOLS OF BEING THE CHURCH

I don't believe we'll ever impact or transform our cities by expecting its inhabitants to come to our buildings and be participants in our programs. Such church-centrism is a defensive stance, not a proactive one. While there is nothing wrong with having a building, as we have discussed before, too often when we do, we tend to anchor activities within its walls instead of getting out "among the masses" to be the church. From what I have seen, God is currently reversing the direction of the flow of the Church from "cloistering" to being "godly catalysts" in their neighborhoods and cities. Just as the waters from Ezekiel's temple (see Ezekiel 47:8-12) flowed into the Arabah (sterile land) and brought life and healing to its banks, so God seems to be calling the Church today *out into* society to be salt and light again rather than letting us withdraw into the safety of creating our own subculture and defenses against the darkness of the world around us.

So, if outward is to be the flow, what does this river look like in the life of the Church? Our first responsibility is not to *do*, however, but to *be*. We cannot be catalysts of transformation until we, ourselves, have been transformed (or at least, are already along the way in the process of being transformed). In his foreword to

To Transform a City, Reggie McNeal contends that the Church needs to emphasize the "who" of what we are more than the "what." The "what" are silos—self-centered, marketed, seeker-friendly locations—versus the "who"—a people dispersed throughout all of society *being* the Church.

> Jesus is identified as the head not of a corporation but a body. He is not a senior partner in a corporation; he is a spouse in a marriage. In other words, the church is *people.* Missional followers of Jesus see *themselves* as the church. I am the church if I am united with Christ; so are you. I am not *all* the church and neither are you, but we *are* the church nonetheless. That means everywhere you and I go, the church is present.[23]

The Church as a *who* should see its relationship with culture very differently: We are the Family of God deployed across all domains of culture. These life-place assignments have been made by a God who desires to plant the incarnational presence of His Son everywhere, because God loves His world as well as His Church. "Whereas 'doing church' builds the church silo (a *what*) . . . 'being church' (as a *who*) . . . releases the church to impact the world—right where God's people already are."[24]

This means that the Church doesn't have a mission; the mission (of God) has a church (a people). The scorecard can no longer be about how well our individual congregations and programs within the church walls are thriving. Now, "the condition of our communities is the scorecard on how well the church is doing at being the people of God."[25]

The move of God in the first church was of house Christians—of everyday people taught by their leaders to live out the Gospel in the repressive atmosphere of a hostile religious culture and a global, godless empire. In light of the great barriers facing this young movement of rabid believers, the revelation that John the apostle passed on to the believing Family was beyond remarkable:

> The seventh angel sounded his trumpet, and there were loud voices in heaven, which said: "The kingdom of the world has become the kingdom of our Lord and of his Messiah, and he will reign for ever and ever."
>
> —REVELATION 11:15

This is our primary purpose then, not to be whisked away to heaven, but to advance the dominion of Christ over all creation during our time on earth until *"the kingdom of the world has become the Kingdom of our Lord and his Messiah* [Christ].*"*

This New Covenant mandate contains three delivery systems for re-establishing the rule of Christ. This is the "work" and priorities of *being* the Church (none of which, oddly enough, seem to necessitate that we have a building—neither are they necessarily hampered by having one, if we have the right mindsets). Since we're God's tapestry, let's look at these three protocols in light of the tapestry pattern being revealed on the Weaver's loom.

The First Protocol (Our Ultimate Purpose): Manifesting the Image of Christ in All Creation

What is the biblical understanding of the meaning of the word "transformation?" (The Greek word is *Metamorphoo*, from which we get the word *metamorphosis*.) We know the community of faith is to *"be* transformed *by the renewing of our mind"* (Romans12:2, emphasis added), and that all of creation is pregnant with *"the earnest expectation of . . . the revealing of the sons of God"* (Romans 8:19 NKJV).

What is creation hoping will be manifested? What are we to be transformed into? The full image of Christ in the Church, that we would have *"the mind of Christ"* (1 Corinthians 2:16) and be able to *"test and approve what God's will is—His good, pleasing and perfect will"* (Romans 12:2). This is where transformation starts—at His pleasure to convert creation from the image of Adam to the image of Jesus.

> And we all, who with unveiled faces contemplate the Lord's glory, are being **transformed** into his image with ever-increasing glory, which comes from the Lord, who is the Spirit.
>
> —2 CORINTHIANS 3:18 (emphasis added)

The "ultimate purpose" of redemption is an intimate love affair, a marriage between God and humanity that reveals the Father's ultimate goal for His creation—that we would be *"conformed to the image of His Son"* (Romans 8:29). In a parallel text in Ephesians, Paul reiterates this ultimate purpose, *"Instead, speaking the truth in love, we will grow to become in every respect the mature body of Him who is the head, that is, Christ"* (Ephesians 4:15). We see here that the "ultimate purpose" is to be shed of our old identity and be formed in Christ, our life-source. A stunning transformation of existence!

For all the good works that the Ephesian church did, the Holy Spirit's evaluation of them in John's revelation was that they had moved away from that which would manifest their "ultimate purpose":

> "I know your deeds, your hard work and your persever-ance. I know that you cannot tolerate wicked men, that

you have tested those who claim to be apostles but are not, and have found them false. You have persevered and have endured hardships for my name, and have not grown weary.

"*Yet I hold this against you:* **You have forsaken the love you had at first.** *Consider how far you have fallen! Repent and do the things you did at first. If you do not repent, I will come to you and remove your lampstand from its place.*"

—REVELATION 2:2-5 (emphasis added)

If they were not loving God as their primary love, as this text indicates, then there was no possibility they were being fully formed into the image of His Son. Somehow their "deeds" and "hard work" had supplanted Jesus as the centerpiece of their affections. It was repentance time for the Ephesians—and for us in His twenty-first century church that have been diverted from becoming like Jesus in similar fashions.

Howard Snyder, in *The Community of the King,* explains the heart of God's plan for our transformation into His Son's image:

> The Church is not an inanimate tool in God's hand which He uses to accomplish His ends. This would violate the very concept of the Church. . . . The Church *is* before she *does.* Christ loved the Church and gave Himself up for her. (See Ephesians 5:25.) Therefore, the Church has value for it is the object of Christ's love. . . . God's will is that the Church and each member within it attain to "*the full measure of perfection found in Christ*" (Ephesians 4:13). . . . As the Church thus grows, it will accomplish God's plan to make known through the Church the manifold wisdom of God . . . "*to the rulers and authorities in the heavenly realms*" (Ephesians 3:10).

So the Church is not to be understood primarily as a means to the end of transforming society. . . . [T]he amazing and profound fact is that the Church most transforms society when it is itself growing and being perfected in the love of Christ. . . . We assume the battle for right and justice can be won by force, by technique, by doing. It can't. . . . Truly Christian transformation of culture comes through Christlike (and hence sacrificial) love, community, and being.[26]

Ray Stedman expounds on this theme in his excellent book, *Body Life*,

Note that the Supreme purpose of the Church is not the evangelization of the world. I know that is often held up to us as a supreme aim and purpose of the Church. Certainly, there is a Great Commission in the Bible and Jesus has sent us out to preach the Gospel to every creature. This is a most important thing, but it is not the supreme thing, not the final goal. Romans 8:29 ESV speaks of God predestining His own to be *"conformed to the image of his Son."*[27]

So, what is our ultimate purpose of our pilgrimage on planet earth? Paul explains the reason for his birth to the Galatian church, *"But when God, who set me apart from my mother's womb and called me by His grace, was pleased to reveal His Son in me so that I might preach"* (Galatians 1:15-16, emphasis added). Why was anyone, including ourselves, "set apart from birth" in the first place? So that the Father could "reveal His Son in us." That "Adamic guy" has no place in the equation anymore!

The Second Protocol: The Great Commission

As this beautiful image of Christ is formed in us, it then

radiates out from us into the newly formed and transformed community of Christ. The power of transformation is the Gospel and the delivery system of Gospel-infused believers to *"Go and make disciples of all nations, baptizing them in the name of the Father and of the Son and of the Holy Spirit, and teaching them to obey everything I have commanded you"* (Matthew 28:19-20).

Nations—*ethne* in this passage—are not geopolitical entities, but ethnic groups, racial and cultural families in particular, the "Gentiles"—all non-Jewish peoples. (The assumption being that the Jews had already been included in the mandate for hearing the Gospel in Acts 2.) We have traditionally called this "The Great Commission."

Missiologist David Hesslegrave gives excellent insights into a proper biblical understanding of this command to Christ's disciples:

> Despite its widespread use as a challenge, however, exhorters seldom take the time to exegete the passage carefully and compare it with parallel passages. As a result, the essence and method of mission are often lost in exhortations to undertake it![28]

Hesselgrave explains further that the word *"go"* is "a participle in the original and not an imperative"[29]—i.e., "going" or "as you go," not "You—go!" To *"make disciples"* is the sole imperative and the central activity referred to in the Great Commission. Converts and cultural Christians, as popularly conceived, might do their own thing, so to speak, but disciples obviously must do the work of their Master. Disciples make other disciples as they go about the business of being alive.

Here is where a slight disparity comes in, however. It is where we distinguish the difference between the Great Commission and the Great Commandment, and the order in which Christ would have us prioritize them. Hesslegrave gets to this in his assertion that there is a vast difference between loving and serving *"all creatures"* (Mark 16:15) and making disciples of them. This begs the question: *Is there a higher goal for us as believers than "loving our neighbor"?* As the Church, what is our highest obligation to our fellow human beings? Loving them or making disciples of them?

> Now there can be no question but that believers are created in Christ for good works (Eph. 2:10) and that they are to *"do good unto all men, especially unto them that are of the household of faith"* (Gal. 6:10 KJV). If one is disposed to say that all things that believers are commanded of God to do constitute their mission in the world, there is a sense in which we can agree. But to say that good works constitute the Great Commission, or the heart of our mission . . . is to fly in the face of sound exegesis and clear thinking.[30]

Hesslegrave asserts that loving others and helping them become disciples are two different sides of the same coin. While both are needed, the Great Commission must be our focus as we walk out the Great Commandment.

Have you wondered why Paul was so successful in seeing whole cities and peoples impacted with the Gospel? He clearly understood this priority.

> There were many reasons [for Paul's success], of course. But one important reason was that Paul considered the preaching of the Gospel and the establishment of churches as his primary task. The biblical record leaves no room for thinking that either Paul or the members of his team were basically engaged in raising living standards, ameliorating

social conditions, imparting secular knowledge, ministering to medical needs, or dispensing aid from previously
established churches. There can be little doubt that allegiance to Christ on the part of converts in the churches
entailed these effects as by-products of faith even to the
sending of needed aid back to the Jerusalem church (a
kind of reverse flow). That the missionaries were concerned about social relationships, and about minds and
bodies as well as souls, is patently true. But Paul's primary
mission was accomplished when the Gospel was preached,
people were converted, and churches were established.[31]

So what motivated this disciple-making, church-planting
movement? Harry Boer builds on Hesselgrave's assertions,

> According to Acts 1:8, he had told them that when the
> Holy Spirit came upon them, they would 1) receive needed
> power or strength, 2) testify regarding the Christ whom
> they had seen and heard and in whom they believed, and 3)
> go to Jerusalem, Judea, Samaria, and the ends of the earth.
> After the Holy Spirit came, they discovered experientially
> that the Holy Spirit is also the missionary Spirit. He car-
> ried out the commission in and through them.[32]

We can see that the command to make disciples then is in
direct correlation to the Spirit's arrival to make the church "witnesses," and these witnesses made disciples and planted churches.
Though they served their respective cities and did "good works" as
they went (the Great Commandment), their mission, nonetheless,
was to make "hair-on-fire" disciples, gathering them into communities that would continue to be "witnesses" to the indigenous
peoples in each locale, fulfilling the Great Commission and passing
on the image of Christ to Adam and Eve's sons and daughters.

This, then, is the imperative to "make disciples" and teach them to be obedient to the words of Christ. What is an "image bearer" but a disciple? And what do disciples do other than pass on that genetic to "infect" others who will follow in the DNA of Jesus, the genetic Source of their new life. Ergo, *baby Christians!* We saw how this plays out in the Scriptures as passing on His image—discipleship—and teaching the community of faith how to obey and be formed into missional families that propagate the Gospel. This is the foremost activity we are called to. It is the command and call to every believer to make other disciples by passing on His image and form them into "redemptive communities" who will pass the life of Christ on to others. "Ministry" that does not include these two ingredients—making disciples and forming them into local church families—cannot be considered truly "missional," but falls in the category of the Great Commandment, which focuses on serving and loving others, not on turning them into disciples of Christ.

The Third Protocol: The Great Commandment

Jesus said it,

> "'Love the Lord your God with all your heart and with all your soul and with all your mind and with all your strength.' The second is this: 'Love your neighbor as yourself.' There is no commandment greater than these."
>
> —MARK 12:30-31

The second part of this "two-pronged" commandment is often used to explain our commitment as disciples to serve and love the broken world around us, as we should. However, the command is predicated on loving God as our "first love" and loving our "neighbors" as a byproduct—an "overflow," if you will—one commandment, yet two connected and inseparable parts. Paul expands on Jesus's words by saying,

> Let no debt remain outstanding, except the continuing debt to love one another, for whoever loves others has fulfilled the law. The commandments, "You shall not commit adultery," "You shall not murder," "You shall not steal," "You shall not covet," and whatever other command there may be, are summed up in this one command: "Love your neighbor as yourself." Love does no harm to a neighbor. Therefore, love is the fulfillment of the law.
>
> —ROMANS 13:8-10

"Loving our neighbor" is not simply that we love God and the poor, but that we love all of our fellow human beings—believers and unbelievers alike. The *whole* law is relationship based—and thus Jesus specified through the Great Commandment that we are to embrace love as the supreme interface for all human interactions.

We see non-believers and nominal Christians fulfilling the second part of this command in a spirit of "human benevolence," yet have ignored or discarded the first part of the command: "*to love God* with your whole being." Loving people, even for true believers, is not the same as making disciples, but is a byproduct of our love for God as His disciples. The Great Commission only works through the first part of the Great Commandment. To punctuate his summation of these two imperatives and their interplay, Hesselgrave wrote: "Obedience to the Great Commandment to love one's neighbor was part of the Commission to teach all things Christ commanded. But good works were the fruit—not the root—of Paul's mission."[33] Good works are part of disciples establishing the Kingdom.

When Paul and Barnabas were sent off by Peter, James, and John as apostles to the Gentiles after the Jerusalem Council of Acts 15, they received "the right hand of fellowship" for their calling to the Great Commission and were then given a final charge, *"All they asked was that we should continue to remember the poor, the very thing I had been eager to do all along"* (Galatians 2:10). Here we see the confirmation of the primary calling to "make disciples" (the root) and injunction not to forget the poor (the "fruit").

Operating in this "Trinity" of Protocols

So in these three protocols, we have both the "work" and the priorities of *being* the Church:

1) We are to manifest the image of Christ in all creation;

2) We are to transfer that image—make it "infectious"—wherever we go, "as we go" about our daily business, which will result in making other disciples; and

3) We are to love all and do good—establish justice—to align the activities of earth with the government of heaven, establishing God's Kingdom, and extending His grace to all, whether they would receive it and become disciples or not.

I wanted to bring these protocols out here near the beginning of Ken's story because it would be easy to see a different pattern in how he walked things out through The Friary as well as in how I talk about transforming cities in the rest of this book. "Stewarding dreams" as we have already seen and helping solve community problems could be construed as exactly the opposite order of priority—1) serving the community first and foremost, 2) making disciples, and then 3) manifesting the image of Christ.

But we mustn't forget God's first instructions to Ken as he prayer-walked the streets of his New Haven neighborhood: "You know you're My son." God was first establishing the image of His Child in Ken, then showing him how to walk out that image in his neighborhood so far outside the walls of a church that there wasn't even a church.

Manifesting the image of Christ is our ultimate purpose and the Great Commission is the delivery system of that high calling to both manifest that image in ourselves and transfer it to those around us, but we fall short if we leave the society we "disciple" unjust, uninspired, and lacking empowerment as we walk those things out.

Some divide out a "social Gospel" from "the Gospel of salvation." That poses a touch question that might sound something like this: "Is it better to lift a person out of poverty and leave them unsaved, or is it better to convert them to Christ, but let them remain in poverty?" Such things ought not to be, however. It's like saying, "Who should we owe the greatest allegiance to? The Father, the Son, or the Holy Spirit?" I can't help but think Jesus's answer to this would be something along the lines of His condemnation Israel's religious elite:

> "Woe to you, scribes and Pharisees, hypocrites! For you tithe mint and dill and cumin, and have neglected the weightier matters of the law: justice and mercy and faithfulness. **These you ought to have done, without neglecting the others.** You blind guides, straining out a gnat and swallowing a camel!
>
> —MATTHEW 23:23-24 ESV (emphasis added)

While there is a definite order, you don't get one without the other. These three protocols are a "trinity" of church function. We cannot do one and neglect the others. Transformation into the image of the Son and discipling people into that process leaves no room for injustice and a lack of spiritual fruit.

In this we see that the Gospel has intensely social implications—that it is part and parcel of our disciple making on the earth. That is why our calling as ambassadors and vice regents to the earth is a call to be benefactors to all of society. The Church, the culture, and God must all interface to bring transformation to the earth and its vast populace. We are the instigators of the Kingdom now that Jesus sits at the right hand of the Father. Where there is a "church" planted, it should always be spreading roots that the kingdom should be blossoming wherever the ministers of that body go.

KNIT TOGETHER

The members of The Friary committed to living a lifestyle around what Ken calls the four "mutualities." These rhythms—sort of basic tenets of faith—were reminiscent of Patrick and the Celtic communities of the fourth century: 1) mutual Christ, 2) mutual spiritual rhythms, 3) mutual support, and 4) mutual mission. These four mutualities framed their "order."* In more detail, they were:

---

* Note: many of us have associated monasticism with the Catholic tradition of religious adherents sequestered out of sight of society and living under the conviction of various "sacred" vows. The nature of Celtic monasticism was juxtaposed to the Catholic traditions and championed a community of faith imbedded in the local community, committed to spiritual rhythms, engaged in the economics of society and missional in all that it sought to do. Friars and Friaries were "missionary" in nature and sought to reach the community they lived in with the Gospel. There is a healthy resurgence of this form of "church" today being labeled "Neo-monasticism." Believers are again being "friars" in their communities, only without anything to distinguish them but their love.

1. *Mutual Christ.* As it grew, those who gathered as The Friary all came from very different spiritual backgrounds. To grow together, they had to take the time to listen to each other's faith stories as well as tell their own. The one thing they all held in common was Christ, so they built around that as their center. They needed to be able to be sensitive to each other on the journey, have grace for little disagreements, and build on each other's strengths and contributions. As they did this, they became willing to submit to each other in the areas where each needed to grow and mature, giving each other permission to call them out, or forward, as people belonging to each other, into a deeper walk with Christ.

2. *Mutual rhythm* became a practice of sharing meals together, gathering, opening the Word together, working together out in the community, and breaking bread and sharing the cup of Christ in communion on a regular basis. (See Acts 2:42 once again.)

3. Being *mutually supportive* means to be willing to *"bear one another's burdens, and so fulfill the law of Christ"* (Galatians 6:2 ESV). They began to define community around a total availability regardless of their weakness and responsibilities. In a sense of, "Listen, you and I have liabilities. Let's just be honest and let's share those and not be afraid that we're going to run off on each other and abandon each other just because we have some areas that need work." They found strength in supporting each other's frailties, and in that way grew and matured both as individuals and as a community.

4. They committed themselves to *mutual mission*—not all doing the same thing, but all engaged in some way in the community. Some had specific passions. For example, one woman was a teacher. She knew all the kids that didn't

have enough for a Thanksgiving meal, so on her suggestion, they prepared boxes for them and went to their homes to bring what was needed. She was able to open the door into those homes because she was a teacher at their school and they knew her. As The Friary was focused on resourcing dreams for maximum community impact, they all worked together on projects like this, even though it was one member that had championed the particular "mission."

The Friary was thus imbedded in this neighborhood to "be the Church" and became a life-giving missional community reminiscent of an early "book of Acts" church. Just as the move of the Spirit in Jerusalem came from the life emanating from the homes of God's people, so too the beautiful move of God through Ken and The Friary was from believer's homes, without any of the trappings of a church building or even a rented community space for gatherings.

Ken and the Friary didn't expect their neighbors to come to them, but took their house church to the neighbors. They didn't bring a program; they brought a helping hand and the Gospel. It was a pretty interesting transition for a man whose experience was in building a megachurch in a suburb, but he did it anyway because it was God was leading Him to do. In the process, his neighborhood was starting to change in some remarkable ways.

They were just getting started, though.

NOW WHAT?

Question #1: "Who" not "what," then, is the question for our church-es—a focus on people more than on structures and activities. How can you and your church family better mobilize members into all of society to complete His mission? How are you walking out the "three protocols"?

Question #2: Discuss the "Ultimate Purpose," the "Great Commission," and the "Great Commandment" (see pages 244-250).

Do you agree with the premise of each of these sections? Why or why not?

In what ways can you and your church family better align your values and practices to build the Church into Christ's image, make disciples, and love God and your neighbors as the pattern and order suggests?

Question #3: Consider Ken's "mutualities" (pages 253-254) and ask the question: "Do you and your team have clear mutualities—biblical values and practices—that inform your decisions, commitments to one another, and mission?" What are, or should, your mutualities be?

COMMUNITY DREAMING

Be careful to live properly among your
unbelieving neighbors. Then even if they accuse you
of doing wrong, they will see your honorable behavior,
and they will give honor to God when he judges the world. . . .
It is God's will that your honorable lives
should silence those ignorant people who
make foolish accusations against you. . . .
Respect everyone, and love the family of believers.
Fear God, and respect the king.

—1 PETER 2:12, 15, 17 **NLT**

ost of the streets in Fair Haven hadn't been cared for or invested in for years, but parents dreamed about their kids going outside and feeling safe. They wanted to see their neighborhood be open for walking and cycling. So Ken's team and their local Alderman launched a campaign to raise money in order to entice a skilled city-street planner to meet with them. They used jars to collect as many pennies, nickels, and dimes as they could. After contacting several people, one of the top planners in the country finally came and met with them, looking at areas in their neighborhood that they wanted to see redesigned and reimagined.

There was no way they could ever afford to hire this well-respected gentleman, but when he heard "the dream" for the neighborhood and the fact that they had saved jars of coins, anxious to contribute, he decided that he would come and help recreate Fair Haven—*pro bono*.

Ken remembers walking with him and looking at the intersections where cars would drag race down the streets. Together, they brainstormed ideas on how to slow traffic, how they could create bicycle paths, and make it safe so people wouldn't be afraid their kids would be hit by a car if they let them out of the house.

They convened several community meetings with this planner and then he left with all of their ideas and dreams. Some weeks later he came back with a proposal: a full-scale redesign for their community. Everyone was so excited everyone to see what he had come up with.

Then, a few weeks later, together with his neighbors, Ken helped presented the plans to city planning officials. "This is what we want our neighborhood to look like!" they told them. The community spoke as one. They were told there wasn't money for it at that time, but someone from the city would let them know if that changed. So they all chorused in unison, "When the day comes that the city has the finances to invest in our neighborhood, then this is what we want done." Their plan was summarily put on file with the city and they waited.

And they waited.

And they waited.

Despite all the excitement, nothing happened. This left the community frustrated. Not only were the streets continuing to decay, but the sidewalks were a mess. Over the years, roots had grown up and buckled the concrete pathways. There were many elderly who could hardly navigate them. While they persisted in asking the city for help, their pleas continued to fall on deaf ears.

Then one of the neighbors had a brilliant idea. They suggested throwing a party in the neighborhood akin to the Boston Tea Party—only instead of dumping tea into the harbor, they'd bring their kitchen tables, replete with chairs, cups, saucers, etc., and hold their "tea party" in the middle of the street. When they did, it blocked all traffic.

As horns honked, they sat at their tables festively drinking their tea and shooting the breeze. Eventually reporters showed up and asked them what they were doing. They told them they wanted to raise awareness regarding the fact their elderly could not navigate the sidewalks because of their disrepair. They informed the press that they had been asking the city and the mayor repeatedly, yet nothing had happened. Then they introduced the reporters to the neighbors that couldn't walk the sidewalks sitting next to them.

They still didn't hear anything from city hall, but within a few weeks, a construction team showed up and started working on the sidewalks, putting in new curbs, and resurfacing the streets—*all according to the plans they had submitted to the city commissioners.* Fair Haven was getting its much-needed face lift!

SERVING OUR COMMUNITIES IS SACRED WORK

Ken likes to call himself a "dreamweaver." He came to Fair Haven as a servant, asking his neighbors about their dreams, and then acted as a Kingdom emissary to help make them a reality. As we explored in the Navah story, Jesus's whole *modus operandi* was to play the part of a servant—and He expects His Family to emulate being fellow-servants to the *"least of these"* (Matthew 25:40)—in other words, to serve in helping fulfill their dreams. But that's not as easy as it used to be.

The sacred/secular split in many nations today teaches us to draw strong lines between the social work of churches and the good works of nonprofits, NGOs, government agencies, and businesses. It is not difficult to see the positive effect the private sector and privately-owned businesses can have as they engage in our communities with a heart towards being a blessing. At the same time, the goods and services provided by local, state, and federal government agencies are growing more limited in the midst of expectations for them to do more and more. Then there are the benevolent activities of the social sector and volunteer not-for-profit organizations that parallel the work done by religious groups. With "church and state" constantly being called into contrast in courts both in the US and Europe, it feels like the work traditionally done by faith communities is being handed over to organizations with more secular and political motivations. The poor and dispossessed seem to have new champions.

This all leaves me wondering, "Where does this leave us with respect to what used to be considered 'Christian work' and was the domain of faith organizations?" Where, for centuries, we were the ones reaching out to the "least among us," it can now feel like we're on the outside looking in. In an increasingly secular world, those with belief in God are looked at by many with suspicion, especially when it comes to our motives. How do we be city transformers when it doesn't even feel like we have a seat at the table for addressing the same problems we used to be the point of the spear for solving?

When working with civil and religious city leaders in Europe, Africa, Asia, and North America, I learned they all had one thing in common—they had a dream for a better city! So how do God's dreams for His creation, man's dreams for His society, and the Church's dreams for the "salvation for all," coexist, or perhaps even cooperate, for the good of everyone?

Members of my former team in Amsterdam once sat on silk pillows with leaders of the Turkish community and asked them how we could serve their needs as foreigners in the Netherlands. Not surprisingly, none of them mentioned "salvation in the name of Jesus." It just didn't come up.

When we asked the leaders of the LGBT population or the Satanic Church in Amsterdam how we could help them, again salvation never showed up on their "must have" list. The desire to "become Christians" simply wasn't first and foremost for the majority of the residents, organizations, and leaders in our cities. However, when we asked instead what their dreams were and if there was a way we could help make them come true, they jumped at the opportunity. As Swanson and Williams wrote in *To Transform a City*: "Cities resist being 'reached,' but they love being served, loved, and blessed."[34] Service is where the dreams of God, the Church, and the community intersect—and service is *our* specialty as our King is *the* Servant-King of the "if you want to be great be servant of all" Kingdom. The world around us has no shortage of "felt" and real needs. Ken and his crew recognized this in their "hood" in New Haven and became the "go to" people for solving the issues that would eventually bring transformation to the entire city.

Not long ago where I live in Douglas County, Colorado, officials were reeling from reports that they had the highest teen suicide rate in the state. A group of church leaders, school principals, and social services directors were summoned to help remedy the situation. It reminded me of the time God brought Daniel on the scene just as Babylon faced an impossible situation. King Darius recognized his impotence and summoned Daniel who received his strategy from God.

Like Daniel, one of the Douglas County pastor was asked to pull a team together to address the problem, and they, in turn, formed a compassionate response to suffering families and explored ways to provide suicide prevention services to students. Evening trainings were held at the schools for the parents utilizing materials provided by Focus on Family. This endeavor had the blessing of the county and was led by local believers and even some believing teachers from the two main high schools. Serving the real needs of a hurting community resulted in the opportunity to live and proclaim the Gospel to numerous families and opened the hearts of the county leaders to more active engagement by the churches in their area.

At one of these events, a lawyer tasked with helping the county deal with underprivileged families had a little girl with big brown eyes come up to him while her parents were in a consultation. He was struck with the realization that county programs couldn't meet the fundamental needs of this wee girl and her precious family. With tears in his eyes, he told one of the pastors, "We can't take care of their real needs, you have to do that. In fact, you can even talk about Jesus!" As a result, the doors were wide open in Douglas County for the Church to do her work of serving the dreams of the community. Mobilizing our own families to become servants of the Kingdom enterprise is both great fun and highly critical to the future of our cities.

WHERE DREAMS COLLIDE

Eric Swanson and Sam Williams have developed the excellent graphic you see below to show the interface of God's dreams, a city's dreams, and the Church's dreams.[35]

Here we see three concentric circles each representing a unique "field of dreams." God, the rightful owner to creation's purpose, has mandates and desires that motivate His plans and purposes. Likewise, every city has dreams for her citizens, for their economic wellbeing, protection, and future. Then there is the Church that has dreams commensurate to her capacities and her calling from God to bring salvation to all people. In the intersection between the City and the Church there are significant control issues, each feeling it is better to help others from their own worldviews. (There is a bridge between these circles we will discuss in the next chapter). When these collide, neither makes fruitful headway. Their respective sacred/secular viewpoints are often inherently incompatible. (They aren't necessarily which I'll explain in chapter 24.) Swanson and Williams suggest "We don't go there"—that we steer away from the "control" or governing quadrant. The Kingdom won't go where any party insists on control over all others—unless we can create a bridge into their dream zone.

Where the dreams of the City and God intersect are the issues of social justice and community wellbeing. This is where all those kind and benevolent activities seem to pop up without the help of the Church because those outside of the Church care about these matters as well. This is the area where common grace is the catalyst between God and culture. Common grace is a way of talking about God's beneficence toward all people, a concept reflected in the works of Jesus, but in the overall society, not just among the people of God. As Jesus instructed us:

> "But I tell you, love your enemies and pray for those who
> persecute you, that you may be children of your Father in
> heaven. He causes his sun to rise on the evil and the good,
> and sends rain on the righteous and the unrighteous."
>
> —MATTHEW 5:44-45

In the same light, Barnabas and Paul, having just been deemed the
"gods" Zeus and Hermes, pleaded with the residents of Lystra to
understand the ways of the true God for all of His creation,

> In the past, he let all nations go their own way. Yet he has
> not left himself without testimony: He has shown kindness
> by giving you rain from heaven and crops in their seasons;
> he provides you with plenty of food and fills your hearts
> with joy.
>
> —ACTS 14:16-17

God desires that all people would live in safety with justice. The
common grace of God includes good things such as schools, street-
lights, sewers, roads, bridges, police and fire protection—all things
municipalities strive to provide without prejudice or bias.[36]

God has never turned His back on earth's citizens, even when
they have rejected Him, but instead has chosen to repay their evil
with good, furnishing them with a beautiful, functioning planet
to live on. Our God displays the cosmos's greatest gift of hospitality—all are invited into "temple earth" and its beauty, though
some have polluted and scarred the land with their pantheon of
defiled "gods" in return. The greatest pollutant on earth is not car-
bon emissions or oil spills, it is the sin of rejecting Creation's Host
by ungrateful guests in the Creator's very own "house." Despite
the ungrateful response of His creation, Luke wrote that our God

"*is kind to the ungrateful and the wicked*" (Luke 6:35). God interacts with the world through earth's natural functions and the kindness of His people.

God's and the Church's dreams intersect in the desire for salvation—in the fullest sense of the word—*for all*. This is the Church's calling: to bring the Gospel of the Kingdom to the community she has been assigned to. Paul told Timothy that prayers for governmental leaders would result in "*peaceful and quiet lives*" (1 Timothy 2:2). Furthermore, these prayers were to be motivated by one wonderful fact, God "*wants all people to be saved and to come to a knowledge of the truth*" (1 Timothy 2:4).

In Luke 6, there is a beautiful hint that reveals the difference in the good works the Church does and the good works found in the culture. It is found in the character of God. Luke tells us (vs. 35) that we are to "*love your enemies, do good to them.*" There are two key words for "good" in Greek. The first, *kalos*, refers to the intrinsic goodness we acquire as a result of our salvation—we become like Jesus in our motivations. The other word used here is *agathos* and refers to works that we are to do that will benefit our enemies. The rationale for doing beneficial things to our enemies is because that is the way God is. He is merciful and has extended His mercy to us so that our works towards the culture (*agathos*) are a result of His good work on our behalf (*kalos*). Luke ends this section by saying that God is "*kind to the ungrateful and wicked. Be merciful, just as your Father is merciful*" (Luke 6:35-36). We serve in the arena of our cultures by doing "good works" (*agathos*) that benefit those around us because we have obtained an intrinsic goodness (*kalos*) from the God who is good by nature.

How then do we serve the needs of our society, yet still proclaim and demonstrate the Gospel? This is where Ken "dream-weaves" the best. As we we've discussed several times already,

Jesus, the Servant-King, has mandated us to serve one another and the "least among us." Championing the unfulfilled dreams of the people around us is a natural onramp to the Gospel and "making disciples" of all—even as we serve in the fulfillment of their dreams. Yet these two—serving dreams and making disciples—seem to be in tension with one another in the heart of many of God's people. How do we go beyond just serving our cities as the community leaders we've invited to become, and also be about the business of the Kingdom as mandated by Jesus? They are not mutually exclusive The Church is called to function as a "benefactor community" to the culture.

I have participated in and am aware of an increasing array of transformational endeavors being lived out in our cities through the partnership of churches, communities, and civil government leaders across the globe today, but it was Ken's story that grabbed my attention the most. It is a beautiful example of a grassroots movement containing many of the ingredients necessary in seeing our personal lives, churches, and cities transformed—it's all about serving in a way that gives dignity and purpose to the dreams of those around us while also making room to introduce them to the Ultimate Dreamweaver Himself.

NOW WHAT?

Question #1: Reflect on the chart on page 269 and its implications. How do you—or would you—hold the tension between serving the city in the realm of common grace, proclaiming the Gospel of the Kingdom, and staying true to the correct priority of the three protocols of the church as we discussed them in the last chapter?

Question #2: Are you cognizant of the fact that you are a minister in *your* sphere of life? As a "minister," do you value your work as a sacred calling from God?

> **Exercise:** Consider taking prayer walks in your neighborhood and in and around your business communities. Report the results of these prayer walks to your friends and family. In fact, invite them to walk and pray with you. Watch what God does!

CHANGING CULTURAL CONVERSATIONS

They reside in their respective countries, but only as aliens,
they take part in everything as citizens and put up with
everything as foreigners. Every foreign land is their home and
every home a foreign land. They find themselves in the flesh,
but do not live according to the flesh.[37]

—EPISTLE TO DIOGNETUS

from a 2nd century Christian

As the sidewalks and streets grew more navigable for people again, Chatham Square Park came to the forefront. It was a center of drug dealing and prostitution and dangerous territory, even at midday. It was one thing to send kids out to ride their bikes, but where could they go to meet their friends besides each other's homes, especially when parents were still at work? It wasn't a matter of more police patrolling the streets, either. There were plenty of patrols, but too much acreage in the parks for those officers to make an impact. The real question was, how could the community rise up to take back what should be a place of playgrounds and picnic lunches?

Ken and his crew got an idea. They approached and recruited top-notch photographers who wanted to build their businesses and asked if they would take pictures of people in the neighborhood. They shot beautiful black and white portraits of individuals in the community: a dad that's all rough and tatted up holding his sparkly, precious baby; a neighbor working in the school gardens pulling up carrots with a big grin; the friendly face of a local bodega owner standing in his doorway; and other similar shots. Then they had the best photographs blown up on four-by-four-foot banners they could hang from the sides of buildings around the edges of the park. If you came into dark bypasses formerly covered in graffiti, you would now see them covered with bright, beautiful portraits of people who lived in the neighborhood. These were the faces of the community, the true beauty of the neighborhood. The uniqueness of their collective identity was beginning to redefine them.

They then organized clean up days for the park, clearing it of debris and removing all the graffiti, followed by organizing community events there. This central park became the place where the community started gathering for their annual Easter egg hunts. Soon, the neighborhood people began to get familiar with each other. As ownership of their community grew, an informal "neighborhood watch" started to form. Where people live in fear and isolation, they don't get to know each other; now, because people became friends—real neighbors—they started looking out for one other, and miraculously (in a manner of speaking) crime and violence began to decrease.

After only five years of this kind of planning and working to steward dreams, Fair Haven was beginning to be looked at by the city as an empowerment zone that was truly being empowered. But Ken and The Friary crew had only scraped the surface.

DUAL CITIZENSHIPS

Ken understood his dual citizenship: The call to carry "passports" from both heaven and earth as he walked New Haven's streets. He wasn't plagued by a sacred/secular paradigm, nor was he either a "social Gospel" warrior or an "all that matters is to be born again" guy. He was neither a political "activist" (disruptive of political life) or a "quietist" (withdraw from public life). He was a *politeia*—a Greek word referring to "a public life as one that wields influence by virtue of a life well lived in the public forum that marries his love for God with his love for his neighbor."[38] He was also a "son" of the Father, a member of the Family of God called to plant himself in a dark neighborhood to live out a godly life and quietly affect the affairs his community.

Without this transformative DNA of dual citizenship restored to the Church, there is little hope for true systemic transformation in our cities through the Church.

Being born of American parents in Japan, I hoped to enjoy the benefits of dual citizenship. No dice; I wasn't ethnic "Japanese." I later discovered, being one quarter Danish, I could apply for Danish citizenship and be entitled to some of their social perks (I'm not sure what I was thinking when I did so!). I was summarily rejected by my Viking brethren. I have always thought it would be spectacular to have two passports to allow me to sneak around flaunting various persona in my global travels. I am a spy at heart and was looking for an outlet for my fetish for clandestine activities. Then I discovered my dual citizenship between my American heritage and the Kingdom of God, and my secret agent predilections found a home.

This is God's norm for the Church—to be "in the world, but not of it." (See John 15:19.) In fact, it was God's norm for Israel as He laid out His intentions to Jeremiah,

> This is what the Lord Almighty, the God of Israel, says
> to all those I carried into exile from Jerusalem to Babylon:
> "Build houses and settle down; plant gardens and eat what
> they produce. Marry and have sons and daughters; find
> wives for your sons and give your daughters in marriage,
> so that they too may have sons and daughters. Increase
> in number there; do not decrease. Also, seek the peace
> and prosperity of the city to which I have carried you into
> exile. Pray to the Lord for it, because if it prospers, you too
> will prosper."
>
> —JEREMIAH 29:4-7

God's plan for His people was that they would be observed by the nations and many would come to them to see God and His ways. Instead, they disobeyed incessantly and found themselves captives in the Babylonian Empire. God did not leave them unattended, nor did He tell them to maintain a fortress or enslaved mentality, nor to complacently wait to return home. Instead He told them to find their peace and wellbeing in the land of captivity. They were charged to be active: build houses and plant gardens, to imbed themselves in living a godly life—all while looking towards home: "next year in Jerusalem"—if for no other reason than to make God known by simply being His people, wherever they were scattered.

They were called to dual citizenship.

Daniel was raised up in captivity always mindful of the primacy of following God, but also being loyal to and supportive of the king who ruled them as a captive nation. His vision of the times terrified him. He was tasked to serve three world rulers including a kingdom that was destined to be eradicated. As a foreshadowing of who Jesus would be, he was placed in captivity to be elevated to influence and leadership in a demonized and godless society. This was God's appointment for him—dual citizenship.

As resident aliens and pilgrims on this earth, the New Covenant also describes our role as engaged and embedded citizens with tasks to perform for the Kingdom of God.

> But our citizenship is in heaven. And we eagerly await a
> Savior from there, the Lord Jesus Christ.
>
> —PHILIPPIANS 3:20

As citizens of heaven and ambassadors of the Kingdom, we must be mindful of how we think and act—and how the surrounding culture sees us. How does the current culture perceive the Church? They often see us as separate, part of a politically conservative force, judgmental, isolationists unwilling to truly enter the conversation regarding problems in our cities, and not all that important to the welfare of our communities. That makes us sound more like bearers of "bad news" rather than the "Good News" of the Gospel. Jeff Reed states that, "How we think about our citizenship will affect how we work with the city."[39]

In this same spirit, the early church leaders realized that the disciples were citizens in a "foreign land," aliens and captives of a wicked society. Peter puts their calling in perspective,

> Peter, an apostle of Jesus Christ, To God's elect, exiles
> scattered throughout the provinces of Pontus, Galatia,
> Cappadocia, Asia and Bithynia.
>
> —1 PETER 1:1

Disciples are "exiles"—aliens—and are to keep their behavior excellent in the unbelieving world. As aliens and foreigners in our own captive nations, like Daniel, we are to imbed ourselves to be positive forces in the affairs of our communities and cities.

In the light of being dual citizens in a captive land, Paul told the Thessalonians to continue loving each other, yet do even more beyond the comfort of the church family,

> ...yet we urge you, brothers and sisters, to do so more and more, and to make it your ambition to lead a quiet life: You should mind your own business and work with your hands, just as we told you, so that your daily life may win the respect of outsiders and so that you will not be dependent on anybody.
>
> —1 THESSALONIANS 4:10-12

The church in Thessalonica had learned to love the Family, but not the surrounding culture. Here Paul is encouraging them to extend their love into the social arena. He was admonishing them to make an impact in their culture, not withdraw from it. At first glance, it may sound as if he was advocating they sit back and not make waves. Understanding the historical and cultural context of this passage reveals his actual intent. Leading *"a quiet life"* was the opposite of activism, which some in the Church were engaged in. "Mind your own business" was a warning to not engage in mobs and demonstrations that were common in the city. His charge to them to *"work with their hands"* was inviting them to do what he himself exemplified—not to be a burden to anyone, but make a contribution to the culture God placed them in. The Church was not to be a welfare state. It was to contribute to the community, not take from it.

Winning the respect of authorities and outsiders is prevalent in Paul's writing, where he emphasizes living out the life of Jesus in the *politeia*. This strong admonition not to depend on the welfare of others was due to the Church's calling to be caretakers and benefactors of the earth and its inhabitants. They were to provide for themselves and those around them, not be dependent on welfare or become proverbial "couch potatoes."

> Whatever happens, **conduct yourselves in a manner worthy of the gospel of Christ**. Then, whether I come and see you or only hear about you in my absence, I will know that you stand firm in the one Spirit, striving together as one for the faith of the gospel without being frightened in any way by those who oppose you.
>
> —PHILIPPIANS 1:27-28 (emphasis added)

The word "conduct" (*politeuomai*) is from a family of words meaning city, citizen, citizenship, conduct, commonwealth (including the word *politeia* that we have discussed already). "The term referred to the whole of life in the public domain of a city, in contrast to private existence in a household."[40] It is also fair to deduce from this text that if you are being opposed, you are most likely engaged in the affairs of the culture you are in. This call by the apostles to engagement in public life was normative for the early church.

The text immediately following a similar injunction in Philippians 2:1-4 is in the context of interaction in the legal arena of the community (*polteuomai*)—civil rights and civil suits—where Paul admonishes them to handle their own disputes. In underscoring the need for them to settle their own differences and not resort to the court system, he was demonstrating that as benefactors to the culture, their unity was essential to their witness in the public square.

When he wrote to Titus, Paul made it abundantly clear that the Church was to engage in the "good works" of public life as those who have been saved *"by grace and not of works."* Check out this bombshell Scripture!

> Put them in mind to be subject to principalities and powers, to obey magistrates, **to be ready to** [do] **every good** [*agathos*] **work** [*ergon*], To speak evil of no man, to be no brawlers, but gentle, showing all meekness unto all men [living in the *politeia*]. For we ourselves also [followed by the nasty stuff we've done]. . . . But after that the kindness and love of God our Savior toward man appeared, **Not by works** [*ergon*] of righteousness which we have done, but according to his mercy he saved us, by the washing of regeneration, and **renewing of the Holy Ghost**; Which he shed on us abundantly through Jesus Christ our Savior; That being justified by his grace, we should be made heirs according to the hope of eternal life. [The Gospel!] This is a faithful saying, and these things I will that thou affirm constantly that they which have believed in God might **be careful to maintain good** [*kalos*] **works** [*ergon*] **These things are good** [*kalos*] and profitable unto men. . . .
>
> *And let ours also* **learn to maintain good** *[kalos]* **works** *[ergon] for necessary uses [*"daily necessities" niv*], that they be not unfruitful.*
>
> —TITUS 3:1-8, 14 KJV[41] (emphasis added)

In the last chapter we considered two words for "good" in Greek, *agathos* and *kalos*. In verse two, Paul is instructing Titus to teach the church to do the work of "benefactors" *(agathos)* in society like others in the culture. He then launches into a celebration of our salvation that was not gained by our own works. He ends the section in verses 8 and 14 by changing the language and highlighting the difference between the works of benevolent people in any culture to those saved by this amazing grace. He tells the church to maintain *kalos* works. This can only be accomplished by those who have been changed by the work of grace—it is intrinsic goodness that emanates from the same God who stood back from his own works in Creation and called them "good."

Thus *agathos* refers to anyone who brings benefit or improves the state of people and the city, while *kalos* is reserved for those who have inherited His life and dispense it freely in the city under the guidance of the Holy Spirit. A stunning distinction! This tandem of *grace* and *works*—being *found* in the image of Christ and *doing the work* of *"loving your neighbor"* as a result of loving our God—combine to produce the template and the fruit of biblical discipleship.

My friends, practice and teach this in your churches. It is this transformational thinking and practice in the Church that our broken world is waiting for—and the Church has been so ambivalent about embracing. Only as we are transformed by this magnificent plan of God, will we be enabled to transform our communities and cities in like manner. There are no real transformational works without the grace of being found in the Father—we don't do works to merit salvation, we are saved so that our works might matter and make a real difference.

THE HOUSEHOLD ORDER

The apostles received instructions from Jesus Himself regarding the conduct and order of the household of faith. The teaching that laid out this framework was called the *didache*, and the particulars of how to carry it out are found in the word *administration* (*oikonomia*, "the management or administration of the property of others"[42]).

> Surely you have heard about the **administration** of God's grace that was given to me for you.
>
> —EPHESIANS 3:2 (emphasis added)

This word—translated *dispensation* in the *King James* (a word that escapes most of us) and *administration* (a scary word for some) in the *New International Version*—simply means that Paul was given, by Jesus, the stewardship and care over God's household or estate. Beautiful! He was shown the order of the house of God in order to maintain order in, and the beauty of, the house.

Two of the main tenets of the *didache* are: #1) it gave instructions for how to conduct ourselves within the context of the Family of God; and #2) in the context of society—how to behave as heaven's citizen among the earthly citizenry. Paul refers to the Church citizenry as *ambassadors* (see 2 Corinthians 5:20), as we found in our discussion of the work of the Spirit in forming our Gospel Identity. What is our identity in the Spirit? Ambassadors, intermediaries between heaven and earth, reflectors of God's image, and His emissaries to the culture we are assigned to (which is by default the one around us unless God sends us to another).

Could we perhaps say that the state of our cities is a reflection of the Church's impotence as servants and benefactors to the communities and authorities around us? Could individual believers, families, house groups, churches, and networks of churches be more convinced of the biblical mandate to "seek the welfare of the city"? If we did, how might that impact nursing homes, unwed mothers, the homeless, foster care, broken homes, and broken finances? This might also put a new twist on modern evangelism practices. Instead of being removed from the culture and taking forays into it with various short-term endeavors ("outreaches") to "preach the Gospel," what if we were to dedicate ourselves to "own" the broken cisterns of our communities and train God's people to be benefactors to the broken and the helpless? What if we availed ourselves to community and governmental leaders ready to do any "good work" armed with prayer and the power of the Holy Spirit? I'm sure we would be able to give a good account of the hope that is within us and to let our neighbors see our good works and glorify the Father who is in heaven.

PRAYING FOR GOVERNMENT LEADERS

As of this writing, there have been many significant elections in a number of nations in the last decade. Political partisanship in the Church seems high and battle lines seem drawn around various political ideologies. On the one hand, activism in the Church is increasing, while on the other, some are withdrawing because of a sense of hopelessness and confusion. Praying for leaders seems to be at a low or cursory level at best. I have heard vitriolic and disparaging comments made about certain elected officials that tell me the speaker has engaged in very little prayer and certainly doesn't seem conversant with heaven's perspective. While they talk of so many things, what they are really saying is that this leader simply doesn't conform to their predisposed political agenda, preferences, or sensibilities.

The admonition to pray for civil leaders has its roots in being ambassadors and benefactors of a greater King and His Kingdom, a greater perspective on the eternal purposes swirling around us and the proper manner in which we navigate our dual citizenships. Here's what Paul said about it to Timothy:

> I urge, then, first of all, that petitions, prayers, intercession and thanksgiving be made for all people—for kings and all those in authority, that we may live **peaceful and quiet** [*eremos*: "'tranquility arising from within,' causing no disturbance to others"[43]] lives in all godliness and holiness. This is good, and pleases God our Savior, who wants all people to be saved and to come to a knowledge of the truth.
>
> **—1 TIMOTHY 2:1-4** (emphasis added)

The result of living as non-political activists armed with dangerous, prayerful lives under the rule of dubious leaders is that people get saved! If we are serving and participating in meeting the felt needs of our civil leaders, they will come to see us as safe "contributors" and benefactors and not combatants of the city's or nation's best interests. If Joseph could serve Pharaoh and Daniel could serve Nebuchadnezzar from their states of captivity—and I'm sure, surrounded by political disagreement—we, the Church, must find the grace to live above political discord in the culture and find a greater grace to be servants of God's agenda.

With one wee caveat! The condition for these results is always unity in the Church. If we were more dedicated to gather in His name, cease our palaver, and be emboldened by His perspective on current affairs, He would manifest Himself in our midst, in our cities, and in our nations in a more tangible way. It's His earth, His opinion, and His rule that He is longing to reveal to His ambassadorial entourage on earth. Our aggression, passivity, and general lack of heavenly perspective is killing our witness and His Name in our nations. What is God's perspective on the current national and political landscape in your city or nation? Ask Him—together as His Body!

Peter confirms this rationale for submitting to "every authority instituted among men," for the Lord's sake (and I know we just looked at this Scripture above, but it bears repeating):

> For it is God's will that **by doing good** [*agathapoeio*: "to be a well-doer"] **you should silence the ignorant talk of foolish people**. Live as free people, but do not use your freedom as a cover-up for evil; live as God's slaves. Show proper respect to everyone, love the family of believers, fear God, honor the emperor.
>
> —1 PETER 2:15-17

Remember that we are talking about Roman Caesars here! Peter is calling the Church to be benefactors (*agathapoeio*) to the worst of rapscallions, and by doing so we can *"silence the talk of foolish people."* Thank God for that!

I love how Ken submitted to laws and governmental leaders around him as a benefactor and servant-contributor to New Haven. Both the mayor (and eventually the governor) came to him for help, which resulted in a transformed neighborhood, economic renewal, the return of innovation—and most of all *hope*—to a community, all in the name of Jesus.

NOW WHAT?

Question #1: How should we embrace the idea of *politeia* without falling into one of the two extremes of "activism" or "quietism." Is the mindset of *politeia* in your own mind and heart? In that of your church or ministry?

Question #2: Do the beliefs and behaviors of the leaders and people in your church reflect "good deeds" as a necessity in your everyday lives? How could you better further the idea of becoming a "benefactor" person, family, or church?

Question #3: How would you evaluate your level of understanding and your practice of praying for leaders in the public arena? What more could be done to hear the Father's heart for your nation and receive His instructions for implementation in the culture around you?

> **Exercise:** Paul and the early church were praying for leaders in a system that they not only disagreed with, but was persecuting them. Reflect on your attitudes towards your current political leaders and ask the Father to give you His perspective above your own political leanings. Be open to being surprised!

Question #4: How is doing "good deeds" as Jesus did a means of discipling both people and nations?

> **Exercise:** Discuss together the two different meanings of "good works" from Titus 3:1-8, 14.

Question #5: Did this chapter put your current evangelistic "beliefs and practices" in a different light biblically? In what way(s)?

MARKETPLACE DREAMING

*So he reasoned in the synagogue with both Jews
and God-fearing Greeks, as well as in the marketplace
day by day with those who happened to be there.*

—ACTS 17:17

Another part of New Haven's dream for renewal was to improve
its economic landscape. One of the programs for this was called
"project storefronts" in downtown New Haven that envisioned
refurbishing one of its central business areas. Inspired by all they'd
been able to accomplish in their neighborhood, Ken and his friend,
Slate Ballard, decided to write a business plan for an idea that had
been bouncing around in the back of their minds. What if they had
a space where small businesses and entrepreneurs could gather to
work and share resources in a similar way to what they had been
doing in Fair Haven with their dream stewarding? They would
allow people to rent space—anything from conference rooms to a
single desk space—and then use the power of networking they'd
employed in transforming Fair Haven to help small businesses and
solopreneurs get off the ground. While such co-working spaces—
like the one Navah moved into in Kansas City—are everywhere

today, it was a model Ken had never seen anywhere in the US before. His driving question was: "Why wouldn't dream stewarding work in the business domain as well?"

Ken described it this way: "We were created to weave our dreams together, not in isolation, but by working as a network to support each other. What if a strategy like peer-to-peer production, a powerful engine that helps people spark things inside of each other—the same kind of energy we've started tapping into at The Friary—were suddenly available to entrepreneurs who usually get started all alone? What if such people were given access to resources, people willing to partner with them, and the teamwork needed to get things off the ground?"

Ken wanted to see what would happen if they put people who needed each other (even if they didn't know they needed each other) into close proximity and then coaxed them into the process of stewarding their own dreams as well as helping steward the dreams of others. In this way, they could open the door to things that were only found through collective work and collective impact. It was a powerful idea.

Ken decided to call this shared space "The Grove" because New Haven is called "The Elm City," and he liked the imagery of meeting in a grove of trees to do this work. "When I visited in Colorado, I was blown away by the beauty of the Aspen groves and I remember learning that the Aspen grove is one of the largest living organisms in the world. Each grove is actually one large organism because underneath the soil every Aspen tree's root system is interconnected with the root system of the entire grove. This is what makes Aspen groves such a strong forest entity. I remember thinking, "Wow! That's a beautiful picture of what we are doing in stewarding dreams, because that is what it looks like to help people be so interconnected and so tight with each other that they give strength and resource to the new root system in their lives. That's how they create new things as they follow the dreams of God and grow up into oaks of righteousness."

Ken had seen this idea of co-working spaces in London, so he borrowed their economic model of "collaborative consumption": the idea that people could collaborate together by sharing resources so each wouldn't have to buy their own things, but instead could own them in common. This was the same "sharing economy" concept that has given us things like Netflix and Zip Car.

Ken remembered when he bought his first cell phone, he bought a plan based on how he wanted to use the phone. If you owned a phone, you bought a plan priced according to how you would use it. So, they built their "rental" packages like a cell phone plan or a gym membership, where people could pay a small amount of money and choose how they wanted to dip in and out of their emerging community of entrepreneurs.

ENTERING THE DOMAINS OF LIFE

In 1981, I remember sitting on that pile of unfriendly lava rocks in Kona, Hawaii, not just mulling over past mistakes, but also Loren Cunningham's "seven domains of society"—what in some circles have come to be known as the "seven mountains of culture." (It is interesting that the Church in China and in other Asian nations have also adopted this language.) These seven domains were identified as 1) family, 2) education, 3) media, 4) arts & entertainment, 5) government, 6) business/commerce, and 7) religion.[*]

---

[*] Note: Each of these domains are cultural influencers or "foundation stones." As such, each influences what is "normal" in a society, from moral and legal issues to beliefs to justice to how we interact with one other. Thus, the domain of religion is not about the Church or houses of faith as much as how they influence the spiritual and moral thinking of their society.

Over the centuries Christians have lost our influence in most all these domains of life, including religion, because the institutional Church organization has so often isolated itself from many of the other arenas of society. What's said in the pulpit doesn't carry the weight in the community it did when I was a boy. The secular/sacred and clergy/laity splits have further made us think that what we discuss on Sunday should only influence our spiritual existences and not how that spirituality affects the other six days of our weeks. We've forgotten our call to be salt and light and that the Kingdom of God should have impact beyond converting people to our beliefs. The local church as an organization can't really do much to changes this, but the church broken down into smaller "collectives" focused on influencing where the individuals in them work and live can.

Much of the rebuilding of Nehemiah's wall in Nehemiah 3 was done by appointing *"watches of the inhabitants of Jerusalem, everyone in his watch, and* everyone to be over against his house" (Nehemiah 7:3 KJV, emphasis added). A protective wall wasn't the only goal of the rebuilding, it was also rebuilding the people and households themselves as the order in Nehemiah 1:3 shows: *"Those who survived the exile and are back in the province are in great trouble and disgrace. The wall of Jerusalem is broken down, and its gates have been burned with fire."* People before structures: check!

In the figure below, I've created a diagram that shows the family household (which could also be a missional community) as the center of the Kingdom paradigm in each domain (slice) of life.

The practice of "building against our own homes" as was done in Jerusalem under Nehemiah (where people worked where they lived and lived where they worked) holds true for the individual family as well as the Church: the "Family of families (missional communities)" and "Household of faith." Until the exiles built the wall of God's promises around their own homes and missions, the enemy would still be able to penetrate the city of God. Nehemiah's summary statement then applies for building our "families" and individual households today as the first wall of defense: *"So built we the wall; and all the wall was joined together unto the half thereof: for the people had a mind to work"* (Nehemiah 4:6 KJV).

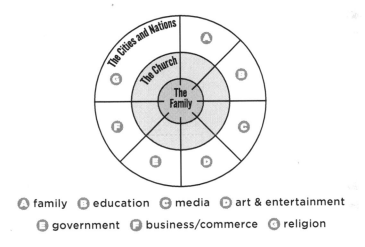

Ⓐ family Ⓑ education Ⓒ media Ⓓ art & entertainment
Ⓔ government Ⓕ business/commerce Ⓖ religion

We should be *"joined together"* with *"a mind to work"* in "place" in our cities until we are linked heart to heart and house to house with other believers to secure the circumference of our city walls and restore the "gates of authority." The "families" of God, and then the Church, are the first concerns of God's transforming power.

In order to understand this, perhaps it would be good to look at this in terms of what happened at Believers and Navah. Pulpit to pew interaction alone did not supply either enough time or relationship to either the church members, their families, or their communities. Values within the church looked about the same as those without, even if the way they talked about them did differ somewhat. Only when the churches were broken into smaller groups as well—into families, collectives, missional communities, etc.—that could then be infused with sound biblical dialogue, did things start to change within the churches, and then begin to influence those church members touched in the worlds where they worked and socialized. Strong "walls" in these groups eventually connected to form strong "walls" for the church, which created safe havens—true "sanctuaries"—for people to grow and from which to reach out to affect their communities. These stronger individuals within these stronger "families," then, in turn, bring the result of that transformation to their respective workplaces, community centers, and cities.

We are summoned as ambassadors of this Kingdom to emulate Abraham, the father of faith, who, *"was looking forward to the city with foundations* [the Church], *whose architect and builder is God"* (Hebrews 11:10). Isn't that what God wants to do in our day—laying the foundations of the Church as its Architect and Builder according to His very own blueprint?

In their seminal book, *The Drama of Scriptures*, Craig Bartholomew and Michael Goheen beautifully summarize this engagement of the Church in all of culture: "Through Genesis 1 the repetition of the word 'good' is a reminder that the whole creation comes from God and that in its initial state it beautifully reflects his own design and plan for it."[44]

> God himself is revealed or "imaged" in His creation
> precisely *as* we are busy within the Creation, developing
> its hidden potentials in agriculture, art, music, commerce,
> politics, scholarship, family life, church, leisure, and so on,

in ways that honor God. As we take God's creative commands of "let there be . . ." and develop the potentials in them, we continue to spread the fragrance of His presence throughout the world He has made.[45]

It was always what the Church was on the earth to do, *"Be fruitful and increase in number; fill the earth and subdue it. Rule over* [created things]*"* (Genesis 1:28).

Church and city transformation then is merely a furtherance of Creation's intent, and a precursor and shadow of the great City of God that we will someday enjoy with Him. When God's people rebuild a unified spiritual environment around their own homes, they become purveyors of blessing to the domains of life and the city they have been assigned to by God.

DEMONSTRATING THE KINGDOM

The Spirit empowers the local church to demonstrate the supremacy of Kingdom authority in all of the domains listed above. The Church of each city was being summoned to demonstrate the Gospel in all walks of life. Ed Silvoso, in his book, *Anointed for Business*, points out,

> Jesus's parables show that He was thoroughly familiar with the marketplace and its operation. His allegorical stories dealt with
>
> » Construction (see Matthew 7:24-27),
>
> » Wine making (see Luke 5:37-38),
>
> » Farming (Mark 4:2-20),
>
> » Treasure hunting (Matthew 13:44),

- » Ranching (Matthew 18:12-14),

- » Management and labor (Matthew 20:1-16),

- » Family-run businesses (Matthew 21:28-31),

- » Hostile takeovers (Luke 20:9-19),

- » Return on investments (see Matthew 25:14-30),

- » Futures markets (see Luke 12:16-21),

- » Crop yield (Mark 13:27-32),

- » Management criteria (Luke 12:35-48),

- » Research (Luke 14:24-35),

- » Bankruptcy (Luke 15:11-16),

- » Leverage (Luke 16:1-13) and

- » Venture capital (Luke 19:11-27).[46]

These are all subjects that ironically—and tragically, I would say—are not taught in most seminaries today!

Likewise, when Paul preached the Gospel, it became the basis of the faith for all those that had become disciples and their spheres of influence (both vocational elders in the church and those ministers out in business, nonprofits, and government as well as home with kids!). He preached the *kerygma*—"the proclamation"—and then passed on the *didache*—"the teaching"—from Christ. These were not mere words or a treatise on systematic theology, but were given by Jesus to the apostles and prophets to be lived out in a demonstration of the Spirit's Kingdom power by *every* believer.

When we connect the *"all"* and *"anyone"* in Acts 2:44-45 to the *"all the people"* in verse 47, it becomes evident that the *ekklesia* in Jerusalem was, by simply being the Church, affecting systemic poverty, not only among its members, but in the city as well. This new social order resulted in the Lord adding *"to their numbers daily.*" A summary of this demonstration of this new society later in Acts 4:34 was that, *"there were no needy [poor] persons among them. For from time to time, those who owned land or houses sold them, brought the money of the sales and put it at the apostles' feet, and it was distributed to anyone who had need"* (Acts 4:34-35).

What were some of the other mechanisms then for living out and injecting the Gospel of Jesus Christ into their society? What was the early church bringing to the culture that the culture could not provide for itself? How was the reconstruction of their "new life in Christ" beginning to result in the early signs of transformation in the city?

Despite our love for and commitment to social change, transformation will never be fully realized in our cities by merely serving the social needs themselves (protocol #3); it will ultimately take place when the Church's primary passion is to reveal the image of Christ in all of life (protocol #1) by making disciples and forming them into reproducing families that carry the Kingdom Gospel from their hearts to their spheres of life (protocol #2). As the Great Commission to *"make disciples . . . teaching them to observe everything I've commanded you"* (Matthew 28:19-20) becomes a main focus of the Family of God, the Great Commandment will *not* become a matter of isolated acts of benevolence, but the great demonstration of our "loving the Lord our God with all of our hearts" (see Matthew 22:37) which results in His image manifesting in us.

A TRANSFORMATIONAL STRATEGY

As the Grove was being birthed, they began to realize that there were key things that were important for them. The first thing it had to do was providing people with access to the resources they needed to birth their dream and realize their ideas. So the shared space would provide all the amenities people needed in order to launch a business or project—everything from staplers and whiteboards to workstations and conference rooms.

The second thing that they needed was to provide people with credible mentors and coaches. Sometimes that could be their own peers, but they also mobilized "stakeholders" from the city to invest their knowledge and understanding as coaches and mentors.

The third thing The Grove needed was ongoing education. At the end of the day, people needed to keep learning in order to keep moving forward. So the team created workshops, learning projects, and provided tools and training that people could easily pick up such as, "How do I optimize being found by search engines?" Or "What are the nuts and bolts of setting up a website?"

The fourth thing needed was to access seed capital. Ken felt they were called to steward, but not to own, dreams. The Grove made a policy that they would never take ownership or shares of any businesses started there—staff input would always be a free gift of facilitation. At the Grove, they would do two simple things. First, they would create an atmosphere where investors could come to see what was being created inside The Grove. They would ask those investors to operate within The Grove under a code of ethics where they agreed to observe the community values and ethos. Secondly, they'd ask potential investors to make at least a $25,000 investment in a project or an individual within a one-year period from when they were given access to The Grove. This ensured that people weren't coming to The Grove with no intention to ever invest, but instead to see what kind of ideas that they might want to act on and engage in. It was somewhat like the *Field of Dreams*. Ken had no idea that "if he built it, they would come," but the reality was if you created a space like The Grove, it would attract not only the dreamers, but also the resources to see their dreams manifest.

The fifth thing that every group had was an "accelerator" who worked to help each enterprise build a system that would assist in graduating it to the next level. This individual would be someone who could facilitate an idea, validate a business plan, make sure a given pipeline was developed, or give advice on acquiring resources and investment capital per the business's needs. The "accelerator" inside The Grove needed to be able to take people from business plan validation all the way up to funding their concept. That kept people from getting stuck. That helped the Grove team ensure that people made the necessary adjustments early in their development before they got too far down the road, realized they were off course, and would be tempted to abort their dream.

All of these things would operate inside a space where they had community animated by members who watched over the space, provided spiritual hospitality, including the conversations, coaching, and mentoring that everyone needed to stay encouraged and move forward.

THE MAYOR GIVES THE GO-AHEAD

After working through these various steps and submitting his proposal to all of the right officials, the mayor's office finally said, "We are ready to start this program. We have a storefront, and you can move in there." And so they did in September of 2010. The first Grove was not a big space—around 1,200 square feet—but had room to expand around it (by 2016, the Grove's shared offices had grown to 12,000 square feet).[47]

Ken remembers the day the doors opened. Standing across the street, it was like the first time he held one of his children in his arms. "So, that's what you look like," he wondered to himself.

It wasn't long before they began to sign up members, and locals began coming in and working as the first Grove community.

When The Grove finally launched, Ken and his team were firmly positioned to speak into the marketplace of New Haven, Connecticut: "'Firmly ensconced to speak into the marketplace' is a beautiful description of God's goal for us as 'benefactors to the culture,'" Ken told me.

So how are you becoming "firmly ensconced" in your world? As Ken shared about the five "accelerators" at the Grove, I couldn't help but wonder what wisdom he would impart in how to reach the domains we've each been placed in. Just as Daniel had a dream that no human wisdom could decipher, I pray the Spirit will give you similar wisdom for the impossible situations in your world.

NOW WHAT?

Question: Look at the chart on the "domains" on page p. 284 and discuss the following:

Do you or other "marketplace ministers" in your church family feel that they are adequately encouraged and equipped to carry the Gospel into your domain?

How might your church services, programs, vision, and direction change to redefine and equip these gifted people as the "Church in society"? The *politeia*?

A PERSON OF PEACE

Whatever house you enter, first say, "Peace be to this house!"
And if a son of peace is there, your peace will rest upon him.
But if not, it will return to you.

—LUKE 10:5-6 **ESV**

A t first, they didn't have much furniture at the Grove. In fact, most of their original desks were doors Yale University was throwing out that they used as tabletops and built into cubicles. Most of the chairs and other things they found discarded along the roadside. Despite some good finds, the space was still sparse and had the feel of someone's first college apartment.

One morning Ken walked out of the building, praying, "You know, Lord, you got us this far, but we don't have enough furniture. I don't know what you want to do." As he got to the corner still praying, the Lord said, "I want you to turn left here." After turning left, he walked a little bit further and the next thing he knew he was standing in front of what looked like a deserted building. Its sign read, "Acme Furniture." He was perplexed, so he pushed on the door, found it open, and went in to see an ocean of old furniture, recycled, reused, and stacked from the floor to ceiling.

He got halfway in and heard a rustling. He looked over to see a man sitting at a desk, staring at the ceiling.

Ken went over to him, introduced himself, and asked him about his business. The man said, "Well, my father started this business—you know, we just have a lot of furniture."

Ken laughed and said, "Well, it so happens that I need a lot of furniture. I'm opening a business not too far from here, just around the corner, but I don't have any money at the moment."

The man looked at him squarely as if considering something. Then he replied, "Take a look around and see what you need—and don't worry about the money, just pick out what you want and take anything."

Ken was shocked, "Wait a minute, what do you mean 'take anything'?"

The man shrugged, "If your business is successful and you make it, someday just remember me."

All Ken could say in response was, "Okay."

And like that The Grove had furniture.

Several weeks later, Ken went back and gave him a check.

After that, he ended up visiting this fine fellow every few months to have a cup of coffee and talk. Ken refers to him as a "son of peace," like the ones Jesus told His disciples to look for in Luke 10:6.

"He turned out to be another piece of the puzzle," Ken told me. "The mayor was like that too. I think God is constantly placing key men or women of peace in our pathways who can open a door and accelerate something for you. We need acceleration because many dreams die in the birthing canal. They take so long to get born and people get discouraged. Unfortunately, many people aren't aware enough or have a mindset that keeps them from noticing these people of peace, and they miss their breakthrough."

GOD DOESN'T ALWAYS SEND ANSWERS; HE OFTEN SENDS A PERSON

The mayor and this furniture guy weren't the only people Ken met who became "people of peace" for he and The Grove. From the day he and his family moved in, it had been grandmothers, the *pro bono* city planner, photographers, and neighbors that carried the dreams that became the gateways of peace into the Janke's neighborhood. They were placed there by God to accelerate His plan for the community and each individual's dream. The Father opened the doors through these "persons of peace" who knew more locally and contextually than Ken and his crew did. God always opens up "highways of favor" in the land He has called us to navigate, but we too often fail to look for or recognize them.

For years, I've trained pioneer church planters to look for these "persons of peace" when entering a new city. In Mindy's and my church-plant with hippies in Grants Pass, Oregon, the Lord brought "natives," Chris and Phil Hyatt to us as "a couple of peace." Without their opening the doors to twelve beleaguered and hungry hearts, our work at The Barn Church would have either not happened, or at least, not moved forward with such evident blessing.

When my friend Paul and I arrived at the airport in Sofia, Bulgaria, we observed an individual jumping up and down, nearly hyperventilating, behind the glass window with my name on a white sign. He had met me years earlier in Frankfurt, Germany (I don't remember the encounter at all) and dreamt of me the night before; he was told to rush to the airport in the dream to intercept me. Talk about a Godsend! My animated Bulgarian friend opened doors to Sophia and national church leaders and led us on a prayer journey in the city-center that resulted in the communist headquarters being burned to the ground and the founder of communism in Bulgaria's body being unceremoniously stolen from his mausoleum—all in forty-eight hours! False idols that stand in the way of propagating the Gospel don't do well when God activates His people. He was a true man of peace!

Jesus taught this "man of peace" principle to His disciples.

> After this the Lord appointed seventy-two others and sent them two by two ahead of him to every town and place where he was about to go. He told them, "The harvest is plentiful, but the workers are few. Ask the Lord of the harvest, therefore, to send out workers into his harvest field. Go! I am sending you out like lambs among wolves. Do not take a purse or bag or sandals; and do not greet anyone on the road.
>
> **"When you enter a house, first say, 'Peace to this house.' If someone who promotes peace is there, your peace will rest on them;** *if not, it will return to you. Stay there, eating and drinking whatever they give you, for the worker deserves his wages. Do not move around from house to house."*
> —LUKE 10:1-7 (emphasis added)

It is fascinating to see what operating through a person of peace accomplishes. First, a person of peace is a setup by Jesus, a plant in any city where *"he was about to go"* (vs. 1). Second, His disciples ensured that the way would be paved by the Lord Himself by responding to His command to go into "the harvest." Third, He sends them without defense, helpless as lambs, into the wolves' den—a norm for Kingdom emissaries. (I have a sermon on this subject I like to call, "Little White Fuzzballs in the Land of Fangs." It always helps to address such things with a sense of humor.) Fourth, the disciples were to pronounce the peace of the Kingdom upon those who received them with open arms. It was at this point that coming in the Spirit of peace would unveil the person of like spirit as a "son [or daughter] of peace."

What ensues after these four steps is very straight-forward: *"Heal the sick that are there and tell them, 'The Kingdom of God has come near to you'"* (Luke 10:9). The effects of working through the people the Lord has already established in your workplace, in your neighborhood, and in your city is key to the proclamation and demonstration of the Gospel of the Kingdom.

The New Testament has many examples of "persons of peace" being in place for the entry of God's ministers into a new location or new assignment. Paul, blind and uncertain about his new standing with Jesus after being zapped on the road to Damascus, is visited by Ananias, who prayed for his blindness and gave him his first glimpse of the ministry Jesus had designed for him. (See Acts 9:10-18.) Later, as the Church was in fear and uncertain about the reliability of this legendary "murderous" persecutor, Barnabas came alongside Paul, introduced him to the apostles and advocated the legitimacy of his conversion. (See Acts 9:27.) Likewise, when Paul, Silas, Timothy, and Luke came to Philippi on his second missionary journey, it was Lydia, *"a dealer in purple cloth"* (Acts 16:14) who was the "woman of peace," took them into her home, saw her family converted and later received the team again after their brief foray in a Roman prison. (See Acts 16:14-15; 40.)

In many cities Paul visited there were locals there who hosted him and opened the doors of the community for the furtherance of the Gospel. Leaning into this principle also assures us of God's ability to arrange His plans on our behalf, and therefore keep us from trying to pull off our missions in ignorance of local customs or roadblocks—without the help of these divinely placed "mystery" people. Much damage has been done because we thought we were supposed to do this kind of stuff on our own, but that's just not the way God likes to work.

MIXING BUSINESS WITH BLESSING

Every church and ministry leadership team will benefit by a biblically informed discussion on the role of our churches in society. That would help us identify what the sacred-secular mindset has done to our effectiveness in our communities and to what degree our people have been seduced to believe that their neighborhoods and workplaces are not sacred spaces destined for the blessing of King Jesus.

We saw in our discussion of the sacred/secular dilemma in the Church in the first section of this book that God has sanctified the life/work/home balance of all believers. We observed that wherever God has His people, He is committed to display His "workmanship" in them, created to fulfill their destiny in every aspect of their lives.

When we speak of the "marketplace," we aren't simply referring to the business community. We are speaking of the primary domain that humans traffic in to do life: the marketplace of ideas, services, and solutions. Most of God's people know the domain they live and work in—they are good at what they do and whether they realize it or not, it is at least part of the assignment for their mission on earth that God has given them. Then these hugely competent, clever people go to church, and they feel a massive disconnect. Many of them are leaders in their domains outside the church building, but they feel helpless and unprepared to bring the influence of the Kingdom into their workplace. That's probably because the Church is still too focused on the point-of-sale conversions they so often mistake for raising up a transformative people of God—rather than fully engaging hearts and minds that is the making of disciples. Most successful people who work "outside of the church" know something of recruiting people and organizing them to be successful, but we allow them to believe those skills have little to do with "ministry." But dream weaving for our communities requires people who understand how to do develop resources as much as how to pray and hear from heaven. We should be working to put all of our talents together—that's why we are called the "Body" of Christ, not the "index finger" of Christ—and why no one gets excited about their liver until it's not functioning. We need all the different parts of the body to thrive.

Most if not all in our church pews, despite feeling misunderstood or unappreciated by their church leaders, are ripe candidates for training and deployment into Kingdom enterprises in their workplace and communities—not to convert necessarily, but to exemplify and recruit. Discipleship looks a lot like making friends—*because it is*. The sermon on Sunday is great, but it often has minimal effect on how we train up Kingdom ambassadors to affect change throughout their weeks. I often ask people if they have ever been commissioned and anointed as "ministers of the Kingdom" in their neighborhoods or workplaces. The most common response is the ole "deer in the headlights" stare.

I remember asking one church congregation how many of them were *missionaries* (I could sense that "buzz word" rattling around their heads) and three people out of 600 raised their hands. By the end of the service, however, most of them came forward to have their elders commission them into Kingdom service in their workplaces and neighborhoods.

Missionaries are merely "envoys" or "sent ones." Words like "the ministry" and "missionary" have been so reduced that it has left many of God's people outside the high calling of being trained and released by their leaders to serve in the "field"—whether at work or in the home—they are already assigned to.

345

Paul the apostle was a businessman—a tent-maker/tanner—who understood the importance of the role of business as a partner in Kingdom endeavors. Abraham Mahlerbe beautifully describes Paul's marriage of his business and missionizing endeavors in Thessalonica. He suggests that the household provided the primary context for Paul's evangelization in Thessalonica, raising the question: "In what way would such a household have been appropriate both as a workshop and a setting for preaching and teaching?"

> The residence in view was most probably an "insula," a type of apartment house that served the vast majority of people in the large cities of the Roman Empire. Insula's contained shops on the ground floor with space for manufacturing of goods sold in the shops and living accommodations for owners, families, visitors, employees, and servants on the top floors. Such households were part of an intricate social network, being linked to other households by ties of kinship, friendship, professional advantage, and so on. Paul's strategy of initiating his tent-making work in such households was a sound one, because the household provided him with a relatively secluded setting for his business and a ready-made audience (to lay foundations in the Church) as well as a network along which his influence could spread.[48]

This should inspire each believer to seek the Lord for culturally relevant strategies in their workday for blending their business and missionizing endeavors—for gathering and discipling hungry hearts. We should be asking, "What in our culture lends itself to an integration of Kingdom business and redeemed community? How do we speak and live the Gospel at work and serve the Lord in our life assignments?"

As we become salt and light and our co-workers respond to our acts of kindness and our attractive lives, what do we so often do with them? Bring them to a Sunday service? Maybe, but is that the optimal strategy? Let's say I develop a personal relationship with Jill and invite her to a church service. She then finds herself in "my world," sitting in rows with strangers, introduced to a very unfamiliar religious culture, singing songs she doesn't know and shuffling a basket along with money in it (*Should I put something in that thing?* she wonders). Surrounded by strange new words that have never been introduced into her vocabulary, she glances to her left to see some guy over there with his hands raised, eyes closed, and beatific smile on his face—*weird*.

We have been trying for some decades to get people into our "culture," while Jesus whole *modus operandi* was to enter theirs. The first century church met their neighbors at the temple, in the marketplace, and in the neighborhood—they went *to* them. Only then did they take them, not to an impersonal religious meeting, but to their homes. There, they were received and treated like royalty, witnessed people living out of the words and teachings of this Jesus life-on-life, then actually conversing with Him as though He were in the room—and of course, they were surrounded by an abundance of yummy food. It feels like family.

Those of you already in the marketplace every day are in your assigned place from God. Embrace it fully! See it as your calling and your "ministry," reject "sacred/secularitis" and invite the Lord to give you His perspective of the work and the precious people He has assigned as your "sheep."

I often find myself encouraging my business friends to see themselves as the Church in action, the people of God with a Kingdom mandate in the marketplace. They speak readily about doing the work of the Kingdom in the "marketplace," yet seem to be standing back and pointing at their church as "that religious place over there where I attend once or twice a week." I have frequently heard them refer to the word "Kingdom" to define the endeavors they are engaged in for the Lord in their patch of the marketplace, but rarely if ever as them being "the Church."

With so much verbiage around the word "Kingdom" these days, it is critical to discern the difference between Church-centrism and Kingdom-centrism. The error many make is to separate the two. Many are using the word "Kingdom," but do not include the "Kingdom works" of those in the pews as an extension and calling of their church. Some folks, in essence, don't fully identity themselves as *the* Church, under God's mandates for the Church's function, as they carry out what they call "Kingdom" endeavors. You cannot separate the Church from the Kingdom—it is, though, a matter of order, as we are told in Matthew 6:33: *"Seek first His Kingdom."* The King speaks, the subjects respond, and light displaces darkness.

To have the mark of God's Kingdom, a human life, a church community, or an assignment has to manifest three things:

> First, Jesus has to be sole owner and ruler of that life and that enterprise. All previous ownership has to be relinquished, all decision-making placed into His hands and all credit for success must result in praise to Him and none other. (He has to be made the Chief Shepherd and Chairman of the Board.) What makes a "thing" a "Kingdom thing" is that its origins come from the mouth of the God-King.

> Second, that a life or an endeavor will be committed to extending the presence of Jesus into any realm, industry, people group, or any "territory" where He was heretofore excluded by His created ones. He is here to claim what

is now rightfully His as the King who paid the price to have His whole earth returned to Him—*"This gospel of the Kingdom will be preached in the whole world as a testimony to all nations"* (Matthew 24:14).

Third, those that have accepted His sacrifice for them have been invited to return His earth to Him as His Kingdom emissaries—heaven's ambassadors on earth—what we call the Church. The subjects of the Kingdom, in essence, are the disciples of Jesus, the ones that have been invited to "come," to "follow," and to "be made into His image." These disciples are formed as a family, shaped by the Word and the Spirit until they begin to be fruitful and multiply themselves into every sphere of society. These Kingdom ambassadors "can do nothing" unless they hear it from the Spirit.

Works of the Kingdom, then, are those that originated in the mind of the King and extend into an area or domain that He Himself is leading His people into. Those same people are helpless to move as individuals, but are formed into a family by the Gospel proclamation *kerygma*, and the apostolic teaching *didache*, which leads them to be like Him and follow His leadership—together! (We will see shortly how discipleship is a key component of any "Kingdom enterprise.") To call something "Kingdom" and *not* include the directives of the Spirit, the people of God (the Church), the making and establishing of disciples, and leaders who carry the "genetic of Jesus" into society's unredeemed arenas will fall short of the Father's original plan and intention.

Another word that has come into common usage is that word *apostolic*. To call something "apostolic" is usually to describe the work of leaders with a big vision and pocket book that falls short of the plum line for biblical apostleship—as does its description of a leader who establishes a large church or missionary organization. Any work that is truly "apostolic" will be aligned with the blueprint Jesus established for all "church work" (note: all "Kingdom work" is "the Church at work," though not all "church work" as we know it today is in line with the Kingdom framework or mindset.) The apostles of the first century were commissioned to get revelation from the ascended Christ, to lay foundations that make and establish disciples and "equipper/leaders" to take the Gospel of the Kingdom into every aspect of life on earth. Two additional key aspects of the apostolic ministry as we see it in the Scripture are:

a) they are made "spectacles for Christ" through suffering and carrying *"in our body the death of Jesus, so that the life of Jesus may also be revealed"* (2 Corinthians 4:10), and

b) they also became fathers in the Church replete with sons and daughters—fathers like Paul, who identified his sons and daughters, trained them, deployed them, and turned over the enterprise to them as he was coming to the end of his life.

They got no "jollies" for doing big "stuff" for God, but reaped their reward by creating a family legacy that passed on the image and message of Christ to future generations.

Christian business and professional leaders are in need of a conversion to the Church as the Family of God, of being healed of their "church wounds," forgiven, and then taught to operate out of a family paradigm in their Kingdom callings. "Going to church" pales in the light of learning to "be the Church" and forming the community of faith in the context of the marketplace, home, and surrounding society.

On the other hand, and in the same way, church leaders are in need of a conversion to the marketplace—of moving away from "building my church" to "equipping *the* Church" to be the Family of God on *His* mission out in the community around them. It would behoove us as church leaders to swiftly remove the "I-need-your-money-for-our-building-program" bull's-eye from off the pocketbooks of the wealthy business leaders in our midst. They are not targets of the Church's "agenda," but rather arrows themselves to be launched as worshipful and dangerous sons and daughters against mammon's minions—a much higher calling than we have assigned to them up until now.

ORIGINAL INTENTIONS

As The Grove was established and began to grow, Ken continued to prayer walk and ask the Lord about the redemptive purpose of New Haven. In his prayer wanderings, Ken had taken up the habit of going to East Rock, which is the highest point in the city. Here he could look over all of New Haven and pray. As he did, he grappled to understand the city's redemptive purposes within the context of its many needy communities. His heart yearned to know more about what his contribution could be in the light of God's historical plan for the city.

It was time to do some research.

NOW WHAT?

Question #1: Have you ever utilized Luke 10:1-7 as a framework for entering a new field of life or ministry? Do you primarily work through church contacts or are you open to seeking the Lord for a "person of peace" to be the source of a "door opening" ministry? Give it a shot!

Question #2: What is a "missionary?" Does the modern-day usage of the word reflect the biblical definition? (Some even think of missionaries as apostles. How does and doesn't that description fit?)

Question #3: What is a "Kingdom" work or ministry focus?

> **Exercise:** Ken offers some "marks" that define a Kingdom endeavor. Discuss his three points on page 301 and see if you agree. If not, what would you add or subtract? This will help clarify the difference between a Church-centric mindset and a Kingdom-centric mindset.

DISCOVERING THE REDEMPTIVE ROOTS OF OUR CITIES

*Now if it pleases the king, let a search be made in the
royal archives of Babylon to see if King Cyrus did in fact issue
a decree to rebuild this house of God in Jerusalem.*

—EZRA 5:17

Ken hit the local museums, historical societies, and libraries, looking for whatever he could find on the original roots of New Haven. One of the first things he discovered was that the city had many nicknames, one of them being "first city" because it was a city of many "firsts." For one, it was the first planned city in America. There was also a time in New Haven's early history when it was known as a "seedbed of innovation"—perhaps as we think of Silicon Valley and similar areas today. Many Inventions of the Industrial Revolution that became useful tools to the rest of the nation were birthed in New Haven.

The Lord gave Ken a picture of water-wells throughout the city becoming stopped up. Ken recognized these as "wells of innovation" and was deeply impressed that it was part of his work and The Grove's to unstop these wells and reinvigorate this city of firsts. Ken started asking the Lord, "How can I be a part of seeing this innovation reborn?"

The Grove staff started being even more intentional about this becoming a space where innovation could flourish, where ideas could be accelerated, where dreams could be realized to bring about solutions to systemic problems in the city. In the light of these musings, and much to his surprise, an article on their work appeared in their local newspaper not long after this. The first line read, "A river of innovation now flows in the streets of New Haven and it all begins at the door of The Grove."

SEEING OUR CITY THROUGH GOD'S EYES

When people ask Ken how they could get something like The Grove started in their own city, his reply is always, "First, you've got to know your city." We may live in our cities, but do we *know* them? Why should we care? Because we are called on this earth to *"seek the welfare of the city"*—each one of us! It is your geographical assignment from God. Your attitude and commitment toward the city effects how you order your life and contribute to the Church's love and desire to implement God's strategy for it.

What are the spiritual origins of your city? What were the earliest prayers and covenants made on the land? Who and what kind of people sowed the DNA of the Gospel in your city? (They are your spiritual predecessors after all.) To what degree has their legacy been faithfully carried on? How do we recover the spiritual roots of our own cities?

A phrase popped into my mind when I was doing "redemptive research" in Sacramento, California: *The strongholds in the city lie in the shadow of a broken covenant.* The common approach in the '90s to researching our cities was termed, "Spiritual Mapping." Unintended by the authors of that approach, the research often degenerated into mapping what the enemy was doing in the city and what strongholds had been established through ancient or modern-day sins. This would be followed by intense "warfare prayer" by certain leaders and intercessors to "tear down strongholds" and evict powers and principalities in the city.

That got me thinking about ways we could focus our research on what God was doing rather than the enemy, when it hit me: *You can't have a stronghold if someone didn't break a covenant.* The enemy has no power unless someone gives him jurisdiction in that area. So who broke the covenant? And what were the covenants anyway? How did the church in the city come under these strongholds and why did they allow them? *"Ah,"* says I, *perhaps they need to know what the promises and prayers of the earliest inhabitants on the land were first. Perhaps the redemptive story will attract "redemption-focused" people of the city to embrace the city's sickened state together, reclaim the dusty promises of old, and stand in agreement for the restoration of God's original intent for their city.* This is what Ken did so beautifully in New Haven.

Back when I was in California, I learned that as Sacramento City was reeling from the effects of the Gold Rush that turned it from a small settlement into a city nearly overnight, God was laying foundations. Four friends, all pastors, had arrived just before the Gold Rush by divine assignment and began praying for the city. As the rush was in full flow in the fall of 1849, a mining engineer named Dr. Grove Deal would stand at the bottom of the gangplanks of the steamships coming up the canal from San Francisco and ask one question of every miner: "God or gold?" If any happened to answer, "God," he would direct them to a small stand of trees on the banks of the Sacramento River that just happened to also be called "The Grove." There they would be received by these four pastors and a small circle of believers who were determined to make Sacramento City a "sacrament" to the Lord.

In twenty-five years, there was no record of dissent or disunity between these four leaders. They went on to establish city-wide prayer discouraging the use of denominational distinctives—they saw themselves as "the Church of Sacramento"—and were the epicenter of charity and encouragement during the repeated floods that ravaged the burgeoning mining town.

Years later, in the late 1990s, the full story of Sacramento's redemptive history was discovered and rehearsed in the ears of hundreds of believing residents who rejoiced, repented, reclaimed, and agreed to break the "claim-staking" spirit over the city by prayer and unity, inviting God's blessing back into the city. It was an amazing time.

While I was in Amsterdam, we discovered that a priest had established a church in this raucous port-side town 800 years before at the harbor front, a strategic location to preach the Gospel to sailors arriving to gratify their pleasures. We also discovered that the remains of this church were on the very block where the Salvation Army had established a beachhead in the "Red Light District" and was now occupied by yours truly and our band of merry YWAMers. Needless to say, we repented for losing ground, reclaimed that land, and God responded to our prayers by sending hundreds of Dutch Christians to stand and agree with us. It was a powerful show of unity that had the effect of "a rock thrown into a still lake" for years to come.

When meeting with the Navah group one time, I shared that one of the redemptive roots of Kansas City was "advocacy." The early French fur-traders advocated for the local native tribes as though they were their own families. A French settler named Madame Berenice Chouteau surrendered the beautiful lace of her wedding dress to function as shrouds for the Native-American babies that had died from the ravages of fever. Isaac McCoy was a Baptist pastor who led a campaign of other spiritual leaders to host over fifteen tribal people groups from the Northeast and across the Mississippi after the US government mandated their removal in 1815. McCoy and his "cohorts" in the Gospel set up a church at Shawnee Mission that saw an outbreak of the Holy Spirit among a congregation of local Native-American tribes, African Americans, and white settlers. The descriptions of these meetings are hair-raising. Isaac McCoy, Baptist missionary and a founding spiritual father of Kansas City, gives this report of those meetings at Shawnee Mission:

> On many occasions, the power of God was so strong in the meetings the Indians would begin shouting with joy, other times the translators and preachers had to stop because the power of God was so strong. The glory of those meetings spread to many of the Indians and many were saved.

McCoy's friend and co-conspirator, Methodist missionary, Nathan Scarritt, corroborates the power of those same meetings with high emotion:

> There seems to be something electrifying in the mutual effort of two souls [interpreter Charles Bluejacket and the preacher], thus struggling in holy, loving rivalry, to elevate the Cross of Christ before a wondering people. How often have I seen both preacher and interpreter so filled with the divine Spirit, and so overcome by the ecstasy of joy, that they would break off from their discourse, and in some way, give vent to their feelings. Sometimes they would greet each other with embraces, and with shouts of praise to God. Sometimes they would leave the pulpit and make their way through the congregation, scattering the

holy fire as they went, until almost the entire congregation would be on its feet "praising and glorifying God." [49]

The church in Kansas City went on to host the migration of freed slaves after the Emancipation Proclamation (though not without some rancor), emigrant workers, and pioneers streaming into Westport to be provisioned on their journeys to California gold, Santa Fe trade, or the good life along the Oregon Trail. Their benevolence and advocacy of the city's most downtrodden resulted in over twenty-two charitable organizations being established in KC funded by wealthy Christian business leaders and the formation of two universities to train students to "spread the Gospel and minister to the poor."

These and many other stories formed the spiritual legacy and redemptive wealth for the church in Kansas City to build upon. Together with the Navah leadership and various other churches in the area, we uncovered five redemptive roots in that city that had gone unnoticed by the people of God for over a century and a half. Armed with this spiritual knowledge, God's people started becoming "dangerous" again, visiting the key redemptive spots in the history of their city, repenting, reclaiming, and re-covenanting with God to take up the threads of the city's divine tapestry again to see His purposes restored. In 2006, they went on to hold a "Year of Prayer" where over 200 churches participated in casting a canopy of blessing over the city.

RE-COVENANTING WITH GOD

This journey of rediscovering God's promises by uncovering the hidden covenants and prayers of God's people is imperative for being able to know our cities, uncover its dreams, and re-reveal

God's intentions for the people there. If we are not seeing and actively reclaiming God's redemptive roots in the city, we are either living in disconnected isolation or falling prey to a Christianized version of the American dream for our own wealth and prosperity with little regard for those outside our immediate families.

The Church's mandate in a city is almost always based on these old, buried covenants God made with our forbearers in the faith for those places. Over the years, I've learned a few things that I hope will help you see your city with "redemptive eyes."

1. The "You can't change what you don't love!" Principle—Loving the places where we live and work entitles us to receive the authority needed to bring change. Without the "love of place," we'll be grumpy, critical, and ineffective—judging what we see with our eyes and unable to perceive what God sees with His.

2. The "Turn the Lights On!" Principle—Society has removed God from any interpretation of the past and the Church has often accepted these secular limitations along with their shortcomings. We tend to see our city through its sins and faults. We are either ignorant of the past or are misinformed about it—in either case we are not believing the truth. Darkness can't release the light of truth; that's what we Christians are here to do. When we see the truth and originally intended purposes of our city, we begin to see the city as God sees it, and He will always show up in the midst of truth. (To aid in this in Amsterdam, we renamed The Red Light District, "The Promised Land.") As Bob Waymire wrote in *Discovering Your City*:

    > Many pastors and spiritual leaders don't feel they need more information. Instead they should seek for the "light" [in city history]. If light can't convince

them—they will go astray. One of Satan's schemes is aimed at keeping the Body of Christ ignorant and deceived.[50]

3. **The "Thumbprint" Principle**—Because God was always the "first settler" in any geographical coordinate on His planet, He put his DNA in each city (even if there is no apparent "Christian" history).

   Through thorough research and "spiritual forensics," we can determine the origins of a city and what its genetic patterns and toxic tendencies are.

   We came to realize that the centuries of prostitution in Amsterdam were actually revealing the "thumbprint" of God in its DNA: hospitality, for example! "What?" you say, *"Hospitality?"* Yes, prostitution, is simply hospitality gone wrong, a redemptive gift that became obscured by the breaking of a covenant. If you follow that shadow back to its inception, you'll find a city that was founded for the purpose of providing hospitality and trade with people that visited the banks of the Amstel River.

4. **The "Title Deed" Principle**—*"The earth is the Lord's, and everything in it"* (Psalm 24:1). Just as Isaac re-dug his father's wells to unstop the flow of water to his inheritance (see Genesis 26), redemptive discovery helps reveal the things in a city that block the flow of the river of blessing that is the inheritance of the church in that city from her forbearers.

   Ezra found that the permission to build the temple was hidden in the archives of Babylon's secular power. (See Ezra 6-7.) In the same way, much of the city church's redemptive history is buried in the dusty archives of our city and county libraries.

5. **"The state of the 'temple' determines the state of the city" Principle**—*"Then he entered the temple courts and began driving out those who were selling. 'It is written,' he said to them, 'My house will be a house of prayer'; but you have made it 'a den of robbers'"* (Luke 19:45-47). The goal in any city is the return of God's glory to the "temple," the people of God. The blessing flows from God's people to the city, and from the city to the nations. The city church, then, is under a mandate to become the "temple of the Lord" there in order to carry and reveal *His* presence. As we become "the dwelling place of the Spirit," we will be able to affect our cities in a way that reveals Christ to its inhabitants—for good or bad. (See Ephesians 2:18-20.)

The purpose of this book is not to focus on the deep details of city transformation strategies, but to encourage each believer to consider their attitudes and mindsets concerning their city. I often hear believers speak ill of their community leaders. Some will advise you "don't move to that neighborhood, it is run down and dangerous." Some still haven't gotten the memo that they are geographically placed in their city or neighborhood saying, "I can't wait to get out of this place." Huh? This, isn't the American dream, this is "captivity"—a temporary assignment on earth meant to reveal the heart and purposes of the Lord to those around you.

I invite you to adjust your thinking and mindset (with God's help) to embrace the beauty of God's plan and intentions for the city He has placed you in (even though it is in "captivity"). Jeremiah had it right:

> Seek the peace and prosperity of the city to which I have carried you into exile. Pray to the Lord for it, because if it prospers, you too will prosper.
>
> —JEREMIAH 29:7

JOBS TURN AROUND

Within its first year, the Grove had been named "Small Business of the Year." In its second year, it was featured in *Fast Company* magazine. After just two or three years, the mayor and other city leaders were partnering with The Grove on a broader level. It didn't take long before people began to realize that using collaborative, collective, and social dreams to solve the city's issues could also be leveraged by the city for creating new jobs.

During the economic crisis in 2008, more and more people in New Haven were finding themselves unemployed. Whole sectors of the city that once employed many vanished—they simply didn't exist anymore. People would come to The Grove and say, "You know, I've been unemployed now for some time, but my unemployment is going to be running out soon. I don't know what I'm going to do. The type of job I used to do doesn't even exist anymore." To this, the team would simply say, "Just come work at The Grove, join us and we guarantee you within a week or two you'll have an innovative idea of something you can do or start." It was a true statement of faith that almost always turned out to be a true statement in the natural as well!

So The Grove began stimulating and reimagining employment and growth. People were starting businesses, and those businesses began to employ the citizens of the city as they grew. People in Connecticut began to see that The Grove was an economic engine for New Haven that was fueling an incredible economic turnaround. There were a lot of really amazing and good people doing a lot of good work in the city alongside the Grove community, including Yale University.

A MODEL TO THE STATE

At the time they started the Grove, Connecticut ranked somewhere around forty-third in the nation in entrepreneurial startups, due perhaps to its historical profile as a predominantly manufacturing state. However, state leaders really wanted to push new startups and entrepreneurism in their biggest cities. They began to discuss what it would look like to reproduce New Haven's entrepreneurial ecosystems in other key cities. What it came down to was creating more Grove-like entities which served as one aspect of an emerging entrepreneurial ecosystem.

The Grove never pretended to be the one and only source of all the integral ecosystems that were emerging. They knew what they were uniquely contributing—and helped others to bring that "secret sauce" to their "kitchens" as well. This openness had fed New Haven's ecosystem and received the attention of the governor. It wasn't long before they were giving him and other state officials tours of the facility. When the governor came, he said, "We need to create more of what New Haven has in other areas of the state." He even declared at a press conference, "We are going to invest state dollars to help launch entrepreneurial ecosystems like New Haven's in three other areas of the state."

So they chose to create a Grove spinoff in Storrs, which is where University of Connecticut is located; one in the state's capital, Hartford; and the other in Stamford, a bedroom community of New York City just outside of the I-95 corridor. They asked The Grove to be one of the contributors in launching these other three ecosystems in the state. The Grove soon became a key player in stimulating these three other regions.

As of today, the state of Connecticut has four internal ecosystems: New Haven, Storrs, Hartford, and Stamford. Although they did not put a Grove in each of those cities, centers for entrepreneurialism were established using many of the principles learned and developed at The Grove in New Haven. Ken was happy just to provide coaches, mentors, and helpers as a part of the governor's plan to launch this transformation throughout the state.

In the end, what was started to transform a neighborhood became a transformational tool for the whole city, and eventually, for the entire state. As Ken says when asked about how they did it: "You know that old saying about, 'How do you eat elephant?' One bite at a time."

Then he just smiles and laughs.

NOW WHAT?

Question #1: What is your speech and your attitude toward your workplace, neighborhood, or city? Would you say it leans redemptive or critical?

Question #2: How could you better reflect more "redemptive" attitudes and practices regarding your town or city? What has the Spirit shown you about the purposes of your city and do you love your city having seen it through God's eyes?

Question #3: How could you encourage your church family to erect a prayer canopy over their respective neighborhoods, workplaces, and city officials?

Question #4: How has "redemptive discovery" been initiated in your city?

A TRANSITION TO NEW TRANSFORMATION

For we are the temple of the living God.
As God has said:
"I will live with them
and walk among them,
and I will be their God,
and they will be my people."

—2 CORINTHIANS 6:16

While the Grove was growing, thriving, and fruitful, Ken got a call from a pastor friend in Dallas: "I am going to plant an urban church in downtown Dallas and I need help. Would you come back and help me?" It was one of those things where, in prayer, Ken felt the Father tell him, "This is a dream I want you to invest in stewarding." So he agreed and handed his responsibilities at The Grove over to his partner, packed up the family, and returned to Dallas.

It had been an exciting time in New Haven, and Ken had some regrets about leaving, but his time there was finished. The day the family was to leave New Haven, Ken went to East Rock again.

There, one last time, he thanked New Haven for opening her doors to him and for allowing him to invest his contribution in her. Ken reflected, "You know Father, when we came here almost eight years ago, we came saying we were going to plant a church. I'm sorry that I never got around to doing that."

The Lord's gentle correction came firmly to his mind: *"What do you mean you never planted the church?"*

It was that day, for the first time, Ken realized The Friary and The Grove actually *were the Church.* Oh, that we would be that innocent to what God is doing through us as we simply follow and obey.

A CHAPTER CLOSES, A NEW ONE OPENS

Ken looks back on his journey with the New Haven Grove with gratitude.[*] "The reason I tell the story of how The Grove got started so often is because there are so many great lessons from the journey—the biggest being to start with people's dreams. It's been great to reflect on it and not merely talk from a place of information, but a place of a 'life lived out.' I've had people try and steal The Grove business plan, and at times it looked like we wouldn't have the resources to carry on, but I've seen the power of God time and again, as well as the power of people working together. That was more than enough to make the venture worthwhile."

One of the beautiful lessons of Ken Janke's story is how one man affected the Family who in turn effected a community. That local community then partnered with the business community and finally the government wanted in on the deal—the state began

---

[*] In the years following this, Ken would plant another Grove in downtown Dallas, "But that," as the saying goes, "is another story."

championing similar initiatives to re-invigorate other urban areas throughout the region. Although many look to government to address their particular needs, government can really only help empower those "boots on the ground" willing to coordinate those closest to the problems. Ultimately, if the social fabric of a community is threadbare, no amount of political surface work is going to make lasting positive change. God hardwired us to connect to one another for a reason. Networked communities strengthen and protect neighborhoods and cities—and although government should help address emergencies, they aren't very effective at replacing the day-to-day work of "loving our neighbors."

Fair Haven crawled out of "disgrace" because it was being honored, loved, and supported in its dreams. The partnership between governmental leaders and agencies in Ken's story are stunning, but until there was a connector like Ken, such services working in their own silos would do little good.

Ken's story also reminds us that the continuity of the "Gospel of the Kingdom"—the revelation that His Kingdom is both eternal and superior to all other kingdoms—is still alive and well. Believers Church, Navah Church, and The Grove are each answers—each fulfilling their unique destiny—in addressing the prophetic promises of the Father to establish the Kingdom of His Son in the city through the Church.

One of the remarkable aspects of Ken's story is that he and The Friary influenced nearly every worldly domain we discussed earlier: family, education, media, art & entertainment, government, and business/commerce as well as religion. It makes me wonder what the impact would be on the churches in our cities if we committed ourselves to these transformational principles at a more collective level. Ken was one guy. What if we emulated his heart and values together? The possibilities blow the mind!

TRANSFORMATION BEGINS WITH US

There are numerous excellent books on city transformation. The focus of this discussion, however, is aimed at church transformation, helping the disciples of Jesus and their communities to become transformed in their own thinking and practice as a precursor to tackling justice and innovation their cities on God's behalf. However, much of the discussion these days has jumped to city transformation and has often minimalized the crying need for the city church herself to be transformed into the primary agent of reconciliation in each region. It's like trying to revive a patient without dealing with the fact that the heart's not beating. It isn't ultimately works of social justice that bring transformation to a city. What transforms a city is first and foremost the power of a community forged together in living out of the life-force of Christ and observing all that He commanded us to do.

The idea that we can transform our cities without first undergoing a transformation in the community of faith is just not tenable. *The Church, the way she is, cannot transform the city, in the way she dreams.*

The earth needs more Kingdom mischief at the hands of folks like Ken Janke, Adam Cox, Roger Nix, Gyle Smith, and those who walk with them. Anyone else up for joining in on the joy of such mischief?

PART FOUR:
AN INVITATION TO KINGDOM MISCHIEF

One day, when the kingdom of this world

becomes the kingdom of our Lord

(Revelation 11:15), the city will finally

be fully transformed. Since complete

transformation is not entirely possible

until that final day, we should remember that

city transformation is more like

the North Star than the North Pole—

a direction to pursue rather than a

destination we arrive at.

—ERIC SWANSON AND SAM WILLIAMS,
To Transform a City

EPILOGUE
PRAYING AND DREAMING . . . ANEW

*"You are the salt of the earth. But if the salt loses
its saltiness, how can it be made salty again?
It is no longer good for anything, except to be
thrown out and trampled by men.
"You are the light of the world. A town on a hill
cannot be hidden."*

—MATTHEW 5:13-14

As I sit here in my "rolling office" (my car) in Castle Rock, Colorado, aided by my mobile phone, Kindle, and laptop, I'm at one with the universe. As I survey my domain, as it were, I can't help thinking about all the doors that have opened by simply waiting for the Father to give me my next assignment. I'm helpless anymore to partake in anything that He doesn't serve up at my table. It's from my "office" that I Skype with friends in Europe, Asia, and across the US, set appointments in an array of coffee shops and eateries, while engaging in Googling and searching all manner of trivia related to my life and passions. But the one thing that dominates my attention? *My friends*—my "co-conspirators" in Kingdom mischief.

I think of Roger and Gyle and their faithful journey from deconstruction to reconstruction at Believer's Church. I get all warm and wiggly when I think of Adam and David, two green-horns in Kansas City, that have matured into purveyors of the Gospel's power and are now building and multiplying a vibrant Family of families. And of course, there is "I love you" Ken Janke. (He never ends a conversation with me that he doesn't say, "I love you.") His commitment to do the impossible as the Lord's servant is a constant source of inspiration to me. These are just some of my friends who I can't imagine doing life without. What would be the point? In working with and helping mthem, I've found meaning in what God is doing through them.

When the Lord spoke a simple phrase to me in Georgetown, Colorado, "Move down the hill and engage the Church," I had no idea I would find myself in the vibrant little Front Range town of Castle Rock smack in the middle of another of God's plans for my destiny. Today I'm still being detoxed of servitude to an organi- zation—or even sustaining a movement as beautiful as the Boiler Room Network and 24-7 Prayer—and am left overwhelmed by the privilege of a Kingdom calling alongside the network of ambas- sador/friends that are bringing reformation to the Church, the Family of God, and seeking to impact every domain of society in all that they do.

As I'm watching the increased momentum of reformation and transformation of the Church across the globe, the implications are massive: Cities and cultures are being revitalized through disciples in "all walks of life." I can see that all the lessons we've learned at Believers, Navah, and The Grove have led us to see a new vista laid out in front of us: the transformation of cities and nations.

I've spent numerous hours with my business friends dreaming about the release of the Spirit through the business community—the

Church in the marketplace. Man-devised strategies, however, from impatient, unbroken hearts, will result in lots of "Christian" activity with few disciples in their wake. Strategies, released by God to patient, broken, "lost everything" hearts, will witness the image of Jesus transferred to "faithful men and women" who are solely committed to "observe everything" that He says—things *"no eye has seen, what no ear has heard"* (1 Corinthians 2:9). Until we've lost everything, we will see nothing of lasting value. This is the blessed season I and my friends are now experiencing, idling our engines, careful to avoid the "Ishmael Syndrome" of trying to fulfill the promise of God in your own strength, and waiting for Father to say, *"Let there be...!"*

Meanwhile, I find myself invited into the world of "laying foundations" in church elders, pastoral staffs, and a gaggle of business leaders all intent on discovering the joy and pain of the journey into deconstruction, reconstruction, and transformation. From traditional churches and new church plants to global "marketplace" leaders, the template is still the same: *The seed of the Kingdom is friends, together, praying and dreaming, stumbling and growing.*

People constantly ask what I do, what I have achieved, and what are my *bona fides.* I guess I could give a long list of achievements that might look rather impressive to some. I'm not impressed, nor do I calculate any success by the things I've accomplished. Neither is my greatest treasure in my rather unique story, but in the wealth that resides in my spectacular family and friends that are serving Jesus around the world. I'd rather brag as Paul did,

> Are we beginning to commend ourselves again? Or do we need, like some people, letters of recommendation to you or from you? You yourselves are our letter, written on

our hearts, known and read by everyone. You show that you are a letter from Christ, the result of our ministry, written not with ink but with the Spirit of the living God, not on tablets of stone but on tablets of human hearts. Such confidence we have through Christ before God.

—2 CORINTHIANS 3:1-4

NO LONGER ALONE

I can't think of a better inheritance, a better treasure, than this. It drives me to wish this for the many leaders who long for the same, but may feel entrapped by the expectations and demands of a construct that leaves them isolated and lonely. It motivates me to invite leaders of all stripes to enter the reformative journey that runs through the cross—*deconstruction*.

Many of the mindsets that we've inherited from our church traditions are not our friends. They have caused us to be beholden to build churches at the expense of extending God's Kingdom, chasing "our" vision at the expense of building up "the ministers" to do the work of ministry and leaving us exhausted and discouraged because, in the end, we make such little impact for our King.

The six competing mindsets of the Church and the Kingdom we discussed in Part One must be addressed with our teams in God's presence if we are to see the Church align herself with the mind of Christ. At Believers Church, the deconstruction of these old ways of thinking was long and painful, yet increasingly fruitful. Getting the DNA to align with God's specs has taken nearly fifteen years now, but the multiplication of new "house groups" (missional communities) and the increase of influence in new neighborhoods is underway—in many ways it feels as if we have only just begun. But the *reconstruction* has had a strong start.

The Lord is encouraging His Church to shift from revival-mindedness to reformation-mindedness; out of longing for a visitation (making converts) to us partnering in making earth a place of habitation (making disciples). This is a relational journey—not buying into certain "models" of alteration or adaptation—but a journey that reconstructs us and brings us back into alignment with God's original design for His creation.

We saw through Adam, David, and their crew's journey at Navah Church that there is no greater power for salvation and reformation than the Gospel and the ensuing righteousness that produces our Gospel Identity. The righteousness available through the Gospel is the main ingredient in the recipe that moves us from deconstruction to reconstruction. Our Gospel Identity provides a framework, a grid for us as leaders to ask the pertinent questions of ourselves and our teams:

> » Do we know Him as Father, Son, and Holy Spirit?
>
> » Do we know what each person of the Godhead has done for us?
>
> » Do we know who we are because of the work of each and what we do out of our new identity in Him?

Just as critical, knowing our Gospel Identity gives us a template for measuring the Church and every disciple according to the beauty and commands inherent in the Gospel itself. Are we disciples that understand and embrace what He declares over us (vs. feeling guilty, ashamed, and believing lies about how short we fall of His love) and do we observe all that He has commanded us (or do we do "what is right in our own eyes" [see Proverbs 12:15; 21:2])?

What kind of culture have we created in our churches? The Lord is longing for the Church to be about the business of being "found in the Father and formed in the family"—a culture of discipleship that passes the image of Christ from one disciple to the next and from the family of God to the culture around us.

I have found an initial desire and willingness in many churches to embrace a culture of discipleship—"It is in the Bible, after all"—but when it comes time to "pull the trigger," the brakes get pressed instead. Only then do they begin to encounter the religious idols standing in their way. They are often shocked to see the "sticker price" of this level of obedience. Such deep work is not easy work, and it tends to be slow. It's much easier to attract a crowd around a set of beliefs than it is to build a Gospel Identity into collective, growing family of families.

One leader told me recently, "We are too busy, too overwhelmed, and lack the 'margins' to be able to move forward in this direction at the present." (Ergo: "Don't call us, we'll call you.") If we're *too busy* to deconstruct our current practices in exchange for His mandates, we are simply *too busy* to pray effectively, *too busy* to hear from God, and *too busy* to build *His* Church *His* way. Not a very good place to be. (My prescription? Start with the "sticky note" exercise.)

It's like the young man who said he was all over this "discipleship thing," but would it be okay if he snuck home to bury his father first? Jesus's answer? *"Let the dead bury their own dead,* but you go and proclaim the Kingdom of God"* (Luke 9:60, emphasis added).

Ouch!

Or how about the guy who said, *"I will follow you, Lord; but first let me go back and say goodbye to my family."* Jesus's reply this time? *"No one who puts his hand to the plow and looks back is fit for service in the Kingdom of God"* (Luke 9:61-62).

Harsh? To converts perhaps, but not to "in love" disciples. We are not mere converts to a religious set of tenants and truths, we are commanded to be Gospel-infused disciples, radicalized by the power of the resurrection. This can't be done when it's convenient for us.

My friends, it's time to raise the bar!

It's no wonder that the Father invited Ken into the spectacular adventure in New Haven—he was and is a Gospel-infused disciple. The guy wears "redemptive glasses," it would seem. He saw everything in his blighted community through the eyes of a God who wanted to restore people's dreams and do the impossible for their neighborhood.

And it wasn't' just New Haven. After returning to Dallas, he started another Grove. Ken tells one of his favorite stories from the Dallas Grove of a destitute young lady he found sitting on the steps downtown there one morning. Though now living on the streets, she had once had a dream of being a chef and had even been featured in a cooking contest on a television series. Not only did she not win the competition, she lost all opportunity to pursue her dream in short order after that. But you guessed it! "Dreamweaver" Janke got her connected into the Grove and soon catering for all the "Grovite's" events, yummifying parties, and building up her own business. She and some "foodies" now run a "cooking school" in a renovated Methodist church building in Dallas. Redemptive eyeballs are the key to transformation!

So, where do we go from here? We need to remember the three protocols of what it means to be a church of the living God. We must embrace the plan conceived from the "foundation of the earth"—restoring the image of Christ to all creation! This is the ultimate purpose of our sojourn here on this planet.

What's the delivery system? Protocol #2: discipleship—the Great Commission—the process of shedding Adam's rags for

Christ's robes, trading the pigsty for the party, *"until we all reach unity in the faith and in the knowledge of the Son of God and become mature, attaining to the whole measure of the fullness of Christ"* (Ephesians 4:13).

And what is the methodology? Protocol #3: We hold fast to the Great Commandment. Making disciples is the fruit of the restored root of revealing the image of Christ, and revealing the image of Christ to our neighborhoods and cities means showing them His love by bringing His dreams for individuals and communities into fruition for all around us. We be like Jesus, the upside-down King, by being servant to all.

Thus we celebrate the birthing process of making disciples into His image and forming them into functioning families on Kingdom mission, pulling people out of despair and injustice along the way. This is heaven's call and our response to it. It's time to get back to being the Church Jesus called us to be.

APPENDIX A
IN CHRIST SCRIPTURES

In Christ (in Him)

Acts 17:24-28

Romans 3:21-26

Romans 6:11

Romans 8:1-2

Romans 8:38-39

Romans 12:4-5

1 Corinthians 1:2

1 Corinthians 1:26-31

1 Corinthians 15:22

2 Corinthians 1:21-22

2 Corinthians 2:14

2 Corinthians 3:14

2 Corinthians 5:17

2 Corinthians 5:18-19

2 Corinthians 5:21

2 Corinthians 11:3

Galatians 2:4

Galatians 2:17

Galatians 3:17

Galatians 3:26

Galatians 3:28

Galatians 5:6

Galatians 6:15

Ephesians 1:3

Ephesians 1:8-10

Ephesians 1:10-12

Ephesians 1:13-14

Ephesians 2:4-7

Ephesians 2:10

Ephesians 2:13

Ephesians 3:4-7

Philippians 3:13-14

1 Thessalonians 5:16-18

1 Timothy 1:12-14

1 Timothy 3:13

2 Timothy 1:1

2 Timothy 1:8-11

2 Timothy 1:13

2 Timothy 2:1

2 Timothy 2:10

Philemon 1:4-6

1 Peter 3:14-16

Because of (by, through, at) Me (Jesus, Christ)

Matthew 11:6

John 6:57

John 10:9

John 14:6

John 14:19

In Me (Jesus)

John 14:20

John 15:4-7

John 16:33

APPENDIX B
GOSPEL IDENTITY SCRIPTURES

THE GOSPEL

For I am not ashamed of the gospel, because it is
the power of God that brings salvation to everyone who
believes: first to the Jew, then to the Gentile. **For in the gospel
the righteousness of God is revealed—a righteousness that
is
by faith from first to last.** [Gospel Identity.]

—ROMANS 1:16-17 (emphasis added)

These scriptures are descriptive of the "righteousness" we have
received from the Father, the Son, and the Holy Spirit.

THE FATHER

What the Father Has Done: Sent His Son sent to adopt us into His Family

2 Corinthians 6:16-18

Romans 8:22-23

Galatians 4:4-7 KJV

Ephesians 1:4-6

Ephesians 3:14-15

Who we are: A family of sons and daughters

John 14:18

Ephesians 1:3-14

Romans 8:15-17

Romans 9:25-26

2 Corinthians 6:18

John 1:12-13

1 John 3:1

Matthew 12:50 KJV, Mark 3:31

John 8:34-36

What we do: Love one another as family

Ephesians 3:14-19

John 17:20-23

1 John 4:7-21

THE SON: SERVANT

What the Son has done: Established his Kingdom as Servant King *Life, Death, Resurrection, Ascension, and Reign*

Philippians 2:6-11   Hebrews 2:14-18

Who we are: Servant subjects of the King

Romans 6:22 KJV   Philippians 2:3-5 KJV
1 Corinthians 4:1-2 KJV   1 Peter 2:13-18
1 Peter 2:16 KJV

What we do: Serve the least among us and one another

Matthew 5:43-48, Luke 6:35   Luke 19:8-10
Matthew 25:34-45   Galatians 6:10

THE HOLY SPIRIT: MISSIONARY

What the Holy Spirit has done: Been sent to manifest (the image of Christ) Kingdom on earth by His presence

2 Corinthians 3:17-18 KJV   Acts 1:3-5
John 3:5-6   Matthew 9:10-13
John 16:13

Who we are: Spirit empowered ambassadors/emissaries of the King/sent ones

Acts 1:8   1 Peter 2:9-12
Romans 8:14   Matthew 9:10-13
2 Corinthians 5:17-20   John 1:3-5

What we do: Demonstrate and proclaim the Kingdom by manifesting it wherever we are called to go

1 Corinthians 2:3-5   Jeremiah 29:4-8
Matthew 28:18-20   John 14:15-19
Mark 16:15-18   John 17:14-19

ENDNOTES

1   Jeff Vanderstelt, "Sermon Title" (sermon, Saturate Gathering, Seattle, Washington, April 16-18, 2018).

2   John W. Ritenbaugh, "Bible verses about Ekklesia," (from *The Forerunner commentary*), BibleTools.org, accessed: July 21, 2017, http://www.bibletools.org/index.cfm/fuseaction/Topical.show/RTD/CGG/ID/2415/Ekklesia.htm.

3   _____, "The Correct Meaning of 'Church" and "Ecclesia,'"*AggressiveChristianity.net*, accessed May 17, 2018, http://www.aggressivechristianity.net/articles/ecclesia.htm.

4   Trevor Hartwig, *My Sheep Hear My Voice* (Bloomington, IN: WestBow Press, 2013), 141.

5   "Mission and History," *BILD International* website, accessed July 11, 2017, https://www.bild.org/about-us/mission-and-history.

6   Jeff Reed, "The Churches of the First Century: from Simple Churches to Complex Networks," A BILD International Encyclical (November 5, 2009), 2.

7   Ibid.

8   Ibid., 5 [insert added].

9   Peter Lamp, *From Paul to Valentinus: Christians at Rome in the First Two Centuries* (Minneapolis, MN: Augsburg Fortress Publishers, 2003),

10   Reed, "The Churches of the First Century," 9.

11   Frank Voila and George Barna, *Pagan Christianity?: Exploring the Roots of Our Church Practices* (Carol Stream, IL: Tyndale House Publishers, 2010), 193.

12   Ibid., 85-86.

13   Reed, "The Churches of the First Century," 12-13.

14   Adapted from tenets of Jeff Vanderselt, *Saturate: Being Disciples of Jesus in the Everyday Stuff of Life* (Wheaton, IL: Crossway, 2015).

15   Robert Greenleaf, *Servant Leadership: A Journey into the Nature of Legitimate Power and Greatness* (Paulist Press, 1977), 40.

16   Ibid., 38-39.

17   *Episcopal Church Book of Common Prayer* (New York: Church Publishing Incorporated., 1979, 2007), 326–327.

18   A.W. Tozer, *The Knowledge of the Holy: The Attributes of God, their Meaning in the Christian Life* (London: James Clark, 1965, 1961), 4.

19 Chris Anderson and David Sally, *The Numbers Game: Why Everything You Know About Soccer Is Wrong* (New York: Penguin Books, 2013), 224-226.

20 James Strong, *Enhanced Strong's Lexicon* (Woodside Bible Fellowship, 1995), s.v. G3622, *oikonomia*.

21 James Strong, *Enhanced Strong's Lexicon* (Woodside Bible Fellowship, 1995), s.v., G1248, *diakonia*.

22 Philip W. Comfort and Grant R. Osborne, (ed.), *Life Application New Testament Commentary* (Carol Stream, IL: Tyndale House Publishers, Inc., 2016), 83.

23 Reggie McNeal, "Foreword," in Eric Swanson and Sam Williams, *To Transform a City: Whole Church, Whole Gospel, Whole City* (Grand Rapids, MI: Zondervan, 2010), 10.

24 Ibid., 11.

25 Ibid., 12.

26 Howard A. Snyder, *The Community of the King*, (Westmont, IL: InterVarsity Press, 1977), 69-70, in Jeff Reed, *Catching God's Vision for the Church: First Principles from Ephesians*, Series 3, Book 4 (BILD International, 2014), 28.

27 Ray C. Stedman, *Body Life* (Glendale, CA: Regal Books, 1977), 70, 71, 87-88, 122-123, in Reed, *Catching God's Vision for the Church*, 39.

28 David Hesselgrave, *Planting Churches Cross Culturally: North America and Beyond* (Grand Rapids, MI: Baker Books, 2000), 19.

29 Ibid., 21.

30 Ibid., 22.

31 Ibid., 24.

32 Harry R Boer, *Pentecost and Missions* (Grand Rapids: Eerdmans, 1961) in Hesselgrave, 23.

33 Hesselgrave, 24.

34 Swanson and Williams, 143.

35 Ibid., 140.

36 Ibid., 141, 142.

37 *Epistle to Diognetus*, V.5, 8, in Bruce W. Winter, *Seek the Welfare of the City: Christians as Benefactors and Citizens* (Grand Rapids, MI: Wm B. Eerdman's Publishing Company, 1994), 12.

38 Jeff Reed, *Seek the Welfare of the City*, DVD series, 2006.

39 Ibid.

40 C. Meier, *The Greek Discovery of Politics* (E.T. Harvard: University Press, 1990), 13ff, in Winter, 2.

41 See also Luke 6:32, 33, 35, 36, 1 Peter 2:11-15, 17, and Romans 13:1-4, 6, 7

42 W. E. Vine, Merrill F. Unger, and William White Jr., *Vine's Complete Expository Dictionary of Old and New Testament Words* (Nashville, TN: T. Nelson, 1996), s.v., dispensations, *oikonomia*.

43 W. E. Vine, Merrill F. Unger, and William White Jr., *Vine's Complete Expository Dictionary of Old and New Testament Words* (Nashville, TN: T. Nelson, 1996), s.v., quiet, quietness, *hesuchios*.

44 Craig G. Bartholomew and Michael W. Goheen, *The Drama of Scriptures* (Grand Rapids, MI: Baker Books, 2004), 39.

45 Ibid, 38.

46 Ed Silvoso, *Anointed for Business: How to Use Your Influence in the Marketplace to Change the World* (Bloomington, MI: Chosen Books, 2009), 17-18.

47 Kristen VanBlargan, "How the Grove Found It's Groove in New Haven," *The Knowledge Green*, accessed March 5, 2018, http://knowledgegreen.com/how-the-grove-found-its-groove-in-new-haven/.

48 Abraham Malherbe, *Paul and the Thessalonians*. Quoted in Jeff Reed, *Laying Solid Foundations in the Gospel: First Principles from 1 & 2 Thessalonians*, Series III, Book 3, 27.

49 Nathan Scarritt, "Reminiscences of the Methodist Shawnee Mission: an religious work among that tribe," in Grove, Nettie Thompson (ed.), *Annals of Kansas City*, 439-440, http://www.ohiomemory.org/cdm/ref/collection/p16007coll27/id/10493.

50 Bob Waymire and Carl Townsend, *Discovering Your City: Bringing Light to the Task of Community Transformation* (Light International, 2000).

JON PETERSEN is the founder and CEO of CityForce, an organization aimed at revitalizing churches and businesses with the hope of transforming their cities and nations to be more effective in dealing with social justice, neighborhood empowerment, and multicultural collaboration. In many ways, he's a wandering father to younger leaders and an engaging friar in reaching out to communities. Jon's journey of being pastor, missionary, citywide prayer organizer, and advisor started in the late '60s spanning from the Jesus Movement to being part of seeing 24-7 Prayer rooms sprout up around the globe and being a "resident father" to the Boiler Room Network of churches.

Today Jon makes his home just south of Denver, Colorado where he has access to his nine grandchildren and from which he continues to train and be engaged in raising up the next generation of church, business, and "culture shapers" for the work of the Kingdom of God in cities around the globe.

Made in the USA
San Bernardino, CA
01 August 2018